PROSPECT FOR METAPHYSICS

PROSPECT FOR METAPHYSICS

ESSAYS OF METAPHYSICAL EXPLORATION

Edited by

IAN RAMSEY

Nolloth Professor of the Philosophy
of the Christian Religion,
University of Oxford

PHILOSOPHICAL LIBRARY, INC.

NEW YORK

Published in 1961 by Philosophical Library, Inc.
15 East 40th Street, New York 16, N.Y.

PRINTED IN GREAT BRITAIN
for the Philosophical Library
BY UNWIN BROTHERS LIMITED, WOKING AND LONDON

EDITOR'S INTRODUCTION

The papers which make up this volume were read at a gathering of philosophers in Easter Week 1959 at Downside Abbey. How they came to meet is not without its interest and significance. In a review of *The Springs of Morality*[1] I had expressed the hope that on some occasion opportunity might be given for discussion, between Roman Catholics and others, of stubborn problems of common interest and acknowledged importance. Now what problem could be tougher than that of the possibility of metaphysics? Of what problem, too, could there be a more timely discussion? Twenty-five years ago metaphysics was no more than a topic for abuse and ridicule. But in more recent days there has been evidence of a broader empiricism willing to leave room for the possibility of significant metaphysical discourse. Is the time now ripe to take measure of what for some twenty-five years has been a challenge to metaphysics? Are we able to face squarely this critical and empirical challenge and yet to say something positive and constructive in support of metaphysics?

These were the questions which formed the background of the Conference and brought us together. It was to discuss the present prospects for metaphysics that Dom Illtyd Trethowan took up the suggestion I made in the review, and invited me to collaborate with him in bringing together the philosophers whose papers make up this book. Coming together with diverse backgrounds, and approaching the topic from various directions, we were all nevertheless sympathetic to some of the insights of contemporary empiricism.

Common to us all, for instance, is the position that we can no longer view natural theology as a tight, rigorous, deductive system, taking us to God by a process of unmistakable inference. Professor Armstrong condemns, and in the name of Plato, any over-intellectualized concept of metaphysics, any cut-and-dried scheme which claims universal validity. Dr Hawkins shows how metaphysicians could wrongly translate logic into ontology and misconceive their task.

[1] Ed. John M. Todd. Burns and Oates, 1955. The book is the record of another symposium held at Downside Abbey in 1955.

Of the twelve papers, it might be said broadly that the earlier ones delineate tendencies and themes which any contemporary exploration of metaphysics will be wise to take into account; while hinting at possible ways forward, they set out various difficulties which confront any contemporary venture into metaphysics. The later papers, while not shirking the difficulties, try to make more constructive suggestions.

Dr Rees introduces our several studies with an outline of the development of ethical theory since G. E. Moore introduced his concept of goodness as a 'non-natural quality', and he shows how far more complex than Moore ever supposed it to be is the logical structure of the language of morals. With this complexity, however, comes gain. For much more needs saying, and can be said, than Moore ever supposed, not only for a morality of divine commands, but more generally on the kind of connexion there can legitimately be between ethics and metaphysics. Here is a theme—the possibility of more subtle relations between theology and ethics than has sometimes been supposed—which is also touched on in the next paper. Dr Ewing again starts with Moore, and rejecting any rigorous view of natural theology, seeks to show, in particular, how impossible is the task of constructing a natural theology which leads deductively to ethical conclusions. At the same time he allows for what he calls a 'blending' of ethical and religious concepts. In these ways then both Dr Ewing and Dr Rees, by special reference to the links between ethics and theology, hint at the kind of 'reasoning'—not, in their view, deductive—by which talk about morality could be linked to talk about God.

Mr Dickie's paper sets out to discover the kind of bridges (if any) there can be, not only on the road between ethics and theology, but on that between theology and science. What he shows, and by particular reference to Greek science and philosophy, is that the concepts of science and the character and limits of metaphysical thinking are closely linked; and that with contemporary science arises the possibility of a new concept of metaphysics. Nor is he endeavouring to deduce theological conclusions from scientific conclusions, as has often been done with disaster to both. His major point is rather that the epistemology of the one must be the epistemology of the other; 'authentic science' shares a common epistemology with 'authentic theology'. With such reflections, he hints at possible connexions between scientific and metaphysical schemes, a theme which is later approached from another direction in my own paper.

The alternative to a natural theology conceived as a deductive system is not (as some might suppose) irrationalism. This is the important point made and developed by Mr Smart and Mr Root. Mr Root examines critically both those who in the name of religion, and those who in the name of empiricism, have tried to make the Christian faith immune from all philosophical enquiry; and he finds both positions unsatisfactory and inadequate to what Christians have said and done. His conclusion is that a metaphysical theology must do justice not only to our desire for a natural theology, but also to our religiously inspired distrust of natural theology; and he suggests that this delicate balance may possibly be struck if we ground our theology in some kind of 'basic apprehension' which is a 'point' of 'worship'. Already we have our first explicit hint as to where a constructive approach to metaphysics might begin. It is a hint which we find Mr Smart developing in the next paper. Mr Smart sees philosophical theology as concerned with the working out of a theological scheme by which to express some kind of 'intuition' to which a religious man appeals. His paper can be seen as a bold and vigorous attempt to travel along a middle way between a tight deductive natural theology and sheer irrationalism. Taking the view that the intuitional basis of religion comes most often with complex and corrigible interpretations, he shows us the kind of reasoning that on his view is possible not only about one religion but even between different religions. Here is a 'soft' natural theology.

The possibility of any alternative approach to natural theology, the possibility of metaphysics, seems bound up, then, with the concept of intuition. Professor Armstrong makes this point by special reference to Plato's Forms which (he argues) are no abstract ideas, and Dr Hawkins appeals to an intuition of 'Being' and claims that metaphysics should begin by asking what is involved in an existential judgement, and that it is from such a beginning that a metaphysical theology could be constructed.

Dom Mark Pontifex shows us, by discussing a specific question, viz. 'Does the existence of evil disprove God's existence?', the kind of reasoning that is still possible within a theology of this new brand, empirical rather than *a priori*, though he clearly envisages a rather tighter metaphysical setting than (say) Mr Smart contemplates. If God is spoken of as the source of all being and value, it looks as if this makes God a responsible source of all the evil there is. But Dom Mark claims that it is possible to avoid this conclusion by giving a man a negative causality, the choice of initiating failure, and so by referring evil to himself.

It is the concept of intuition, both its relevance for metaphysics and the problems it brings with it, that forms the topic of papers by Dom Illtyd Trethowan, myself and Professor Lewis. For we do not conceal the fact that problems there certainly are. Indeed, not the least importance of the book is (we believe) to bring these difficulties to the light of day, and to try in some degree to grapple with them. Dom Illtyd Trethowan claims, as against Professor Ayer, that such a statement as 'I am in pain' is incorrigible. The importance of this, he considers, is that it enables us to argue for an intuitive awareness of reality and thus opens the way for a claim to an awareness of God. The content of *that* awareness is, from the nature of the case, indescribable, but this, Dom Illtyd considers, does not make it impossible for us to convince one another that we have it.

In my own paper, I first try to show what is the logical status to be given to any metaphysical scheme, and I then outline the way in which a metaphysical theology of this brand could be constructed on the basis of an intuition, an intuition whose paradigm might be found in the intuition each of us has of himself as more than his public behaviour. Though he is somewhat cautious about intuition, Father Daly makes very similar points, viz. that the possibility of metaphysics is bound up with the recognition that 'I' for each of us relates to more than scientific observables, that metaphysics can be rightly centred on something like a *Cogito* situation. Father Daly continues his thesis by arguing that there is 'mystery' in all being, 'beyond knowing' in all knowing. In this way there is something inexpressible, at least in descriptive terms.

Professor Lewis's paper develops this same theme of mystery from another direction and touches at many points on questions which are inevitably raised when an appeal is made to intuition. He especially considers the recurrent question, faced in so many of the papers, and raised again by Father Daly: how are we to talk of what the intuition, the apprehension is about? how best to talk about what the disclosure is of? He shows in particular that an appeal to intuition need not be the kind of unreasonable irrational appeal which many 'encounter' theologians have made of it, and which in that form has been rightly subjected to severe criticism by contemporary empiricists. Instead, it represents a claim for mystery at various points in experience—one of these points (though not the only one) being found in distinctively personal relationships. So Professor Lewis develops and supplements points made by Dom Illtyd, Father Daly and myself.

Is there now any positive, constructive suggestion which arises broadly out of these papers? Certainly, common to most of the papers is the view that the empirical basis or foundation of any metaphysical theology lies in what may be called, albeit circumspectly, an 'intuition'. What a metaphysical theology does (we suggest) is to elaborate the most reliable scheme by which to talk of what such an intuition discloses. Thus the aim of a metaphysical philosophy should be to cultivate a reasonable currency for, and a due appreciation of, 'mysteries'. In doing this it will somehow relate and bring together, in all their variegation, many diverse ways of reliable reasoning.

We do not claim that all the papers toe the same line or breast the same tape, but they have enough of a common basis, we believe, to encourage those who would start on metaphysical ventures. Such explorers will find discussed in this book many of the questions and difficulties they must face and try to answer before beginning their journey. But they will also find (we hope) some constructive hints which will enable them thereafter to travel hopefully.

CONTENTS

CONTENTS

I

D. A. REES

METAPHYSICAL SCHEMES
AND
MORAL PRINCIPLES

I propose to begin by adverting to that crucial starting-point of twentieth-century British ethics, G. E. Moore's rejection of what he called the 'naturalistic fallacy', and by raising once again the question which has been raised several times in philosophical circles already, what exactly it was that Moore succeeded in proving. Moore in *Principia Ethica* approached his treatment of good by asking whether good was definable or not,[1] meaning by 'definition' an intellectual process of splitting up a complex whole into its component parts.[2] The conclusion he reached was that good was necessarily indefinable, since any definition would involve identifying good with something other than itself[3]— unless, indeed, it was a purely verbal definition, in which case, according to Moore, it would not be a definition in any philosophically important sense at all.[4] In particular, Moore objected to the identification of good with any natural property, since this, he held, must in every case be an identification of two properties inspection of which would show them to be distinct. Where the identification was of this kind, he regarded it as an instance of what he called the 'naturalistic fallacy'.[5] A variant of this, in his view, was the identification of good with any non-natural but also non-ethical property, which was characteristic of what he called metaphysical ethics;[6] while definition (in any but a verbal sense) in terms of another ethical property must be impossible, since good could be seen by inspection to be a simple property, and it

---

[1] *Principia Ethica* (Cambridge, 1903), § 5. [2] *Ibid.*, §§ 7–8, 13.
[3] *Ibid.*, §§ 9–10. [4] *Ibid.*, §§ 6, 8, 11. [5] *Ibid.*, § 10. [6] *Ibid.*, § 25, and Ch. 4.

was in terms of the simple and indefinable that other ethical properties were, if definable, to be defined.[1]

This theory plainly involves a highly special theory of definition, and that increases its vulnerability. In fact, one outcome was that as long ago as 1932 Moore wrote that he knew of no proof that good was indefinable, and that all the proofs he had given in *Principia Ethica* were fallacious, though he still thought it likely that it was in fact indefinable.[2] But, over and above this particular issue, I propose, briefly and without proper discussion, to mention certain points which have been raised by subsequent philosophers and which are either directly critical of Moore's position or relevant to such criticism. It must not be concluded that I think these to be the only or even the most important criticisms, over and above those attaching to his theory of definition, to which Moore's position is open; they are simply those which seem most relevant to what I want to say.

The point to stress here is that firm rejection of the conception of ethical properties which has been characteristic of the main bulk of writing on ethics in this country since 1945 [not to speak of earlier writers, and of the influence from America exerted by C. L. Stevenson's *Ethics and Language* (1944)]. The alternative has been, in one way or another, to think of moral assertions, and value-assertions generally, as having their main function in expressing attitudes and in commending or the reverse. I shall deal a little later with the relevance of this for what may be called the metaphysical relations of ethics. For the moment, I shall merely mention two correlative aspects which can be conveniently, if very roughly, associated with the names of Mr R. M. Hare[3] and Professor P. H. Nowell-Smith[4] respectively. Both serve to illustrate the extent to which the descriptive and evaluative elements (dare one say 'the empirical and the non-empirical'?) are intertwined in the language we use. Mr Hare, for his part, shows

---

[1] We need not discuss the way in which the treatment of 'right' in *Ethics* (1912) differs from that in *Principia Ethica*.

[2] 'Is Goodness a Quality?', *Proc. Arist. Soc.*, Supp. Vol. 11 (1932), pp. 116–31, especially p. 127. For more radical doubts which assailed Moore later, see his 'Reply to my Critics', in *The Philosophy of G. E. Moore* (ed. P. A. Schilpp, 1942), pp. 535–54.

[3] *The Language of Morals* (London, 1952), especially Part II.

[4] *Ethics* (1954), especially Chs. 5–7.

how the word 'good', while fulfilling regularly, in some degree, the function of commendation (in a wide sense of that term) over the whole range of commendations that we may wish to make, has also, within particular fields of subject-matter, in particular types of circumstance and also among particular groups of people, a descriptive content with a degree of precision which may be low but may be relatively high. The term 'good' can have this content because we not only speak a common language but also share a vast number of criteria of evaluation in different fields; within a social group any one individual's ideals and standards will coincide, not indeed entirely, but to a very large extent, with those of most others.

Professor Nowell-Smith, on the other hand, is notable rather for the stress he has laid upon the extent to which the moral judgements we make, and the moral thinking we carry on, are couched not so much in those highly general and, one may be tempted (however mistakenly) to think, more purely moral or evaluative terms like 'good' and 'bad', 'right' and 'wrong', but in terms like 'generous', 'untrustworthy', 'dishonest' or 'callous'. These have a descriptive content which is itself in general— throughout the whole range of its application, that is to say, as distinct from its application to particular contexts—more precise than 'good', but with it are blended overtones, and, as the words are in fact used, ineradicable overtones, of approbation or dis-approbation. To call a man dishonest is to indicate, in a highly general way, the type of conduct which may be expected of him, but it is also to make an attack on his character. This, once again, is possible only because of the large number of evaluations which are shared by those who belong to the same social group and who speak the same language—not only in the wide sense of speaking English, but also in the narrower sense of employing roughly the same evaluative vocabulary, in roughly the same sort of way, within the English language. Now this, in its turn, brings us to a further point, namely that two terms may, where our evaluations differ, have roughly the same descriptive content, though with widely differing evaluative overtones: if I wish to praise what another person dispraises, I shall use a different term to describe it, one which has roughly the same empirical (descriptive or

B

predictive) value, but sets what it is applied to in a very different light. A man described as mean by me may appear to you as thrifty; if I call him courageous you may demur, and, if not actually denying what I say, prefer to call him foolhardy. The language we use, and the standpoint we adopt, are inseparably bound up the one with the other.[1]

In pursuing this theme one may turn to a recent paper by Mrs P. R. Foot, entitled 'Moral Beliefs', in which she develops the point by reference to the concept (among others) of rudeness.[2] To describe conduct as rude (it is to be noticed how naturally it comes to us to use the term 'describe') is to express disapproval of it; and Mrs Foot so presses this point as to question what Moore had widely been held to have shown beyond all cavil, namely the impossibility of a naturalistic analysis of moral terms, or (to put it in words reminiscent of Hume) the radical disjunction of 'is' from 'ought', such that no inference is possible from 'is' to 'ought' without the interposition of some premiss containing an 'ought' either explicitly or implicitly.

But this brings us back to our original question, what exactly it was (if anything) that Moore proved. It may seem, to begin with, that he has proved either too much or too little.[3] For in the first place the arguments in *Principia Ethica*, if valid, would tell against any definition of good whatever, whether in naturalistic (i.e. empirical) or in non-naturalistic terms, and whether these latter were valuational (moral) or non-valuational (non-moral). Again, in the second place, if the naturalist claims that he always uses 'good' in the sense of (say) 'pleasant', and if in fact he does so with perfect consistency, how can he be guilty of a fallacy? It is clear that recourse to Moore's inspection of a non-natural property of goodness will be of no avail, since if the naturalist denies that he is conscious of possessing the requisite power of inspection there is plainly no more to be said. The most that one

---

[1] Cf. S. E. Toulmin and K. Baier, 'On Describing', *Mind*, 61 (1952), pp. 13–38.

[2] *Proc. Arist. Soc.*, 59 (1958–9), pp. 83–104; cf. *id.*, 'Moral Arguments', *Mind*, 67 (1958), pp. 502–13.

[3] Cf. W. K. Frankena, 'The Naturalistic Fallacy', *Mind*, 48 (1939), pp. 464–77; A. N. Prior, *Logic and the Basis of Ethics* (1949), Ch. 1; W. H. Walsh, 'The Autonomy of Ethics', *Phil. Quart.*, 7 (1957), pp. 1–14; R. F. Holland, 'The Autonomy of Ethics', *Proc. Arist. Soc.*, Supp. Vol. 32 (1958), pp. 25–48 (who, however, tends to overlook the positive value of Moore's work).

could do would be to show that his use of the word 'good' did not accord with normal practice and, while some philosophers might treat this as a final argument, and others as a very weighty one, our naturalist might not. Even, however, if the point about usage is allowed, it was not just a point about usage that Moore was anxious to make: he was wanting something more, something which guaranteed that the usage was correct, that it reflected the ultimate nature of things. One might, indeed, make a more hopeful approach by questioning the naturalist not about the use of 'good' but about that of (to take our example) 'pleasant': is it for its part purely descriptive?

Incidentally, what occurs when the naturalist gives such an analysis, and how is he able to give one with any degree of plausibility? It will not do merely to say that, in making 'good' equivalent to some empirical term, he is simply abandoning the word 'good' as we know it and giving to the sound—the phoneme —'good' some utterly different sense, much as 'boot' is used both for an article of footwear and for the luggage-receptacle at the rear of a car. We have to go back to Mr Hare's distinction of the descriptive and evaluative (or commendatory) aspects of 'good', and observe that the naturalist is concentrating on the former and omitting the latter. But, if so, a problem arises for him, since, as we have seen, the descriptive force of 'good' has a wide range of variation over the whole variety of applications of which it is susceptible. One of two things must, therefore, happen; either the naturalist must concentrate on one of these determinations of descriptive content at the expense of the others, in which case his use of 'good' will, outside a narrow range, be widely at variance with the normal, unless, indeed, he fixes on an equivalent such as 'pleasant' which itself has an extended range of application (and here we meet, as already noted, the problem whether 'pleasant', or whatever else is taken, has not itself an evaluative aspect of some importance); or else he must allow a wide range of usages to 'good', in view of the large number of criteria of goodness we may employ, and then the meaning of the term is dissipated throughout these applications and there ceases to be any bond to give it unity. (One may be reminded of the problem which faced Aristotle when he had abandoned the Platonic Idea of the Good, and which he met in *Nicomachean Ethics*, I, 6, by his doctrine of analogy or proportionality.)

On the other hand, as Mr Hare noted, the commendatory aspect of 'good' may in some circumstances be at a minimum:[1] this will tend to be the case, above all, where a speaker is simply reproducing an evaluation current in the milieu in which he finds himself, without committing himself to it in any but a purely perfunctory manner. But the point is, perhaps, of greater interest as applied not to 'good' but to 'ought'; we may distinguish a purely moral 'ought' on the one hand from what we may call an 'ought' of social expectation or again a legal 'ought' (let alone others), and of these the first and the second, especially, may tend to slide over the one into the other, according to the degree to which we are committing ourselves to the standards and evaluations embodied in the second. Where a person has no standards of evaluation beyond those enjoined by the group to which he belongs, or the moral authority to which he submits himself, and where he does not envisage having any standards which might diverge, we may pass over into a purely authoritarian morality susceptible of a naturalistic analysis—as, perhaps, in the case of a tribal morality—though here again one has to make allowance for the presence of imperative overtones.[2] One can, of course, avoid allowing the possibility of this type of morality by denying the title of 'moral' to such an attitude towards problems of practice; and such a narrowing, involving a denial that we have the properly moral where no distinction is drawn between the socially expected and the obligatory, will be illuminating in some ways and will agree with much in our own conception of morality, but social life—and thus *mores*—may perfectly well exist in the absence of morality as so defined.

At this point I should like to turn to a related question about attitude theories in ethics. One motive which philosophers have felt for rejecting moral fact theories in favour of attitude theories has lain in the diversity of moral beliefs throughout the world and throughout history, and on the other hand a motive tending in the

---

[1] *Op. cit.*, pp. 121–6.
[2] Cf. my 'The Ethics of Divine Commands', *Proc. Arist. Soc.*, 57 (1956–7), pp. 83–106, especially pp. 92–3.

opposite direction has presented itself in the feeling that the alternative to a moral fact theory is an extreme individualism, arbitrary and irrationalistic, suggestive of a world in which each agent creates his own moral standards out of a vacuum. This feeling has been encouraged by certain aspects of existentialism; but are attitude theories necessarily so committed? If they were, clearly something would be amiss. On the other hand, one may not feel completely happy about the view that, when all factual elements in moral disagreements have been removed ('factual' being interpreted here in a wide sense to include metaphysical and religious disagreements), those moral disagreements will necessarily either disappear or remain simply as deriving from a failure to apprehend correctly some objective moral truth or fact. Attitude theories escape this conclusion. For them, there will be no one archetypal morality which all actual moralities either copy of fail to copy. But at the same time students of anthropology and sociology may stress—I am thinking of Ginsberg[1] in particular— the extensive identity in moral beliefs underlying a surface diversity, which is to be expected in view of the general character of human life, the common features of what is called 'the human situation', the common nature of human needs and the importance for men of co-operation for common ends. (At the same time, from any one moral standpoint other moral standpoints must seem, if and when they differ from it, to be not simply different but wrong, unless the difference is in some respect which from the former standpoint appears immaterial. Otherwise the standpoints will clash.) It is true that the world contains moral reformers and moral rebels, but their innovations and their rebellions need to be seen against a background of general moral agreement. They arise only within, or (at most) out of, a tradition. Our morality is intelligible only in its social setting (though that is not to say that a social account of it necessarily exhausts its full nature and significance; that is a matter for further argument), and it is embodied in the language we use and the criteria that language enshrines, with its terms of praise and dispraise. We may be faced as individuals with a crucial choice as to our way of life,

---

[1] M. Ginsberg, 'On the Diversity of Morals', in *Essays in Sociology and Social Philosophy* (London, 1956), Vol. I, pp. 97–129.

but in general our moral standards do not present themselves to us as options; nor is it a matter of option for us whether to be moral or not. As Kant put it, as moral beings we find ourselves enrolled in an army not as gentlemen-volunteers but as conscripts. Consideration of this type of point may help to clarify both the relation between the more narrowly moral 'ought' and the 'ought' of social expectation, and the degree of plausibility that naturalism may in certain circumstances possess.

What, however, are we to conclude about Moore's main thesis in *Principia Ethica*? It is clear, in the first place, that in an important respect the type of position which he represents on the issue of naturalism is not one which is necessarily bound up with a particular view of the nature of definition. In a different way it is represented equally by Hume, with his insistence on a radical disjunction of 'is' and 'ought', such that no inference was possible from 'is' to 'ought' without the introduction into the premisses of an 'ought', whether explicit or implicit. Is it possible that what Hume and Moore are alike doing is to give different expressions to a certain common approach to questions of morality, to an approach, however, which does not hold good for all morality whatever? A course of argument somewhat on these lines was followed in a paper by Miss Iris Murdoch a few years ago, in which she applied to such approaches as those of Hume and Moore the term 'liberal'.[1] At least, as has been seen, we need to take account of the ambivalence of descriptive-evaluative terms in our language—of the way in which the aspects of description and evaluation are intertwined in it. But the point I am now making will, perhaps, be confirmed from a different angle if we look at what Moore, consonantly with the corresponding section of Hume's *Treatise of Human Nature*,[2] says about metaphysical ethics; and here I venture to touch upon points made in a paper read to the Aristotelian Society during the session of 1956–7, with the title of 'The Ethics of Divine Commands'.[3]

Moore distinguished interpretations of good in empirical terms (naturalism proper) from interpretations in terms which were non-empirical but nevertheless not distinctively moral (meta-

---

[1] 'Metaphysics and Ethics', in *The Nature of Metaphysics* (ed. D. F. Pears, London, 1957), pp. 99–123.   [2] III. 1. 1.   [3] *Proc. Arist. Soc.*, 57 (1956–7), pp. 83–106.

physical ethics). But he regarded the two as equally erroneous, and in fact thought the difference between them of no great importance for ethics. One may add, by the way, that in his *Ethics*, though he does at one point mention that he sees no adequate reason for believing in any god, the matter is taken up only to be dropped again, and he says that he regards it as of no great ethical importance.[1] Now it is as a corollary of Moore's general standpoint in *Principia Ethica*, though without commitment to his particular theory of definition, that Professor C. D. Broad[2] and Dr A. C. Ewing[3] have rejected the interpretation of 'I ought to do X' as equivalent to 'God commands me to do X', labelling it 'theological naturalism'. But, if this were correct, the possibility so rightly stressed by anti-naturalists of saying 'The state (e.g.) commands me to do X but I ought not to do it' would be paralleled by an equal possibility of saying 'God commands me to do X but I ought not to do it', whereas clearly those who use that form of expression would not admit this. 'God commands X, so it must be right' may be met by 'X is wrong, so God cannot have commanded it'. Why is this so? Plainly it is because God is thought of as a perfect Being, in whose perfection moral perfection plays an essential part; thus moral criteria are relevant to determining what we can ascribe to God, and what we say about God will embody our moral evaluations, though, particularly if we admit a religious revelation, our moral consciousness will not be the sole criterion determining what we say about God even on moral matters—theological dogmas may give rise to moral tensions and predicaments, and there may be a complicated interplay between moral assertions and theological. What I tried to argue in the paper to which I referred was that morality was not all of a piece, but that a morality of divine commands—more than one such, no doubt—could be distinguished, which would differ in its approach to moral problems from a morality of social rules, much as (to adopt a different *fundamentum divisionis*) a pure autonomous Moorean approach to moral problems would differ from one characteristic of an authoritarian morality susceptible,

---

[1] *Ethics* (1912), Ch. 4.

[2] *Five Types of Ethical Theory* (London, 1930), p. 259.

[3] *The Definition of Good* (London, 1947), pp. 106–10. But I gather that Dr Ewing would now wish to modify this.

without any considerable degree of error, of a naturalistic analysis. (Whether the conduct to which these different approaches gave rise would differ, and in what degree, could not be determined in advance of knowing the details of the moral principles advocated in each case.)

I propose now to enquire a little further what is involved in a metaphysical ethics, i.e. a system of morality which is connected with a metaphysical scheme, whether distinctively theological or not. It has been seen already that it is not necessary that a moral system should have such connexions: so far, at any rate, Moore and those like him are perfectly correct. With his position one may also associate that of those who insist on the autonomy of ethics—on an underivative nature in moral principles—in order to have therein a secure and independent basis for the construction of a natural theology of an ethical kind; this seems to be possible only if one adopts a moral epistemology of an intuitionist or at any rate a 'moral fact' kind.[1] A morality, in other words, may be purely autonomous, or it may have purely naturalistic, and not properly or in a narrow sense metaphysical, connexions.[2] On the other hand a morality may be intelligible only when seen in connexion with a metaphysical (or religious) scheme; one may think of a morality in which the concepts of holiness and of sin play a prominent part. Once again, while a metaphysical scheme may or may not make a difference to detailed moral prescriptions, it is inevitable that, if reflected upon, it should set one's morality as a whole in a special light.

I have been using 'metaphysical' and 'theological' (or 'religious') somewhat loosely, as if the latter were simply a special case of the former. This is clearly improper: the terms 'holiness' and 'sin' are theological but scarcely metaphysical; and, while metaphysics aims at being rational, much of theology—some would say properly all—depends not on reason alone but also on revelation. But these differences, important as they are, need not concern us at the moment. It will further be noted that, whereas in general morality (and equally *a* morality) does not, either

---

[1] Cf. H. D. Lewis, *Our Experience of God* (London, 1959), Ch. 18.
[2] One may note the function of such terms as 'normal', 'integrated' and 'objective' in the literature of psychotherapy.

generally or in detail, present itself to the individual agent as an optional matter, he may in a complex culture such as ours find himself having to decide between a theological (metaphysical) and a non-theological (non-metaphysical) way of regarding morality, or between one theological or metaphysical scheme and another.

The second point is that a metaphysical scheme may be expected to embody evaluations. It is one conveyed effectively by the German term *Weltanschauung*. We find here reproduced, at a non-empirical (supra-empirical) level, that close connexion between describing and evaluating which we have already noted at an empirical. The metaphysics may embody the ideal of a perfect Being, an *ens perfectissimum*; this will clearly have moral relevance, though it will be necessary for an investigator to enquire in detail in each case what kind of perfection is envisaged. Again, the metaphysics may present its evaluations in a scheme of degrees of reality, thus maintaining a close correlation between reality and value; one may think of the Platonic and Neoplatonic traditions,[1] and of that of Absolute Idealism.[2]

Beyond this, there are two kinds of relation I wish to touch upon briefly between a metaphysical scheme and the morality with which it is associated, the first of which may be called epistemological and the second practical. The first concerns the kind of inference by which one may pass from the one to the other, and the kind of support that the one may afford to the other. The second concerns the relevance of the eternal and the non-empirical as envisaged to that which is to be done here and now.

(1) Let us take the first of these questions, and begin by asking whether the concept of deductive entailment is of relevance here. We must surely agree with Hume that from a pure 'is'—whether or not it is an empirical 'is'—to an 'ought' no deductive inference is possible. But then, as we have seen, the propositions of a meta-

---

[1] Cf., e.g., J. Katz, *Plotinus' Search for the Good* (New York, 1950), *passim*.

[2] Cf., e.g., the following: 'He [sc. Hegel] thinks—rightly—of the Platonic and Aristotelian philosophy as one in principle. Its fundamental notion that what is most real is *eo ipso* that which is most intelligible and most good is shared by Hegel, to whom it is, in fact, the essential thesis which philosophy must make good' [G. R. G. Mure, *An Introduction to Hegel* (Oxford, 1940), preface, p. xi].

physical scheme may be expected not to be empty of evaluative content, and this fact will seem to open up once again the possibility of deductive inference from the metaphysical to the moral. But in some cases the relation may not be tight enough to appear to deserve the name of 'entailment' or 'deducibility', and in others it may be doubtful whether it does so or not, as when the notion of a perfect Being is held to entail that of the appropriateness of worship or veneration towards it. Of entailment in the reverse direction, i.e. from the morality to the associated metaphysical scheme, one can only say that this will depend on the particular character of the morality in question (i.e. on the mode of its formulation) both for the existence of any such relation of entailment and for the degree of strictness it exhibits. One may instance again a morality embodying concepts of holiness and sin.

If we turn from deductive inference to inductive, we find once again that an induction proper, being based solely on the reports of observations, cannot bring us to a moral 'ought' in the strict sense; the most it could do would be to carry us from particular 'oughts' of social expectation to a general 'ought' of social expectation. What is more relevant here, however, is that clearly a metaphysical scheme could not provide inductive support for a moral principle—or indeed for anything except a generalization about such things as metaphysical schemes. Nor, to consider the possibility of an induction in the opposite direction, could a moral principle provide inductive support for anything, though doubtless the fact that a moral principle was adhered to might. But neither this nor anything else could properly provide inductive support for a metaphysical scheme: if that were possible, it would simply turn the metaphysical scheme into a scientific hypothesis, highly general in character, and susceptible of empirical verification or falsification in the manner appropriate to such.

The notion of inductive support may, however, furnish us with a clue. It has been seen above that a certain morality—a set of moral conceptions—may only be intelligible in the light of a certain metaphysical scheme. It may be said to presuppose that scheme. Conversely, the metaphysical scheme may be said *either* in a more or less strict sense to entail the moral system, *or* to provide it with support—support of a non-inductive kind, as distinct from the support which empirical evidence provides for an inductive conclusion. To put it in other words, the metaphysical scheme may suggest a certain morality, and this way of putting the matter may help in two ways. In the first place, the word 'suggest' conveys a fairly loose relationship; this is important, since it is possible to maintain a metaphysical scheme while at the same time rebelling against it—one may think of the *Weltanschauung* expressed by Hardy or by Housman, or of philosophical pessimism in nineteenth-century Germany. In the second place, to suggest is always to suggest something to someone. In this case, to whom? The answer is that it suggests the morality to those who employ a certain framework of language and of thought, in which the metaphysical and the moral elements interlock. If one stands outside the framework as a whole, one may no longer feel any cogency in the connexions; but then the metaphysical terminology will no longer embody one's own evaluations, and thus no longer possess for one the same evaluative overtones.

More, however, needs to be said on the type of inference involved, particularly as there has been introduced what might be described either as a notion of degrees of strictness in entailment, or as that of a deductive inference which may pass as legitimate without being sufficiently strict for the term 'entailment' to be appropriate. This may be thought to be highly dubious in itself, and further to be dangerous as opening the door to slipshod thinking. But it is now generally accepted that in any non-formal discourse the concepts employed are never perfectly precise; the sharp line between what is analytic and what is synthetic tends thus to become blurred, and we may be liable to find that the question what entails what may not be completely determined or determinable, even though the pursuit of rigour may be carried indefinitely far. Further, the notion of entailment itself, and the relations between the structures of the formal logician and the valid inferences of ordinary life, are by no means easy to determine with precision, and are in fact a good deal more complex than logicians in the past have usually realized; the subject has received some attention recently at the hands of Professors Ryle and Toulmin.[1] But I think that all that my argument requires is that in principle the passage from the metaphysical to the moral could, with the insertion of additional premises, be represented as deserving the status of entailment, and that these should be either premises which in view of the very nature of the language (system of concepts) in question it would be legitimate for its users to take for granted, or premises inductively established.

(2) We turn now to the other question, that of the relevance of the non-empirical, and especially the eternal or supra-temporal, as envisaged in a metaphysical scheme, to the problems of action in particular situations. In a sense, this question has been answered already, since acceptance of an interlocking terminology with both metaphysical and moral sides may be expected itself to provide the necessary solutions for those who work within its framework. But perhaps more can be said, in view of the different forms this relation between the theoretical and the practical may take. For one thing, to say what God is like may have moral relevance in more than one way, for instance if it is thought incumbent on us to strive to be like God;[2] or if on the other hand imitation of God is thought inappropriate for man (even, perhaps, presumptuous or blasphemous);[3] or if in some other way the nature of God is thought relevant to determining what is appropriate for lesser beings—e.g., perhaps, worship. But that this problem of the relation of the eternal to the temporal, of the theoretical to the practical, is not an easy one for the metaphysician may be seen by mentioning a few classical instances in the history of philosophy. How the vision of the Form of the Good is to be related to detailed problems of action is a question to which Plato gives no proper answer in his *Republic*, and Aristotle makes this a point of criticism against him in *Nicomachean Ethics*, I. 6.[4] Again, if we turn to Aristotle himself, while his theology is clearly relevant to the contemplative side of his ethics, there is a wide gap between these and his treatment of moral virtue. A roughly parallel

---

[1] G. Ryle, ' "If", "So" and "Because",' in *Philosophical Analysis*, ed. Max Black (London, 1950), pp. 323–40; *id.*, *Dilemmas* (1954), Ch. 8, 'Formal and Informal Logic'; S. E. Toulmin, *The Uses of Argument* (1958) (which seems at times to push to extremes its depreciation of formal logic). See also P. F. Strawson, *Introduction to Logical Theory* (1952), pp. 230–2.   [2] Pl., *Tht.*, 176B.
[3] Cf. Arist., *E.N.*, X. 1177b31–34 (a view rejected by A).   [4] 1096b35–1097a13.

problem appears in Spinoza, which he attempts to solve in terms of grades of intellectual apprehension. One method of integration, though a method which perhaps few would feel to be fully satisfactory,[1] is on the lines of Plotinus, emphasizing contemplation (θεωρία) and seeing the importance of moral virtue principally as leading to a spiritual purification (κάθαρσις) directed towards contemplation as a goal.[2]

* * *

I propose to conclude this paper with some brief, highly schematic and very amateurish remarks on the differences between a metaphysical scheme and a myth, with some special reference to the relation of each to action. They will be schematic of necessity; and I do not wish to exclude the possibility that a myth which is of a general and all-embracing kind, and which has been rationalized, may approach the status of a metaphysical scheme, so that there can be no absolute disjunction between the two. But, in general, a metaphysical scheme is set out as something capable of rational proof, and the metaphysician regards it as his task to do the proving. Not so a myth: hence the contrast, as old as Plato, between μῦθος and λόγος.[3] One way in which this shows itself is that, while it is an essential characteristic of myth to employ pictorial language, metaphysics tries to remove it; anthropomorphism, for example, from the metaphysician's standpoint, since, or in so far as, it cannot be taken seriously, must be eradicated; or, if the difficulty or impossibility of complete eradication is recognized, it has to be stressed that the pictorial language is being employed in an extended or analogical fashion, and the mode of this extension indicated in principle. One speaks readily of mythological or of religious symbolism, as of artistic, but not of metaphysical—unless one is deliberately setting out to assimilate metaphysics to poetry or to myth, or else suggesting that metaphysical conceptions may somehow be adumbrated artistically. A myth, for its part, may be radically incoherent, as is stressed by Frankfort,[4] and may even have the fantastic quality of

[1] Such a method, it will be seen, is advocated by several contributors to the Symposium.—Ed.   [2] *Enneads*, I. 2.

[3] Cf. especially *Timaeus*, 26E; also *Protagoras*, 320C, 324D.

[4] *Before Philosophy* (*The Intellectual Adventure of Ancient Man*) (1946), Ch. 1.

a dream in which different and apparently unrelated images press and crowd upon one another, and yet it may be accepted with equanimity; but incoherence above all other things is repugnant to the metaphysician. Again, a metaphysical scheme excludes alternative schemes as incompatible with it; but a myth will tend rather to ignore rival myths, and it may be possible to maintain more than one in different contexts, or to mingle two without great concern for the consistency of the amalgam; but these issues will depend partly on the scope of the myth. The metaphysician, once again, aims, unlike the myth-maker, at the greatest possible unification and simplicity in his principles; the myth-maker may embroider his account considerably for artistic reasons. Hence, too, the extreme generality of a metaphysical scheme; whereas the application of a myth may be either general (as in the case of a cosmological or cosmogonical myth) or special (as in the case of a myth explaining the origin of a certain festival); but once again these two classes of myth may overlap—the festival, as in the case of a spring festival, may celebrate some general feature of the cosmos. But I give these instances because the type of myth of particular concern to us here is the aetiological; and in general it may be said that myths have an explanatory function of some sort or other, that they set out to explain why things are as they are and not otherwise, though, except in the sense of providing some such pictorial explanation, a myth is, as mentioned above, something not susceptible of proof; stress on proof might tend to turn it into an empirically testable scientific hypothesis. Metaphysical systems, indeed, may be such that empirical facts of a highly general kind are relevant to them, so that if the most general features of the world were different the metaphysical system would in some degree be rendered false; or they may be such that, if true, they would hold good, as it appeared to Kant that his categorical scheme would, of any intelligible world whatever. Only in the former case will they perform that function performed also by a highly general myth, of explaining why the world as a whole is as it is. One final point arises which is associated with the rationality of metaphysics: myth, and also ritual, of which I shall speak in a moment, may involve the esoteric, the secret formula, the group of initiates; not so a metaphysical theory, which, like a scientific, is in principle open to all who are able and willing to reflect on the world with sufficient force.

It will seem that at this point I can hardly avoid discussing both the legitimacy of metaphysical enterprises and the ambivalent relations of theological dogma to metaphysics on the one hand and to myth on the other. I have, however, space for neither, and for the second I lack any specialized competence, though we may observe briefly that the notion and place of religious authority are here involved, and above all that the theologian finds himself constantly faced with the problem how to express that which cannot be adequately expressed in the concrete language of picturable fact, and yet cries out for expression in such language and can be expressed in no other way. On the other issue I shall observe only that the concept of metaphysics is a polymorphous (shall we say a hydra-headed?) one, and that it may be more helpful to enquire about the function of a metaphysical scheme in a system of thinking and living than about its strict demonstrability alone; its rationality need not be simply, or even primarily, a matter of this.

But (to leave dogma aside) how is metaphysics related to conduct, and how is myth? The connexion of either may in some cases appear fairly tenuous, while in others it may be clearly marked. So far as they have an effect on conduct, both may be expected to affect not simply what we do but why we do it. But a metaphysics will be like a myth only in so far as the latter is a myth of the most general and most profound type, affecting actions and attitudes to life in the most fundamental way. More generally, perhaps, we may associate myth rather with ritual, remembering aetiological myths purporting to explain the origin of a festival or other rite; though at the same time it must be remembered that in a primitive society the whole of life may be governed by a system of ritual and taboo. A myth, I should like to suggest, can only give rise to a fully general moral principle when it is on the verge, at least in respect of its generality, of becoming a piece of metaphysics (perhaps a theological dogma),[1] whereas the intimate connexion of myth with ritual has been constantly

---

[1] What I have called tribal morality lacks, it has been seen, moral principles in the full sense.

stressed by students of the subject.[1] We may compare the observation, frequently made, that for the most part, and for most people, the Greek and Roman religions in classical times lacked any real moral efficacy, and were, in the sphere of conduct, matters of ritual and taboo applying only to a small fraction of life. As for ritual, one may perhaps epigrammatize and say that it is a matter of rules, whereas morality in the strict sense is a matter of principles.[2]

I am not forgetting Parmenides, Empedocles and Lucretius when I say that metaphysics is prose, whereas the kinship of myth is with poetry and poetic drama, with music and song and ritual dance.[3] The term *Begriffsdichtung* has, indeed, been applied to metaphysics;[4] I cannot think it adequate, but in any case *Begriffsdichtung* is a very peculiar kind of *Dichtung*, and there is much to be said for the suggestion that the phrase comes near to being contradictory (but then, some will say, that is the trouble).

[1] F. M. Cornford, *Principium Sapientiae* (London, 1952), Part II. The name of S. H. Hooke is prominent in this field.

[2] By itself this is clearly inadequate; the state of mind of the officiant and participators may be highly important.

[3] One may still, despite its antiquated features, compare G. B. Vico, *La scienza nuova* (first edition, 1725).

[4] F. A. Lange, *Geschichte des Materialismus* (ed. 2, 1873–5), ii. 4. 4.

II

A. C. EWING

THE AUTONOMY OF ETHICS

By the title I mean to express the contention that ethical and indeed valuational concepts generally are quite distinctive and cannot simply be reduced to those of any other branch of thought (or any combination of them). The autonomy of ethics has been defended especially against 'naturalism', which sought to reduce ethical concepts to empirical concepts falling within the sphere of a natural science, usually psychology; but I should, like Kant and Moore, the two most famous protagonists of autonomy, regard it as excluding also their reduction to concepts of metaphysics or theology; and the main reasons for this are on principle, I think, similar to those which tell against naturalism. Good, right, obligation are not at all like non-ethical concepts, and if we try to reduce them to the latter there is always an essential element left out, whether the concepts are scientific or metaphysical, unless indeed it is smuggled in indirectly so that the concepts in terms of which ethics is analysed are after all not really non-ethical. It is unlikely, I imagine, that I shall find here advocates of ethical naturalism in the sense in which Moore rejected it, but theologians certainly should be on the alert against failing as the result of their theology to do justice to the specific nature of ethics.

The most fundamental objection to naturalism is that it reduces what ought to be to what is.[1] No doubt it does not do this in a crude blatant way, at least when it is expounded by a reasonably competent philosopher. It is all too obvious that many things are which ought not to be. But naturalism does it in a more subtle fashion (except in so far as it already implicitly presupposes

---

[1] The relevance of this may not be quite obvious because in combating naturalism here I have spoken of 'good' rather than of 'ought', but 'good' either includes 'ought' in its meaning or at any rate entails a reference to 'ought'.

C

genuinely ethical concepts in its account and is therefore not really naturalistic). It falls back on the actual purposes, feelings, desires, approvals of men and defines 'good' and 'ought' in terms of these. For instance it is maintained that 'good' should be defined simply in terms of human desire. But this will not do. Even if men only desire what is good—and in view of the existence of vindictive cruelty this is very hard to accept—it is quite certain that they do not always desire a thing in proportion to its goodness or even in proportion to the degree of goodness they suppose it to possess, and that is quite sufficient to overthrow the definition. For a definition of 'good' in terms of actual desires would entail a definition of 'better' in terms of 'desired more' and would therefore be incompatible with men desiring the lesser good more than the greater (e.g. with the fact that most men desire a present good more than a slightly greater future good or happiness more than virtue). If on the other hand we define 'good' as what is the object of desire of man *qua* rational, we must either define 'rational' in terms of the way in which people actually think about objects of desire, which need not be always right, or admit the notion of what we *ought* to think or desire in a sense in which it cannot be analysed in terms of the merely actual and therefore can no longer be reduced to the content of a natural science. Similar objections may be brought against other naturalist definitions. Thus the theory popular today that ought-judgements are to be regarded as decisions to act is incompatible, as its exponents are finding, with there being such a thing as sin, i.e. voluntarily not doing what you think you ought, or at least with any sinful decision as opposed to sinning by merely neglecting to make a decision. And there is nothing in the nature of the concept of 'good' or 'ought' which necessarily excludes even all men being mistaken in some point as to what is good or what they ought to do, as all men probably were at one time mistaken about the duty of forgiving their enemies. 'Good' and 'ought' cannot be defined merely in terms of actual attitudes, etc., of men, because no class of these can be specified which is always justified. Other forms of naturalism define 'good' in terms of the things (experiences, states of mind) which are commonly pronounced good, but in that case anybody who disagreed with commonly accepted ethical principles would be verbally contradicting himself, for by 'good' would be meant just those things which are commonly pronounced good. As Hare, a thinker by no means predisposed against the characteristic modern movements in moral philosophy in this country, put it, value-terms have the special function of commending, and if they are defined[1] in terms of other words which do not themselves perform this function there are no means left of performing it.[2]

Modern opposition to Moore's view has, however, not come only from naturalists. According to one very important line of criticism the trouble is indeed that he did not carry the autonomy of ethics far enough. In Moore's form of non-naturalism, as is well known, the fundamental term of ethics was a single indefinable quality, good, called 'non-natural' in order to distinguish it from any quality which falls within the realm of natural science. ('Non-natural' must be sharply distinguished here from supernatural as this term is ordinarily understood. Moore would have been the last person to wish to introduce 'supernatural' entities into his ethics.) Although he denied that the goodness of a thing was part of its description[3] and even suggested that the distinction between natural and non-natural properties might be based on this circumstance,[4] he has been commonly understood as holding that it was as much as any other quality an objective part of the real world, at least of human states of mind and experiences, and objectivists since his time have probably generally thought in this way, though they sometimes have dwelt more on the objective relation of obligation than on the objective quality of goodness or even like myself defined the latter in terms of the former. But to think like this, it is said, is to assimilate ethical and evaluative judgements too much to descriptive judgements and thus to fail to do justice to their own distinctive function, which is not to describe. If an ordinary empirical affirmative descriptive judgement is true, the qualities and relations which it ascribes to its object must exist quite objectively in the latter. Thus if I say that

---

[1] In this article I am using 'define' in Moore's sense, in which it is equivalent to 'analyse', and leaving open the question whether the fundamental concepts of ethics might not be defined naturalistically in some other sense of 'define', e.g. by giving concomitants.

[2] v. The Language of Morals, pp. 92–3. [3] Philosophical Studies, p. 274.

[4] The Philosophy of G. E. Moore, p. 591.

an object is round or that I have a pain, these propositions cannot be true unless the quality of roundness actually exists in the thing and the quality of painfulness actually exists in my experience. But are we to think of goodness as such an objective quality? Judgements that something is good are not descriptive, and therefore their truth need not consist in that sort of correspondence which occurs when in a factual proposition we truly ascribe a quality or relation to some object. They perform the quite different function of evaluating, and to evaluate is not to assert the existence of new special qualities in what is evaluated. It is rather to adopt an attitude for or against it and claim that that attitude is justified by the nature of the object. I have been influenced by this line of thought and am therefore not now convinced that the objectivity of ethics, or of value-judgements generally, requires the existence of what Moore called non-natural qualities. I should still say that an ethical judgement can properly be called true or false, but what it says that is true or false is not that certain qualities or relations exist but that certain attitudes and actions are justified or imposed on us as obligatory by the facts. (Verbally it may be argued that, since 'justified' is an adjective, it does ascribe a quality after all, but it may be replied that it at any rate does not ascribe one in the sense in which descriptive judgements do so.) On such a view the autonomy of ethics goes even further than on the kind of objectivist view to which I have been referring. It is not that there is an objective property existing in what is good quite different from any properties of natural science and that value-judgements ascribe this property, but that they do something different in kind from what is done by factual judgements, which are usually thought of as ascribing properties. This view, to which I am now sympathetic, need not, I repeat, involve a denial of the objectivity of ethics. Ethical and valuational judgements can still be true or false, valid or invalid, in a sense which cannot be reduced to any statement about what people actually think, desire, decide, command or feel. The way in which they are true is not quite the way in which descriptive judgements are. But then are hypothetical or mathematical judgements true in just the same way as straightforward categorical?

If naturalism is false, it follows not only that ethical judgements cannot be *reduced* without residuum to judgements that fall within a natural science but that they cannot be *deduced formally* from any such judgements. There is no valid formal way of deducing the 'good' or the 'ought' from the 'is'. Yet at the same time ethical judgements clearly are in some way based on factual. We judge what we ought to do because of what the situation is or at least appears to us to be; we judge something to be good or bad because of its factual nature. This, I think, is the main truth in naturalism. I do not hold now that we need to interpolate a 'non-natural' property of goodness or obligatoriness actually existing in the things pronounced good or the acts pronounced obligatory, but this does not mean that ethical judgements and value judgements generally are just factual judgements telling us of the existence of certain natural properties. They are based on, but are not themselves judgements about, natural properties.

An important distinction must, however, be made here. We can infer the value from the factual nature of a thing in the sense that, if we know it has certain factual properties, e.g. painfulness in the case of an experience, we can infer (non-formally) that it is in so far good or bad. But from no factual proposition whatever can we infer that things which have such properties will be intrinsically good or bad, and similarly from factual propositions alone we cannot infer that any act of a given kind in a given situation will be morally wrong or right. Perhaps this may be illuminated by a logical analogy. We can infer from the factual premisses that *A* is a man and all men are mortal that *A* is mortal, but that premisses of such a form entail such a conclusion could not itself be inferred from any factual premisses. Similarly we can infer from '*A* is painful' that 'in so far *A* is bad', but the proposition that 'if *A* is painful, it is in so far bad' cannot be inferred from any factual premisses. In this respect there is an autonomy of logic and an autonomy of ethics. This autonomy is violated by supposed metaphysical deductions of ethical propositions. The link between facts and values must be grasped by a specific ethical insight for which no metaphysical substitute can be provided.

I consider it to be involved in the 'autonomy' of ethics that the goodness or badness, rightness or wrongness of anything that is really good or bad, right or wrong, follows from the inherent nature of what is pronounced good, etc., in its context and is necessarily fixed by this. That pain is intrinsically bad depends on the nature of pain as affecting sentient creatures, and being what it is pain could not be otherwise than bad. If an act is justifiably condemned as wrong, that act could not possibly have been other than wrong under the circumstances, its character being what it is. This can be illustrated by imagining somebody who was strongly tempted to do something but realized that it was wrong. Suppose he said—I want to do this very much but I do not want to do what is wrong, so I shall adopt a course of action which is like the proposed one in all other respects but does not possess the additional character of wrongness. In that way I shall both eat my cake and have it, fulfil both my purposes, do what I want and avoid sin. It is obvious that such a suggestion would be utterly absurd; if the act is wrong at all, it *must* be wrong being what it is and the circumstances being what they are. Wrongness is not something that can be thus eliminated, as one might substitute for a course of action one that differed from it in respect of a single empirical quality, and the absurdity of supposing that it could (if not exactly a logical absurdity) is at any rate quite different from the absurdity of believing or planning what conflicts with known causal laws. This feature of autonomy conflicts at any rate with the view which has been held by some theologians and, e.g., the philosopher Descartes, although I think officially condemned by the Roman Church, to the effect that the laws of ethics are fixed solely by God's will. If this view were true, the rightness or wrongness of actions would be quite independent of their circumstances and factual nature.

This relatively lengthy introduction is intended to clarify the position from the point of view of pure ethics before considering the relation of ethics to theology. The reason why theological conceptions are apt to clash with the autonomy of ethics is because it is felt that ethics itself must depend on the nature of God if the concept of God is really to be given the absolute status which theology assigns to it. I am aware that this is a somewhat vague statement: a part of the object of the present paper is to make it a little more precise. In discussing the matter I shall be discussing various views on their own merits (or demerits); I shall not be concerned with attributing them to any particular persons or ecclesiastical body. I am speaking as one who does not see ground for attributing supernatural authority to any Church except in any sense in which a 'supernatural' origin or status may be claimed for all wisdom and goodness in man.

Now the simplest and most radical way of making all ethical principles dependent on God would be to say that their validity just depended on their being decrees fixed by the will of God. In that case it would naturally follow that 'I ought to do *A*' was to be defined as 'it is God's will that I should do *A*'. I have already referred to this view as one to which there are very serious objections. In the first place, if 'obligatory' just means 'commanded by God', the question arises why God should command any one thing rather than any other. We cannot say that he commands it because it ought to be done, for that would have to be translated into 'God commands it because it is commanded by God'. If it were said in reply that God's commands determined what we ought to do but that these commands were only issued because it was good that they should be or because obedience to them did good, this would still make judgements about the good, at least, independent of the will of God, and we should not have given a definition of all fundamental ethical concepts in terms of God or made ethics dependent on God. If what was good or bad as well as what ought to be done were fixed by God's will, then there could be no reason whatever for God willing in any particular way. His commands would become purely arbitrary, and while the idea of God as issuing arbitrary commands has sometimes been welcomed as a tribute to his omnipotence, omnipotence without goodness is surely an idea of no religious value whatever, and the idea of God would be deprived of all ethical content. For to say that God was good would be just to say he was God: he would be good by definition whatever he should do. Since there was no ethical reason for his commands, God might in that case just as well command us to cheat, torture and murder, and then it would really be our duty to act like this.

Secondly, why obey God's commands? Because I ought to do so. Since 'I ought to do *A*' is held to mean 'God commands me to do *A'*, this can only mean that I am commanded by God to obey God's commands, which supplies no further reason whatever. Because God is good? This could only mean on the definition given that God carries out his own commands. Because I love God? This presupposes two propositions as to what I ought to do which could not without a vicious circle be validated by referring again to God's commands, i.e. that I ought to obey the commands of God if I love him and that I ought to love God. Because God will punish me if I do not obey? This might be a very good reason from the prudential point of view, but these considerations of self-interest cannot be an adequate basis for ethics. Even if there is some affinity between command and obligation, a mere command, however powerful the being who issues it, cannot of itself create obligation. Without a prior conception of God as good or his commands as right God would have no more claim on our obedience than Hitler or Stalin except that he would have more power than even they ever had to make things uncomfortable for those who disobey him. It is only because the notion of God (for Christians at least) already includes the notion of perfect goodness that we are inclined to think it self-evident that we ought to obey God.

It should be noted that this theological definition fails for the same kind of reason as do the naturalistic definitions of the fundamental concepts of ethics. It is not subject, indeed, to the same specific objections. We cannot, for instance, argue against it on the ground that God is sometimes wrong, as we argued against the naturalistic definitions on the ground that men are so. But it shares with the naturalistic definitions the error of either reducing ethical statements to merely factual ones, here about the acts of God, or producing a circular definition by presupposing specifically ethical concepts in the terms intended to define them. If God is not conceived as good in a specifically ethical sense but 'good' functions just as an adjective to mean 'what God wants', ethics is reduced to a mere prudent subservience to superior power; if on the other hand in the definition of good or right as willed by God goodness in a properly ethical sense is already presupposed, the definition is a circular one and leaves undefined some fundamental

ethical term. As we can find no necessary relation between goodness and obligation on the one hand and the alleged naturalist
definitions on the other, so we can find no necessary relation
between being commanded or willed by God and being obligatory
or good, unless we already assume the goodness of God, thus
exposing ourselves to the charge of being guilty of a vicious circle,
since we should in that case have defined both God in terms of
goodness and goodness in terms of God. Just as it is a fatal
objection to the naturalist definitions of good that they do not
provide ground for obligation or any ethical reason why we ought
to do any one thing rather than any other, so the theological
definition is open to the objection that a command cannot in itself
be a moral reason for action. Like naturalist definitions the
theological definition would destroy what Kant calls the autonomy of ethics by refusing to recognize the uniqueness of its
fundamental concepts and trying to make it a mere branch of
another study, in this case not a natural science but theology. Both
types of view overlook the gulf between the 'ought' and the 'is' so
far as to maintain that you can reduce propositions about the
former to propositions about what actually is the case. The
theological view is more ethical than the naturalist only in so far as
it covertly reintroduces ethical concepts which it had verbally
tried to explain away by analysing them in terms of commands.
Except in so far as it smuggles such concepts in again, it makes the
fulfilment of duty consist just in obeying the stronger, for if you
once exclude the specifically ethical element from the concept of
the deity God has no claim on us except of mere power, and if you
include it ethics is needed to define the fundamental concepts of
theology and not theology to define the fundamental concepts of
ethics.

Most theologians and philosophers of religion do not go so far
as to accept the view which I have just criticized, but they still
are apt to make ethical principles dependent on God in some way.
Many would no doubt follow in some form the distinction of
Leibniz who held that the laws of ethics (and logic) depended on
God's understanding but not on his will. But is it really more
possible to conceive God as making the laws of ethics (or logic)
by thinking them than to conceive him as making them by willing

them? They would still surely be essentially arbitrary unless God thought them *because* they were necessarily true.

But surely, it may be urged, a believer in God must hold that all things, and therefore the laws of ethics, depend on God? Most theists by no means like the idea of something independent of God limiting him, and it is for this reason chiefly that the laws of ethics have been said to be dependent on God. We must, however, remember that the laws of ethics are not in any case a separate set of *things*. If there were such a set of existing things independent of him, God would obviously be limited in a way very uncongenial to Christian theology (and the theology of most or all religions). The notion of a God limited in this sense certainly does not commend itself to religious experience and is very different from the notion of God held to be derived from the Christian revelation. But we must not confuse laws with existent entities, and when we realize this we can see that we might hold that God created the whole universe without holding that he created the laws of ethics (or of logic for that matter). These laws are just the sort of thing that could not from the nature of the case be created at all. But without having been created, it may be asked, do they not at least depend for their validity on God? Could they be valid if God did not exist? Well, if God has created the whole cosmos, or it is eternally dependent on him, nothing could exist at all without God, and therefore without God there would be no being in existence to whom the laws of ethics could apply. In that sense, if it is a proper sense of the words, a theologian might readily admit that the laws of ethics depended on God. But that is not to say that they are made by God as laws and do not follow from their inherent content. Thus it is surely wicked deliberately to inflict pain unnecessarily because of the nature of pain, and not primarily because God decreed that it should be so. On the contrary, if God forbids it, it is because of the inherent nature of the act, from which its wrongness already necessarily follows. I do not mean to say that the necessity of ethical propositions is the same necessity as that of logic, but, as I have pointed out, there is some necessity here. That being so, it is not the case that the very concept of duty presupposes that of God: it is our duty to refrain from wanton infliction of pain whether God exists or not. (No doubt, if God exists, we have some duties which we otherwise would not have, e.g. at the very least sometimes to think of God, but similarly if a man's parents are alive he has duties which he would not have if they were dead.)

If we do not think of the laws of ethics as if they were separately existing things independent of God, the idea of even God being limited by them need not be offensive to the religious man. Obviously the limitation would be self-limitation and arise because God would just not be good if he did not limit himself in this fashion. Further, if the laws are not made by God, it is not because God is not powerful enough or not wise enough to make them, but because they are the sort of thing which could not possibly be made (or even made valid) by any being.

It has been contended that the concept of law implies that of lawgiver, and this has been made (even by Kant in his *Opus Postumum*) an argument from ethics to the existence of God. I do not myself see much force in this argument. Political laws imply a constituted authority that made or at least sanctions the laws, but moral laws are not laws in the sense in which political laws are, and I do not see that they necessarily imply such an authority. Political laws are laws made and coming into force at a given time; ethical laws do not come into force without having been valid before. To say that something is the law in the political sense is just to say that it is actually commanded in a certain way; to refer to an ethical law is to refer to what is right or wrong whatever the authorities may think about it. No doubt the theologian can say that at a higher remove moral laws too imply a lawgiver, only a lawgiver who is never in the wrong, but in view of the great *prima facie* difference of meaning between 'moral law' and 'political law' I do not see any plausible reason for saying it. We might perhaps almost as well argue that 'moral laws' can never be broken because 'natural laws' cannot be.

At the same time we must not push our argument too far. Even if one cannot argue that, because moral laws are valid, they are the commands of a God, it is clear that a person who for other reasons believes in God may naturally and reasonably think of moral laws as commands of God, not in the sense that God made them valid by commanding us to obey them but in the sense that

God, being supremely good, must recognize their rightness and so necessarily command us to obey them and judge us accordingly. For this and other reasons, such as that he feels himself to offend against the love of God if he breaks moral laws, the religious man, it cannot be denied, will have a somewhat different conception of duty and sin from the atheist or agnostic. So it may quite well be maintained that *his* ethical concepts already include or at least imply the notion of God. But this will be because his ethical concepts are not merely ethical but blended with concepts of religion. One cannot, therefore, say that there can be no ethical concepts without a concept of God. Of course there is a relation between ethics and religion, and a religious man's ethical thinking will be affected by his religion, but it does not follow that we cannot have any proper ethical thinking without the concept of God. We must not say that an atheist or agnostic is incapable of being ethical. It might indeed be argued that, although he does not consciously believe in God or even think of God when he thinks ethically, what he really has in mind is some confused concept which, when analysed and made clear, would be found to include implicitly an idea of God, so that he was inconsistent in denying or even doubting the existence of God and yet insisting on the validity of the moral law, which he could vindicate only by assuming what he doubted or denied. I suppose the most widely accepted line of argument for such a view is to the effect that the notion of obligation includes the idea of a command and a command implies a commander, only in the case of the moral law it will have to be a perfect and not a human commander. For reasons which I have already indicated I am not much impressed by this argument.

Again a theist must be careful how he uses the argument that he cannot be ethical without God's help. Obviously, if theism as ordinarily understood is true, since we could not even exist without God, we could not be moral without him. Further, it is not possible to agree with Kant's view that, whatever his circumstances, a man can display the good will. He cannot do so if he has the brain of an idiot. He could not if he were suckled by wolves and had no human contacts, at least unless he were himself innately a moral genius of a quite transcendent order. He cannot any longer if he falls a victim to certain diseases. Kant argues that, whatever happens to us and whatever our external limitations, we can at least try our best, but to try at all requires some concentration on the idea of what is right and the conditions I have mentioned make even this impossible. In such conditions we should not indeed act immorally, because we could not help ourselves, but we could not do our duty any more than animals. So for us to do our duty we must be provided with at least a certain minimum environment, and on a theistic view environment ultimately depends on God. However, this is not what has been usually meant by saying that we could not lead an ethically satisfactory life without the help of God. It has rather been meant that we can only reach high ethical standards if we are given help by some special supernatural action by God or some conscious experience by us of God. If this activity of God is one of which we are unconscious, I do not see how we can really argue on this topic. It is always possible to maintain that the atheist is unconsciously assisted in his moral efforts by God, but there can from the nature of the case be no empirical confirmation of this or even empirical evidence for this, and I do not see on what *a priori* grounds it could be maintained. If it be held on the other hand that we cannot attain any high moral level without the conscious experience of God, this seems inconsistent with the fact that there have been atheists and agnostics who according to all the criteria at our disposal were extremely good people ethically. We can indeed argue that they would have been still better if they had been religious, or that there are certain heights which none but the religious can attain, but to say that religion is a help to ethical attainment is not to say that the very possibility of any ethics presupposes religion. This distinction seems to me very important when we consider ethical arguments for the existence of God. If it could be shown that the belief in God is presupposed in the very possibility of any ethics at all, this would seem to me a quite conclusive argument for God, since we certainly know some ethical propositions to be valid. But if it can be shown only that the belief is a great help in the ethical life, this weakens the argument immeasurably. I do not myself see any legitimate way of passing from the premiss that a belief is useful to the conclusion that it is true unless some specific reason be produced for thinking that the belief would not have been useful if it had been false.

Are we to conclude from all this that there can be no argument from ethics to the existence of God? Not necessarily, for to say that ethical concepts properly thought out can provide an argument for believing in God or even logically entail the existence of God is not the same as to say that a reference to God is already included in the definition of all ethical terms. Anybody who believes in the 'argument from design' argues to the existence of God from certain features of animal bodies, but it would never occur to him to say that our concepts of these purely biological features must therefore be analysed in such a way as already to include the notion of God. His biology would still be like that of an agnostic and would not be based on concepts of a theological nature. This might still be so even if he accepted the cosmological proof, thus maintaining that the existence of the world logically entailed and did not merely provide probable evidence for the existence of God, at least unless he held the 'analytic' view of *a priori* reasoning, and if he did that I do not see how he could consistently have any *a priori* arguments for God at all. At the same time, although I certainly feel that there ought to be a valid argument from ethics for the existence of God, I unfortunately cannot produce one that seems to me to have any very great cogency. The most superficially obvious arguments at any rate seem to me to be cut off by the considerations I have mentioned above. At the same time I do not think that the belief in God is dependent mainly on argument for its justification.

However, in any case it seems to me that the road should rather be from ethics to theology than vice versa. Indeed even if the moral law were made by God it would not follow that in order to reach moral conceptions we must first have an idea of God. A theist holds that trees and stones depend for their existence on God, but as I have already implied he will not therefore insist that all our common-sense propositions about trees and stones have to be analysed in such a way as to include the notion of God. If God exists he is the *ratio essendi* of the things in the world, but he is not therefore, for us at least, their *ratio cognoscendi*, since we cannot deduce their nature from his, and the same would still hold as regards the moral law even if that were made by God. We should still have to admit that we could only deduce ethics from theology by first deciding what was good or right and then assuming that God, being good, wills that we should further the good and do the right, and such a line of argument obviously presupposes that we have already a conception of ethics, so that to use it to deduce ethics would involve a vicious circle. Even those Christians who accept their theology solely on the strength of revelation can hardly have any justification for doing so if they do not first assume at least that Christ is good, and this would already presuppose ethical criteria independent of theology. On the other hand it is certain that the value concepts are central to theology itself. It would be of no use believing in God if God were not conceived as ethically good in a sense at least analogous to that in which a man is good. And if we grant that God is good, we can give content to the notion of his goodness only by deriving the content from our ethical standards. Thus theology, even if it cannot be deduced from ethics, has at least to derive from this source its most essential ideas.

In conclusion, I turn to some possible misunderstandings which my paper may generate. It was not intended to commit me to saying that there could be no valid line of argument from ethics to God, although it did cast serious doubt on some of the attempts at such an argument. It may indeed be urged in reply to my contentions that what we regard as immediate knowledge of what is ethically right is also at the same time a knowledge of God, so that the good atheist or agnostic really knows God, although he fails to recognize that he does so. This may be true, but I do not see how we could possibly *justify* such a view as against a man who is obviously highly ethical but denies any awareness of God.

Further, I have no objection to admitting that for a theist part of virtue and part of one's duty is to be religious. But it does not follow from this that God makes moral laws in the sense I denied, only that we shall in some respects have different duties if we believe that God exists from any we can have if we do not. If a man is married, an important part of virtue and duty for him consists in being a good husband, but not if he is a bachelor; yet

it does not follow from this that the moral laws governing his matrimonial relations are made by his wife.

At the same time there are two respects in which the position of ethics relatively to God differs fundamentally from its position relatively to any other conceivable being. These points I indeed admitted in my paper but not emphatically enough, failing to realize quite how far my admissions carried me and that they make it misleading to insist without qualification on the full 'autonomy' of ethics.

(1) It is not only the case that for the religious man particular duties are added but that the whole spirit of ethics is transformed by the idea of God. The man who believes fervently in God will regard his duties as incumbent on him not only in virtue of the factual situation and consequences as visible empirically but also because God commands him to do his duty, and respect for the moral law will be supplemented by, or even merge into, reverence and love for God. It may even be said that the 'ought' for him is a different 'ought' because it is now not only an ethical but also a religious concept. But this will not give us new premisses to help us in deciding what our duty is to other men or what things are good in themselves, unless God is held to have revealed them explicitly, a position which I did not discuss. For, apart at least from revelation, our key to God's purposes can only be what we judge ethically right independently of belief in God. Further, I must continue to insist that, if we ignore the distinctively ethical and non-theological element involved, we cannot say even that we *ought* to obey God. This last proposition cannot possibly, I repeat, be reduced to a purely theological one without any specifically ethical content. The concept of ought is unique and cannot be reduced to any factual relation to God. Theism can add a new tone to ethics, but it cannot create ethics.

(2) If nothing can exist without God, then there could be nothing to which ethical laws applied if there were no God. Now a contrafactual conditional may admittedly be true even if there is nothing which conforms to the condition laid down in its protasis. But it may be said that this is only because we assume some things to exist. It is doubtful whether, if nothing at all existed, such a proposition could be true except in the very academic hypothetical

sense that it would have been true if something had existed. I do not wish to defend the notion of subsistent entities or subsistent truths, and if every existent thing depends on God the notion of an ethics which is completely independent of God becomes somewhat tenuous, to say the least. But I want to insist that this is a very different mode of dependence from the one the assertion of which I was criticizing. To assert it is to say that the whole concept of duty would be inapplicable if there were no God merely because there would then be no existents for it to apply to; it is not to deny that our particular, not specifically religious, duties follow from the nature of beings other than God in such a way that they would still be duties even if the atheist were right and there were no God. They still do not require an additional premiss about God. Nor is it saying that they could ever conceivably be deduced from the nature of God without first assuming that God is good and then interpreting his goodness in terms of our best ethical standards. Finally, even if there could be no moral laws if God did not exist, it does not follow that it is good sense to say that God decided what the laws should be. Exactly the same argument would apply to the laws of logic, namely that, if there were no God, nothing would exist to which the laws could apply, yet it is notoriously open to objection to say that it is only the result of God's decision that self-contradictory things cannot exist. It is said that, although God decides what the moral laws are to be, he could not decide otherwise than he does without contradicting his nature because he is good. But what is goodness except doing the best because it is the best, and must not therefore even God's actions presuppose, as logically prior, the recognition of ethical principles?

III

J. S. DICKIE

WHAT ARE THE
LIMITS OF METAPHYSICS?

> There were wise students among the Greeks who brought in
> gods to hide the truths of divinity under the guise of fables. So
> also Plato clothed philosophy in mathematics.
>
> ST THOMAS AQUINAS

What I am proposing is a very modest thing, not to soar the meta-physical heights but to explore the foundations.

I begin with this comment by Father Owens in his *Aristotle's Doctrine of Being*:[1]

'Aristotle is *beginning* his consideration with the individuals, and asking how *they* can be known as *one and the same*. Plato, on the contrary, starts his consideration with the Form, and asks how it can remain one and the same in the numerically infinite individuals. His question is how the Form "must be posited in the infinity of things in generation, either (*a*) as dispersed and multiplied, or (*b*) as becoming outside itself in its entirety—which would seem to be the most impossible notion of all—as at once *the same and one* both in one and in many".'

There is here a radical disparity in the way of approach. The primary consideration for Aristotle is the physical thing, the thing which comes-to-be and passes-away. It is this startling fact of *real change* which has to be reckoned with and studied in all its require-ments. 'This approach throws the question from the realm of logic into the terrain of the *Physics*. Aristotle is looking for a universal form *within* sensible things.'

[1] Joseph Owens, C.SS.R. *The Doctrine of Being in the Aristotelian Metaphysics*, (Pontifical Institute of Mediaeval Studies, Toronto, 1951), p. 132.

Plato is looking elsewhere, not at the physical thing which comes-to-be, but always separated from it and looking instead at a conceptualized image of real change, an abstract mathematical reconstruction of it:

'What puzzles me is that when the units were apart from each other each was one, and there was as yet no two, whereas as soon as they had approached each other there was the cause of the coming into being of two, namely the union in which they were put next to each other. Nor again can I any longer persuade myself that if we divide one it is the division this time that causes two to come into being; for then the cause of two would be the opposite of that just suggested: a moment ago it was because the units were brought into close proximity each to each, and now it is because they are kept away and separated each from each. And for that matter I no longer feel sure that by adhering to the old method I can understand how a unit comes into being or perishes or exists; that method has lost all attraction for me, and in its place I am gaily substituting a new sort of hotch-potch of my own.'[1]

It is to this 'mathematization' of the continuum that the Ideal theory responds. The method of dialectic is devised to cope with the One-Many paradox so construed. It was as such admirably adapted as a weapon against the Sophists, for there is a close and direct connexion between these intractable 'units' and the 'either-or' logomachy which Plato attacked in the *Philebus* (57d).

The new method is a new approach to measurement, a new conception of proportionality and of the 'unit'.

The 'old method'—the Pythagorean theory of proportionality based on discrete numbers—is oblivious to 'the necessary nature of the process of becoming':

'We are saying like them that Measurement is involved in all that is brought into being . . . but . . . we find them confusing these two types of measurement, which are in fact so different, just because they have judged them to be of like nature' (*Politicus*, 285a).[2]

---

[1] *Phaedo*, 97, transl. Hackforth.
[2] *Plato's Statesman*, transl. J. B. Skemp (London, 1952).

Professor Grube summarizes the two types of measurement (*Politicus*, 283d, e) thus:

'You think that what is smaller is naturally so in relation to what is bigger and to nothing else, and vice versa. Yet what exceeds the mean or is exceeded by it we again speak of as really coming to be, and in this way the good among us differ from the bad.'[1]

This recognition, namely that *the nature of things* holds the possibility of 'exceeding or being exceeded by', is the basic recognition of a genuine *techne*.

This broader conception of proportionality is based on the continuous magnitudes of geometry. Plato, unlike the Pythagoreans, must have appreciated the immense implications of the discovery of irrational magnitudes. Imagine yourself for a moment confronted for the first time with the proposition that the diagonal of a square is not commensurable with the side: that they have no measure in common, that no unit of magnitude taken any number of times will measure both of them. And yet—the experiment is easy to set up: take *one* and *one*, and by a simple 'construction' there comes-to-be something entirely new and novel. It would not be surprising if you found here, in this realm of continuous magnitude, infinitely divisible but never divided, a clue or 'model' with which to explore 'the necessary nature of the process of becoming'. The result would be a methodological revolution—something in the nature of what Kant, at a later moment of history, encountered and called a 'Copernican revolution'. Instead of beginning with the 'unit' and enquiring how, by composition or separation, things come-to-be in respect of it, the true method of *search* is the other way round: by what method of systematic and proportionate division does the 'unit' come-to-be out of the continuum of what-is?

The procedure has a counterpart in the method of exhaustion later employed by Euclid:

'In this method we do *not* say that the increased inscribed figure or the decreased circumscribed figure actually reach the limit—namely, the unknown figure (for this, the Greeks thought, would involve them in fundamental difficulties about the infinitely small). We say only that the inscribed or circumscribed figure can be made to approach *as closely as we like* to the figure under consideration.'[1]

What is significant here, and why the method is a notable discovery of the first magnitude, is the new conception of *constructability* which it inaugurated. The device of the construction is not to construct the circle. The existence of the circle is recognized in what the construction enables the geometer to construe, being present as an 'hypothesis' underlying the *possibility* of his performance:

'With this type of exhaustion granted, it can be shown by reduction to absurdity that the area or volume under consideration must correspond to some given formulation, for, if not, a basic contradiction will appear.'[1]

This formal contradiction is available to him—and indeed arises for him at all—because there is finality in the spatial continuum. Were it not so, there would be endless regress and the contradiction would have no decisive effect.[2]

The onus in this Euclidean method is on constructability. And so, too, in Plato's *metretike*.[3] The presupposition of a continuum is common to both: the refusal in each of dividedness, the search in each for a method of division, 'an identical unity being thus found simultaneously in unity and in plurality' (*Philebus*, 15b).

The dialectical method encounters a hazard unknown to the other. Of this Plato is acutely aware. Language easily lends itself to the paradox, as Socrates puts it in the *Philebus*, 'that a pair of completely dissimilar things are completely similar': the paradox being averted by the device of designating the things in question by a name other than their own:

Soc.: You say, I mean, that all pleasant things are good.

---

[1] Marshall Clagett, *Greek Science in Antiquity* (London, Abelard-Schuman, 1957), p. 61.

[2] 'In a very real sense one must know the answer before he begins. He assumes a given formulation and then shows that if it is not true a contradiction follows.' *Ibid.*, p. 61.

[3] Euclidean, but of course Eudoxus could have invented it, in which case Plato would have been acquainted with it.

Now of course nobody attempts to maintain the thesis that pleasant things are not pleasant; but though they are in some cases (indeed in most) bad and in others good—so those who think with me maintain—nevertheless you designate them all as good, although you would agree that they are unlike if anyone were to press you in argument. . . .

Prot.: What do you mean, Socrates? Do you imagine that anyone will agree, after maintaining that pleasure is the good —that having done that he will endure to be told by you that certain pleasures are bad?

Soc.: Well, at all events you will allow that they are unlike, and in some cases opposite to, each other.

Prot.: Not in so far as they are just pleasures.[1]

The geometer, so Plato thought, is saved from this false dialectic by having no dialectic at all. There is no dispute about 'angle' making it available for one geometer to say to another 'Not in so far as they are just angles'. He cannot do with 'angle' what Protarchus does with 'pleasure' for the reason that he cannot construct 'angle'. If it be that he constructs an angle at random, what he constructs is not a random angle. There are three forms of angle, and within these limits there is constructability: there is real possibility, but no randomness. This I take to be Plato's view.

The presupposition of equi-possibility as an overall require-ment would put an end to geometry, precluding the possibility of setting up the experiment which would disprove it; and this, Plato thought, is brought home to the geometer in that he is able to proceed. He is able to *begin* and to go on to do what he does. There is for him a viable field of enquiry given these prescribed limits; and though he is not engaged in 'giving an account' of the coming-to-be of these limits, they confront him in the spatial continuum in a way that he cannot refuse and, in a measure, 'understand'.

The geometer does in that respect take his *arche* for granted. He takes coming-to-be for granted. He does this, Plato is saying, not by declaration or designation—*deciding* merely that there are to be three forms of angle and *agreeing* to work within these

[1] *Philebus*, 13a, b, transl. Hackforth, *Plato's Examination of Pleasure* (Cambridge, 1945), p. 16.

prescribed limits. If Plato is right, the geometer *knows* this; he is made inescapably aware that his threefold division is both exclusive and exhaustive, his certainty of finality being his witness to the continuum.

Plato's philosopher finds here an image of his own method. If he can divide and in so doing acquire the assurance that his division is exclusive and at the same time exhaustive, he will have gained insight into the One; by persistent division (as in the method of exhaustion) he will see the One coming-to-be in the unlimited Many and in the constructability of his dialectic 'construe' the causal efficacy of the Form:

'We ought, whatever it be that we are dealing with, to assume a single form and search for it, for we shall find it there contained; then, if we have laid hold of that, we must go on from one form to look for two, otherwise for three or some other number of forms: and we must do the same again with each of the "ones" thus reached, until we come to see not merely that the one we started with is a one and an unlimited many, but also just how many it is . . .; but your clever modern man, while making his One (or his Many, as the case may be) more quickly or more slowly than is proper, when he has got his One proceeds to his unlimited number straight away, allowing the intermediates to escape him; whereas it is the recognition of these intermediates that makes all the difference between a philosophical and a contentious discussion.'[1]

This dialectic is a supreme achievement, as much in what it refuses as in the new conception of method which it projects. Indeed its very success against eristic is, paradoxically enough, the measure of its failure to engender in itself a continuing existence.

The sterility which afflicts it is easier to see, perhaps, from the first statement of it in the *Phaedo*. The method is there presented as a progressive argument in two stages. (*a*) If the thing has a nature, no unit of explanation ready to hand will take the measure of it. The method is to penetrate to the nature of the thing by

[1] Hackforth, pp. 23-4.

letting the true unit emerge as an insight in the course of systematic search: beginning not by fixing the unit but by taking a stand on the safe *hypothesis*, namely, that there is a coming-to-be in the thing by virtue of which it is what it is:

'Would you not loudly protest that the only way you know of, by which anything comes-to-be, is by participating in the special being in which it does participate' (*Phaedo*, 101c).

(*b*) This first hypothesis, once it has been established, enters into the dialectic as a question; it may then be safely discarded in favour of a second hypothesis, this new unit of explanation being now available because proper safeguards have been laid down for its use:

'Thus if you were to ask me what must come to be present in a thing's body to make it hot, I should not give you that safe stupid answer "heat", but a cleverer one now at my disposal, namely "fire". Again, if you ask what must come to be present in a body to make it sick, I shall not say "sickness" but "fever". Similarly, what must be present in a number for it to be odd? Not oddness, but a unit; and so on. I wonder if you see clearly by now what I want?' (*Phaedo*, 105b, c).[1]

So much is clear. Fire, though hot, can become cold (as 5, though odd, can become even by a process of doubling). But fire does not become fire by the process of taking away cold or of adding heat to cold: 'fire, though not the opposite of cold, will yet not admit cold'. In other words, because primary substance harbours contradictories, a true causal explanation will be achieved not by measuring heat against cold but by measuring both against what comes-to-be, namely, fire: that is to say, not as the coming together of hot and cold in a proportion but as a 'mean' established in the continuum of 'the hot'.

It is important to have this said—assuming, as I am suggesting he did, that Plato got thus far towards saying it. What is not tolerable is Plato's preoccupation even here with the number continuum and the proposal consequent upon this to dispense

---

[1] *Plato's Phaedo*, transl. Hackforth (Cambridge, 1955), p. 158.

with a second-order empirical investigation and to put in its place a linguistic dialectic. It is not merely that this dialectic has nothing to deploy itself *on*: the method of division, as we find it fully articulated in the *Philebus*, is itself the demonstration of precisely this, being in effect a proof by exhaustion that there is no recalcitrant residue and that the continuum is through and through divisible. If only we avoid eristic, escaping at each stage of the dialectic a collapse into paradox, the truth will eventually make *itself* known—a clearly visible Form shining in the light of the Good.

Aristotle, in his frequent criticisms of the Platonic dialectic, seldom acknowledges his own indebtedness to it. I wish now to consider some of these objections with a view to bringing out both the indebtedness and also the important issue on which they are divided.

(1) The dialectic of *diaeresis* is described, in the *Prior Analytics*, as a small part of the syllogistic method: division is a weak syllogism; what it ought to prove, it begs, for it takes the universal as *middle*.[1]

It would be a great mistake to suppose, because this is said in the *Prior Analytics*, that the issue between the two methods is one of logic merely. The Aristotelian syllogism is much more than an instrument of exposition or of instruction. It is presented in the *Posterior Analytics* as a method of *search*. Viewed as *search* a syllogism is the response to a question: 'in all search we are asking whether there is a middle, or what it is; for the cause is the middle, and we are always seeking the cause'.[2] It is for this reason that Aristotle, in the *Ethics*, describes *deliberation* as a 'kind of search',[3] the middle there being the *mean* in action. So too in the theoretical syllogism the true middle is not the middle *term* as such but that *mean* which the middle term enables us, in the syllogistic context, to *see*. And in that context the middle term is crucial in its capacity of defining the major: in response to the question 'Why the inherence of *A* in *C*?' the definition of *A* by *B* has the effect of establishing a viable field of search, in that the minor can *now* be seen as a *mean* within the limits prescribed.

It is precisely this which Aristotle is saying the method of

---

[1] *An. Pr.*, I, 46a, b.   [2] *An. Post.*, II, 90a.   [3] *N.E.*, VI, 9

division fails to accomplish. Because it has no effective middle the cause assigned is not the actual ground in reality of the fact to be explained. The inclination and persuasion of the method has a contrary intention: 'it always establishes something *more general* than the attribute in question. From the beginning this very point escaped all those who used this method of division. And they went on to persuade men that it was possible to make a demonstration of substance and of essence.'

Another way of putting this is to say that Plato had got hold of the wrong continuum, and he was led into this by accepting too readily the mathematical model available to him. The *mean* is thus defined by a division assumed to be self-explanatory on the ground that it is complete. But even if the division were complete, it would not on that ground alone be self-explanatory—though this could be claimed for the geometer's division of angle.

(2) In a famous passage in the *de gen. et corr.* (335b7) Aristotle asks the question, 'if the forms are causes, why do they not always generate continually but only intermittently, since the forms and the partakers in them are always there?'[1]

It is sometimes said that Aristotle is complaining here that the Forms cannot play the part of efficient or moving causes. I think this is to do less than justice to his perception of what is missing. The complaint is not that Plato omitted to consider the efficient cause but that he failed to get within reach of authentic cause at all. 'The nature of the Forms', he is saying, 'are not adequate to account for coming-to-be' (*de gen.*, 335b.10); and in the *Metaphysics* Plato is said to recognize neither efficient nor final causes (988a8).

And this, after all, is only a different way of putting the first objection. Misled, again, by the mathematical continuum Plato mistook the absence of *equi-possibility* for cause; whereas the absence of true cause is *chance*. The two conceptions are poles apart. The application of the one is to a construction; the other makes a statement.

Thus it is possible for things to come *together* by chance, it is not possible that they come-to-*be* by chance. Chance is the refusal of real change; it is the presupposition of a mechanistic

[1] Transl. E. S. Forster, Loeb Classical Library.

universe in which things allegedly come-to-be by the coming together of certain unalterable units.

Aristotle was, it seems, the first to recognize this and to see the implications of it:

'For, according to Empedocles, nothing comes-to-be by their coming together by chance, but by their coming together in a certain proportion. What then is the cause of this? It is certainly not Fire or Earth; but neither is it Love and Strife, for the former is a cause of "association" only and the latter of dissociation only. No: the cause is the substance of each thing and not merely, as he says, "a mingling and separation of things mingled"; and chance, not proportion, is the name applied to these happenings: for it is possible for things to be mixed by chance. The cause, then, of things which exist naturally is that they are in such-and-such a condition, and this is what constitutes the nature of each thing, about which he says nothing' (*de gen.*, 333b).[1]

Professor Waddington, in his recent book *The Strategy of the Genes*, exposes the atomism of the Darwinists in exactly similar terms:

'Darwin's theory was interpreted to mean that all living things, man included, had been brought into being by the collocation of two entirely different factors; on the one hand the occurrence of mutations whose nature was totally unconnected with any ambient circumstances, and on the other a sieving process in which the environment merely selected from among organisms which were offered to it ready-made as units of being, not in any way of potentiality. Any further influence which the environment might have was degraded to the status of mere "noise" in the system of genetic determination.'[2]

And he proposes, alike with Aristotle, a conception of organic Form 'comprising potentialities as well as what is actually realized in any given individual'.

Plato's atomism, on the contrary, was the discrete units of the

---

[1] The passage continues 'There is nothing about The Nature of Things in his treatise. And yet it is this which is the excellence and the good of each thing, whereas he gives all the credit to the mixing process.'

[2] C. H. Waddington, *The Strategy of the Genes* (Allen & Unwin, 1957), pp. 188–9.

Pythagoreans. It was this the *Phaedo*-Socrates refused, not, as it might appear, mechanistic science. Plato viewed the early cosmologists through the eyes of the Pythagoreans, and dismissed them for not quite the right reason.[1]

(3) The proof of this is the *Timaeus*, for there when he comes to the cosmological he takes refuge in myth: such is the failure of the dialectic to implement itself in a physics. It is to the *Timaeus* that Aristotle refers in the following:

'Plato, it is true, investigated coming-to-be and passing-away, but only as to the manner in which passing-away is inherent in things, and as regards coming-to-be he did not deal with it in general but only that of the elements; he never enquired how flesh or bones or any similar things came-to-be, and, further, he did not discuss how "alteration" and "growth" are present in things' (*de gen.*, 315a).

That is to say, he did not discuss physical *action*: how it is possible for one thing to act upon and another to be acted upon. There is no *potency* in his cosmos. There is instead *constructability* in a system or hierarchy of Forms with no prospect of their actualization.

It is most significant that Aristotle in this summary dismissal of Plato's cosmology should at the same time single out Democritus for special commendation:

'he seems to have thought about them all, and from first to last he excels in his manner of treatment.'

The atomism of Democritus is in fact a new manner of treatment, a new conception of the elements. His atoms are featureless particles, possessing none of the properties of the thing. They are not subject to the changes of things, being, like ideal circles, 'the limit of a series of sketches of increasing fineness'.[2]

---

[1] St Thomas, *Summa Theologica* (Ia. xlvii. 3): 'All things are ordered to one another and to God, and therefore all belong to one world. You can assert that many worlds exist on condition that you do not acknowledge one directing wisdom as their cause. You may fancy that everything comes about by chance. Democritus, for example, thought that this world had happened from a collision of atoms, and that there was an indefinite number of other worlds.' Is Plato any nearer to this perception than was Leibniz?

[2] N. R. Hanson. See his *Patterns of Discovery* (Cambridge, 1958), p. 122; also p. 215.

Democritus may thus be said to provide Aristotle with an authentic experiment in particle physics and so to set the stage for his own enquiry. Things come-to-be and pass-away. How are we to cope with the emergence of genuine novelty and with the immutable in what passes away, in face of the dilemma, namely, that either there is nothing new because it was there already or there is something new but nevertheless it *was* already there? If one does not have the unit to begin with, the available alternative would seem to be that it can be exhaustively constructed from infinitesimals.

It is in this context that Aristotle argues the case, in the *de gen. et corr.*, against those who 'construct' everything out of elements. 'In what manner does anything else other than the elements themselves come-to-be out of them?' There is no answer if the process is composition. Coming-to-be requires *mixture*, and the 'mixture' in that case 'will consist of the elements preserved intact but placed side by side in minute particles'. And Aristotle is pressing for an answer. Particle physics, he is virtually contending, is parasitic on the true physics of nature, being unable to establish how it happens that anything is altered, or how it can be that anything is acted upon whether by contact or by action at a distance. It has to be reckoned with that if there are elements they come-to-be in whatever comes-to-be, and they come-to-be in any and every part of what comes-to-be: '. . . not as stone and brick come-to-be out of a wall, that is, each out of a different place and part'.

The requirement for real change is twofold, therefore:

(*a*) It must be possible for the patient to *change into* the agent, for only then is there effective agency. Aristotle comprises this in the formula, that coming-to-be, in its simple essence, is a process into the contrary (the hot becoming cold, the cold becoming hot). The elements enter into the process as 'contraries and their intermediates capable of being affected and of acting reciprocally —indeed it is entirely these processes which constitute passing-away and coming-to-be'.

(*b*) Since the elements enter into mixture as passivities capable of being acted upon, there must be present an active principle in which they come-to-be; and since they enter not as units (*either* ho *or* cold) but as reciprocating contraries, their coming-to-be is by participation and their actuality a *mean* (*neither* hot *nor* cold):

'. . . but out of them flesh and bones and the like come-to-be when the hot is becoming cold and the cold becoming hot and they reach the mean, for at that point there is neither hot nor cold. (The mean, however, has considerable extension and is not indivisible.) In like manner also it is in virtue of being in a "mean" condition that the dry and the moist and the like produce flesh and bones and the other compounds' (*de gen.*, 334b).

This *extensive mean* is the true nature of the thing. The continuum in which it is established is not like the mathematical continuum a construction but the very thing itself, that same thing which comes-to-be and passes-away; and the further exploration of it requires a close attention to the particularity of the thing. Mechanistic science refuses this particularity, attending instead to an artefact of the physical thing in which the potentially active natural elements masquerade as unitary particles, inert and without the potency to be acted *upon*.[1]

The success of particle physics accrues to it from the existential underwriting provided by experimental verification—a physical context in which the atomic model is derelict. Thus, though physicists have tended to put their 'particle' worries into cold storage, even so the paradox of 'action at a distance' has pressed for solution in the inescapable dialectic of experiment and discovery. It is a far cry from the 'contact' of Newton's corpuscles to quantum field theory.

Professor Wilkinson, in an attempt to communicate to the layman the bearing of the Heisenberg Uncertainty Principle, invents what he calls a 'messenger-particle'. The peculiarity of this 'entity' is that (*a*) were it really to exist it would destroy the system:

'These messenger-particles, as they fly between the interacting objects, cannot be intercepted because if they were held up they would not be able to give back to the system the energy they have borrowed, and the conservation of energy would be permanently violated, instead of only temporarily as is allowed by the Uncertainty Principle.'

But (*b*) if we allow them a *virtual* existence then 'we can do a lot of mathematics and show that the inverse square laws of force for electricity and gravitation follow automatically':

'For example: When two electrical charges interact, they do so by the exchange of virtual photons. When a charge is violently accelerated then some of these virtual photons may get a share of the extra energy and become real. This is exactly what happens in an X-ray tube and the X-rays—short wave-length light—are, as it were, shaken out of their virtual into real states when the electrons crash into the anode of the tube. Furthermore, the real X-rays have just the properties we calculated for them on the basis of what photons must be like in their virtual states in order to give rise to the inverse square law of force between electrical charges.'[1]

Aristotle would have found immense satisfaction in this coming-to-be story—as indeed he would at the turn of events in contemporary science generally.

It is worth reminding oneself that the Greeks were essentially a scientific people. The literary tradition in philosophy was not indigenous to them. For Plato, no less than for Aristotle or Archimedes, philosophizing is search for the reality. Call it science, or call it philosophy: it is one and the same.

The thing it is not is theology. The integration of coming-to-be with the creative act constitutes not merely a transformation of the Greek cosmogony but a radical revision of the limits of metaphysical enquiry. The doctrine of primary and secondary causality brings to an end the reign of autonomous philosophy; it is a plea for authentic science because otherwise there can be no authentic theology.

In response, therefore, to the question, 'What is metaphysics?', my own *deuteros plous* is a hazardous passage through very narrow waters—the Scylla of Ontologism on the one side, the Charybdis of mechanistic science on the other.

[1] *The Listener*, May 15, 1958.

IV

HOWARD ROOT

METAPHYSICS

AND

RELIGIOUS BELIEF

There are two mottoes, at first sight contradictory, which could be put at the head of most exercises in metaphysics. They are these: (1) Things are not what they seem. (2) Things are precisely what they seem. The appearance of contradiction is puzzling because both affirmations seem necessary to the metaphysical enterprise. There are times when the metaphysician, in his account of the nature of reality, will wish to cure our blindness or correct our habits of inattention so that we may take in the detail of the picture he is drawing. There are other times when he will wish to direct our gaze upon details of ordinary experience which we have either seen and forgotten or else turned away from. So it is not ultimately paradoxical for him to say that things both are and are not what they seem. If you push one half of that paradox far enough, far enough to see what it is about, you will find yourself compelled to assert the other half as well.

The same mottoes could be taken to characterize the intellectual (or perhaps the more than intellectual) quest of the religious man. *Fides quaerens intellectum* is a quest for what is hidden from unregenerate sight as well as for a right apprehension of what is perfectly open to sight. Yet the fact that these mottoes can be used commonly by metaphysician and religious believer is not in itself a solution to the problem of the relation of metaphysics to belief, even though it may help us to understand the different ways in which that relation is manifested.

For the moment we can leave it an open question whether there is *a* problem of the relation of metaphysics to religion. I want to approach that question by raising a number of other questions. We are all familiar with the claim that religious belief, in so far as that belief is articulate, is tied to some kind of metaphysical view. After all, we remind ourselves, theism is a metaphysical position. If Christian belief is not to be recognized as a type of theism we begin to wonder where we are. Yet this familiar contention, and the situations to which it directs our attention, cannot be taken quite at face value. Though it is no doubt intended to make things precise, it can have the effect of making things blurred and vague. Somehow or other what we also have to identify, accommodate, and account for is the non-metaphysical, or even the anti-metaphysical elements in religious belief. Here I am not necessarily referring to 'feelings' or to irrational elements, to what, for example, Rudolf Otto attempted to isolate in his discussion of the idea of the Holy. What I think we must avoid is the suggestion that the metaphysical aspect of religious belief is to be identified with the rational, while the non- or anti-metaphysical aspect is identified with the irrational. For some purposes it may be useful to distinguish between the rational and the irrational in religion (in accounts, for example, of the causes of belief in particular cases), but whatever that distinction amounts to, it is not parallel with any alleged distinction between metaphysical and non-metaphysical. It may be that in the end neither distinction can stand without extensive qualification; but, however this may be, the two are distinct even if they overlap.

As an introduction to the argument between metaphysical and anti-metaphysical, let me remind you of a few slogans which are often to be heard. It is now quite fashionable in some theological circles to say that Christianity is not a religion at all. This fashion emanates from at least two different quarters. There are those, often followers of Karl Barth, like Professor Hendrik Kraemer, who come to this astonishing-sounding conclusion in their efforts to stress the radical otherness of Christian faith from everything called religion. Religion is fundamentally and inescapably anthropocentric. It is the record of man's quest for his own fulfilment and the establishment of his own values. Hence from the standpoint of Christian faith it is always, in greater or lesser degree, idolatrous. (This applies as much to empirical Christianity

E

as to other religions.) Religions, in Barth's analysis, represent man's wilful disobedience, his denial of the true God. For Barth, one feels, religion (as he once said of the Analogy of Being) is Anti-Christ. No small part of his repudiation is directed at the metaphysical element in (or interpretation of) religion. It represents for him the binding and emasculation of faith by constructs of fallen human reason and feeling. Christian faith, on the other hand, stands over against everything called religion. The Christian revelation, the Word of God, enters the world as a judgement upon all things human, perhaps especially human religion.

But that slogan, 'Christianity without religion', makes itself heard from a quite different quarter. It is no small part of the burden of the theology of Professor Paul Tillich. Tillich is no Barthian, and his attitude to non-Christian religions (in so far as one can find such an attitude implicit in his writings) is at the greatest distance from that of Professor Kraemer. Yet Tillich is, no less than these, quite determined to isolate Christian faith from everything that goes by the name of religion: for example, his notable and very moving sermon on 'The Yoke of Religion',[1] which interprets our Lord's words, 'My yoke is easy', as the promise of deliverance from religion. For Tillich, religion means something like Pharisaism, as much the plague of the Christian as of the Jewish Church. It means everything which men would substitute, by way of religious practice, for that kind of existential commitment which makes possible the New Being in Christ. There is no doubt a common factor uniting even such diverse theologians as Barth and Tillich, a factor expressed in this slogan, 'Christianity without religion'. And plainly there is some connexion between this and Professor Bultmann's slogan 'Christianity without mythology'. In the last few years Bultmann's views have roused far more controversy than Tillich's, the price perhaps of the former's greater clarity. Tillich manages to stay above controversy mostly because of the very high-level ambiguity of his oracles.

The work of a few contemporary theologians may inspire the slogan, 'Christianity without religion', but once loosed upon the

[1] *The Shaking of the Foundations* (London, S.C.M. Press, 1949), pp. 93–103.

world that slogan develops a life of its own and we find it on the lips of many who would be surprised to hear themselves called fellow-travellers with Barth or Bultmann or even Tillich. It has become the symbol of a certain trend in contemporary apologetic. It is not easy to know exactly what it means, but what it suggests is an attempt to make a clean break with traditional ways of expounding the content of Christian faith. What this break amounts to may be something like this. The Christian religion, as it has been called, has traditionally been presented as a closed system of theological (and therefore metaphysical) propositions, moral injunctions, and methods of religious practice. Such closed systems are now out of fashion. They have proved to be intellectually indefensible, morally inadequate or inhibiting, and practically antiquated. The true substance of Christian faith is not a System but a 'way of life'; not a moral code, but a complex of attitudes and dispositions arising from an act of commitment and trust; not a rigid convention in religious observance and worship, but a natural, improvised expression of the shared life of the Christian community. All of this means that Christian faith should be re-interpreted and re-presented to the modern world in a form free from all the undesirable qualities of the Christian religion. One might say that, rhetorically, the method here is for the apologist to identify himself with many of the secular, sceptical, or agnostic criticisms of religion, thereby hoping to disarm the critics. The method has not been without its successes. And in the hands of the skilful it has no doubt been influential. (One thinks, for example, of the writing and speaking of an Anglican like A. R. Vidler and a Presbyterian like George MacLeod.)

We are not concerned, however, with an assessment of tendencies in apologetic except in so far as they throw some light on our question of religion and metaphysics. And the slogan 'Christianity without religion' is of interest to us because one of its offspring is the cry 'Christianity without metaphysics, without propositions'. And this cry has not only a theological but also a philosophical source in contemporary thought. You can compare with it the cry 'Ethics without propositions'. Several years ago a Dutch Calvinist theologian published a remarkable book showing that the philosophical standpoint of the Vienna Circle was in perfect accord with neo-Calvinist thought and ethics.[1] That may seem a strange alliance, but it is not untypical. Professor Donald MacKinnon has illuminatingly written of Karl Barth's 'Christological Positivism', an incisive expression. What requires our attention is the way in which a philosopher or theologian accomplishes this alleged liberation of Christianity from metaphysics or metaphysical propositions.

I will not pursue any further the methods of the Barthian theologians. Instead I should like to turn to one of the preoccupations of contemporary philosophical theology in this country and to illustrate it with a particular example. We hear a good deal these days about 'the logic of religious language'. That phrase reflects a certain philosophical attitude, one which sees the key to many venerable philosophical problems in what Professor John Wisdom once called the 'idiosyncratic platitude'. That is, the assertion that every type of discourse, metaphysical, theological, moral, or whatever, has its own logic. The idiosyncratic platitude is the alternative option if we refuse to accept the Verification Principle, i.e. refuse to accept it as the single key to the meaning or logic of every type of discourse. It is said, and doubtless quite truly, that the Verification Principle, however stated, presents as serious a challenge to religious belief as to any form of metaphysical utterance. If therefore we are to justify such belief intellectually, our first task will be to bring out its character by examining the logic of the language in which it is expressed. What we may find odd is that very often these efforts at analysis, whose purported aim is the discovery of intellectual justification for religious belief, conclude by showing that any such justification—in the literal sense—is neither possible nor even desirable.

As an example we can consider a long essay by A. MacIntyre called 'The Logical Status of Religious Belief'. It appeared in 1957 in a volume of three long essays called *Metaphysical Beliefs*.[2] The argument of MacIntyre's essay is of intrinsic importance; but it

[1] W. F. Zuurdeeg, *A Research for the Consequences of the Vienna Circle Philosophy for Ethics* (Utrecht, n.d.).

[2] *Metaphysical Beliefs*, ed. A. C. MacIntyre (London, S.C.M. Press), pp. 167–211.

also possesses a kind of paradigmatic interest, showing how a particular philosophical (and anti-metaphysical) approach can lead to, and perhaps fuse with, a certain kind of theology, or, if not a theology, an interpretation of the nature of belief. MacIntyre's starting point is the Verification Principle and the problem it raises for Christian belief. He reminds us of the several points made in the so-called Falsification controversy which began with Professor Flew's observations on the non-empirical character of certain religious utterances.[1] MacIntyre notes briefly several of the means which have been used to avoid the conclusion that the unfalsifiability of theological statements is tantamount to a demonstration of their meaninglessness. He rejects the view that theological statements are a special variety of hypotheses. This will not do because the kind of adherence the believer gives to his belief is not hypothetical or tentative. It is one of unreserved, total commitment. He also rejects Professor Braithwaite's view. In his Eddington Lecture,[2] Braithwaite accepted fully the strictures of the Verification Principle and therefore abandoned any effort to understand religious statements literally. Instead, he suggested that they are really declarations of moral policy in the guise of factual and historical statements. Of all this MacIntyre observes, and with some reason, that this is hardly what believers suppose they mean by their assertions. The religious man quite plainly does think that his beliefs have something to do with what goes on in the world.

The substance of MacIntyre's own view comes in the next two chapters of his essay.[3] The first of these is significantly called 'The Religious Attitude'. He assumes the existence of a characteristic attitude and then asks two questions about it. First, what sort of belief does this attitude entail? Second, what sort of justification would be appropriate for this belief? The religious attitude seems to commit the believer to two different things: to the practice of worship, and to the belief that 'God acts in the universe', a belief which is not just metaphorical. As between these two different

[1] *New Essays in Philosophical Theology* (London, S.C.M. Press), pp. 96–130.

[2] *An Empiricist's View of the Nature of Religious Belief* (Cambridge University Press, 1955).

[3] In the following paragraphs I sometimes paraphrase and sometimes quote directly from the essay mentioned above.

commitments there will always be, he says, a certain tension. In worship, the believer manifests what MacIntyre aptly calls a 'systematic reticence' about God, denying that anything truly adequate can be said about God. None the less, he does say things about God, many things. The fundamental claim of the Hebrew-Christian tradition is that the God who is utterly transcendent and beyond the world nevertheless acts in the world. In a careful and often illuminating account of the language of worship, MacIntyre points out that in worship we are for the most part praising God, not describing him. We speak of our hopes, our states, and we only suggest qualities like God's greatness and power. The language is vocative or gerundive, or it falls somewhere between the gerundive and the descriptive. This point reminds us of Martin Buber's emphasis on the fact that God is One whom we 'address', not One whom it is our business to describe as though he were an object, an 'It'.

When we have made all these allowances for the special character of the language of worship, its non-descriptive, non-factual qualities, we still cannot evade the fact that it also has a narrative content, expressed sometimes directly and sometimes allusively. The narratives we can call myths, without prejudicing the question of their truth. What is clear is that they purport to deal with God's actions in the world. They deal with acts which are 'concerned with the central situations in human life', from birth to death. Beyond its narrative content, the intention of the myth is to inculcate an attitude. Hence, 'To accept a sufficiently comprehensive myth is to accept a whole way of living'. This is not, however, to fall into Braithwaite's reduction of the myth to the moral policy it declares. Most perceptively, MacIntyre remarks that 'myths are directive of the moral life at just those points where rules become no longer relevant'. It is a commonplace of experience that 'Time and again we have to take up attitudes, make decisions and so on where there is no clear rule and sometimes no rule at all'. Hence 'we are morally made and unmade in those decisions where there is no rule to make the decision for us. It is a question then of fundamental attitudes to the human and non-human worlds, of those attitudes which receive their definition and their illumination in myths.'

Now of course with much of this Braithwaite would agree. The complication comes when we see that in the Christian scheme one cannot accept the myth while remaining agnostic about its relation to the way things are in the world. For the Christian, 'These stories are . . . stories about a real being, God, acting in the world that we are acquainted with in ordinary experience'. It is just this belief which, to the sceptical philosopher, calls out for justification. It is also the case that the contents of the myth impose certain modes of acceptance upon the believer. They must, for one thing, be compatible with worship. But if Christianity is right, its mode of acceptance must be that of a perfectly free, unforced decision. This point takes us to the heart of MacIntyre's position. For, in his view, to understand this imposition of a mode of acceptance is the pre-condition for discovering what sort of justification of the belief is appropriate or possible. He rules out once again any view which would treat religious beliefs as explanatory hypotheses. But the reason now is that such a view is religiously (or theologically) as well as philosophically impossible. If belief in God could be confirmed experimentally, if God should emerge merely as the conclusion of a rational argument, we should have too much certitude about him. This would mean that a limit was set to the freedom of our decision to believe or disbelieve. And, once again, it is only appropriate to entertain a hypothesis provisionally; but to believe in God provisionally would be 'alien to the whole spirit of religious belief' and would entail a complete mis-description of the content of that belief.

If we want to find a way out of this dilemma, we must ask, 'How are religious beliefs in fact justified by believers?' MacIntyre's answer is that, within Christianity, individual beliefs are justified in terms of such criteria as make up the test for orthodoxy. It is just these orthodoxy tests which give determinate shape to the content of religion. *And there is no going outside them.* This may seem fatally to damage any claim for the ultimate rationality of belief. But MacIntyre's conviction is that such a test is, for example, 'strictly analogous' to the way 'sovereignty' is defined within any political society. That is, e.g., there is no going beyond the statement, 'What the Queen says in Parliament is law'. That rule is ultimate and there is no external criterion for judging it. So, then, 'Every religion is defined by reference to what it accepts as an authoritative criterion . . . the acceptance or rejection of a religion is thus the acceptance or rejection of such an authority'.

Whether we accept MacIntyre's analysis here or not, it is obvious that this account gives us no help with the apparently factual elements in belief. It gives no reason why, for example, we should accept a particular cosmological theory—the doctrine of Creation—as integral to religious belief. MacIntyre's answer to this is that we shall accept such theories because we accept a whole religion on the ground that it issues from *someone* whom we take to be completely authoritative. We judge such theories and factual claims not in their own light or in the light of other knowledge, but in the light of him who utters them. The only person to whom we are likely to ascribe such authority is someone whom we *worship*. He says, 'We accept authority because we discover some point in the world at which we worship, at which we accept the lordship of something not ourselves . . . we do not worship authority; but we accept authority as defining the worshipful'.

The key to MacIntyre's account of the justification of religious belief is this notion of authority, and as he acknowledges, 'This means that religion *as a whole* lacks any justification'. But, he adds, this in no way reflects on the logical status of our beliefs. . . . Every field is defined by reference to certain ultimate criteria. That they are ultimate precludes going beyond them.' It would, for example, be absurd to try to justify religion by excogitating arguments for the existence of God. For one thing such arguments are philosophically inadmissible. Moreover, 'the whole concept of existence is inapplicable to God'. And, further, to say 'God exists' to one outside religion is to speak meaninglessly; to say it to one inside religion is to speak pointlessly. God does not 'exist' because he is not an object. Were he an object the religious necessity of freely choosing to believe would become empty. So much, then, for Natural Theology or for any effort to support religion with metaphysical argument.

In the final chapter of his essay, 'The Quest of the Historical Jesus', MacIntyre turns to the allegedly historical elements in belief. We shall not be surprised to find him saying that 'everything of importance to religious faith is outside the reach of historical investigation'. He arrives at this through his analysis of the nature of belief, of how it happens and how it is sustained. 'To believe', he says, 'that a past event happened is usually only reasonable if historical enquiry warrants the belief. But the essence of the New Testament claim . . . is that certain past events can be part of a *religious* belief, that they can be believed on authority . . . while historical enquiry as to such events would always be legitimate its results are not the ground of belief in any way.' Why? Because, as before, 'religious faith is never provisional'. It is inappropriate to accord more than provisional acceptance to the probabilities vouchsafed by historical investigation.

This is the substance of MacIntyre's position, and what it comes to, he says, is simply this: to acquire religious belief is to become 'converted'. 'There is no logical transition from unbelief to belief.' 'The transition is not in objective considerations at all.' Indeed, to be worthy of the title, believer, means to accept the full burden of free decision. 'There are no reasons to which we can appeal to evade' that need for deciding freely. While some might be dismayed, MacIntyre seems positively cheered by this conclusion. As a result of philosophical criticism and of a deeper understanding of the logic of belief we are now in a far better position to see the gravity of that belief. The old view which saw religion as somehow dependent upon a Natural Theology and which thought that metaphysical argument could take us a long way toward the demonstration of God's existence was no more than 'a sustained attempt to replace conversion by argument'. To do this would be entirely destructive of religion.

I hope that this summary of an ingenious and often penetrating argument does not misrepresent it. But for our purposes the argument exhibits very clearly those tendencies which we have tried to bring out. You might say that given the contemporary situation one might have predicted that someone would be bold enough to try out this line and to press it as far as it would go. Thus, without in any way disparaging its originality and economy, one reads it without surprise. One could put it briefly like this. We are given an account of the logic of religious belief which owes much to two main sources. First, from contemporary philosophical criticism of metaphysics, or from metaphysically sceptical criteria of meaningfulness and particular ideas about verification and the nature of rational justification. Second, from a particular understanding of the 'religious attitude', of what it is like to be a believer. The first source dictates that certain traditional approaches to the justification of belief—and their implicit understanding of the relation of metaphysics to religion—are philosophically unacceptable. Natural Theology is rationally indefensible. The second source, which is closely connected with the slogans, 'Christianity without religion', 'Christian faith without propositions', insists that belief is in essence an act of total commitment. It is an act which must come as a totally free decision to opt for a particular authority. In the end, everything which an anti-metaphysical philosophy rejected is as firmly rejected by an anti-metaphysical theology.

At this point I want to make only one observation about the philosophical source of this view. If MacIntyre's understanding of the relevance of contemporary philosophical criticism is correct, we should have to abandon everything that has traditionally been entered under the rubric of 'rational grounds for belief'. The theistic arguments, however cast, would have to go. Attempts, like that of F. R. Tennant, to work out the basis of an empirical theism, would be pointless.[1] Yet, despite this, MacIntyre shrinks from saying that religious belief is irrational. He takes refuge, it would seem, in something very like the Idiosyncratic Platitude, the assertion that the criteria of belief have their own logical justification. Justification now seems to be identified with description.

What we might well look at more closely is the account of the character of religious belief, apart from any philosophical criticism of its grounds, that MacIntyre presents. At the outset one cannot but welcome any account which begins with actual religious language as ordinarily used. At the same time, any account of the whole nature of religious language—if there be such *a* nature—must make room for all sorts of facts and must beware of purchasing clarity and consistency at the price of making some of the facts unintelligible. (A chief defect of verificationalism, in so far as it claimed to bring out the meaning of

[1] Even a 'soft' natural theology. Cp. Ninian Smart's essay, Ch. V below.

metaphysical and religious statements, is that it failed in just this respect.) With MacIntyre's account we may well feel uneasy. We are now quite used to hearing that total, unreserved commitment is the absolute precondition of true faith. Yet does this mean that matters of independent historical fact are religiously dispensable because in regard to them we can have only provisional, tentative certitude? I am not sure that this is what all believers do say. More than once men have said that if they were obliged, through historical enquiry, to disbelieve the main events of the Gospel narrative, their faith would go. Whether this is a theologically sound view does not matter. It is a part of ordinary religious usage. We can say that in some sense belief is tentative. Nor have we adequate reason for saying that this sort of tentativeness is incompatible with honest and sincere worship. There would be something odd about saying that people do not and cannot ever allow anything to count against their belief. This is the remark which the verificationalists wished to elicit, a remark in which MacIntyre (and some theologians) seem to rejoice. But it is the plain fact that believers sometimes cease to believe; or equally to the point, they sometimes change their beliefs quite radically. It is also the fact they are often ready, even eager, to offer explicit reasons for these changes and are not content simply to point to some authority. Are we then to say that because their belief was not permanent they were never really believers at all? How then should we know that we are believers in this absolute sense? Is the future so open to us that we can never discover that our belief (or some part of it) was in some sense tentative?

Furthermore, whatever the philosophical difficulties, there seem no adequate grounds for ruling out certain hypothetical features of belief. Actual religious language makes it clear that believers explain and commend their belief with statements like this: 'Christian faith makes sense of life, makes sense of the facts, in a way that no other theory does.' Or they say, 'You will never understand Christian faith until you try it and see how it works'. Belief is commended as exploration. No doubt there goes with this the believer's conviction that his 'hypothesis' is adequate, but he could not speak in this way at all unless he regarded belief as in some sense hypothetical.

A more thorough examination of religious language, particularly in apologetic use, might show up defects in MacIntyre's account of the place of authority. How, for example, would it explain the insistence of some theologians that Christ taught what he did because it was true or good, not that it became true or good because he taught it? We should, in other words, be very reluctant to admit that it was religiously improper to commend Christianity on moral grounds. We do it all the time, consistently or not. Nor, perhaps, would religious usage confirm the view that ultimate religious authority can be understood upon the analogy of definitions of political sovereignty. When Anglicans become Papists, or Papists Anglicans; when Quakers become Anglicans, or Anglicans Quakers, they very often suppose that they have reasons, rational grounds, for these changes in obedience. Are these always to be called mere rationalizations? Are they patient of nothing more serious than psychological explanations? In any case, these facts are part of the story of the nature of religious belief. It will not do to ignore them or explain them away. How very difficult it would be, if we did not take them into account, to understand how any changes (or, if you like, developments) could take place within Christian theology or within theological systems. According to MacIntyre it is fitting and proper to take certain cosmological theories on authority. Yet when such theories are modified or discarded by theologians what is happening? Has some non-religious authority—a scientific one, say—intervened to put the religious authority on the right track?

Whatever virtues MacIntyre's account may possess, we still want to say that we have reasons for belief. We are still that far committed to the possibility of metaphysical argument. And we see no cogent case for thinking that such reasons and argument are no more than evasions of our duty to make a free decision. They do not seem to us to entail any limitation upon our religiously significant freedom. In fact, we could scarcely use the word 'decision' at all if we were acting in the complete absence of any reasons. We might even want to say that we are only truly free to decide when we have fully understood the implications of rational argument on all sides. What sort of duty would it be to opt for a belief which we supposed to lack all rational grounds?

And in any case, there is surely a distinction between knowledge of rational grounds and constraint. In MacIntyre's account we hear a curious echo of popular existentialism: we are condemned to be free, but all our choices are inevitably absurd. Moreover, if with MacIntyre we lay so much stress upon the necessity of free and unconditioned decision, how could we reconcile this with his equal emphasis upon the necessity of absolute commitment to some authority? Or is it the case that freedom is important only until we have made that one decision and is thereafter expendable?

There is something else in this account which seems paradoxical. I mean the view—perhaps in itself quite intelligible—that the 'internal' justification of religious beliefs is an orthodoxy test. It is for a religion (or an ecclesiastical authority) to define what is justifiable in belief. Maybe this is reasonable enough. Yet a part of certain orthodoxy tests is the claim that there are rational grounds for belief. I take it that within the Roman Catholic communion you may not with impunity dismiss the validity of Natural Theology. And quite certainly within certain Protestant groups you may not dismiss the literal historical veracity of any of the Biblical narratives. When MacIntyre says that natural theology is pointless or that the results of historical enquiry are of no final importance he seems to violate his own criteria of justification. Or at least he is dealing with a rather uncommon sort of orthodoxy. One example, if I understand it, may bring this out. There is a sense in which, in terms of the definitions of some theologians, one might have to call unbelief (or denial of the existence of God) a sin; even though in an individual case it might not be possible to say whether that sin was formal as well as material. There are a number of interesting things about this, of which I might mention two. First, the impulse to call unbelief a sin would naturally arise if one held that men could, by the use of their unaided reason, come to a knowledge of the existence of God. Second, such a conviction would presuppose the belief that men were free either to accept or reject this knowledge within their grasp. Without such freedom there could be no such thing as sin. The significant thing about this view, for our purposes, is that it takes for granted that there is no necessary incompatibility between this possible, natural knowledge of God and human freedom.

Finally, from the point of view of apologetic theology, this account leaves us with thin prospects. Apologetic could in no circumstances be more than a rehearsal of the Christian story, a pointing to authority, and a hope for conversion. Anything else would be disallowed. MacIntyre may be right. But if he is, he renders unintelligible the great bulk of ordinary apologetic language. Even if we confine ourselves to the New Testament, it is manifest that no small part of apostolic exhortation took the form of intelligible argument: argument from prophecy (which is argument from history as well as appeal to authority); argument from miracle; argument from moral principle. The wisdom of God was foolishness to the Greeks because the Greeks were foolish, not because the apostles eschewed rationality.

If philosophical criticism drives us to abandon the claim that there are reasons for belief, and if the nature of belief is such that no external considerations weigh either for or against it, the religious position begins to look very trivial. But we cannot leave the matter there. MacIntyre's essay may be flawed, in so far as it purports to bring out *the* character of religious belief. But it can be criticized only from particular standpoints. And such criticisms, like the ones I have offered, are not particularly helpful unless they add up to (or, anyway, point to) something like a position or view which can stand on its own feet. It might well be that such a view would incorporate certain features of MacIntyre's view, if differently stated. Perhaps the real centre of MacIntyre's position is that 'point in the world at which we worship'. MacIntyre says very little about this, but I should guess that this 'point' at which he feels so compelled is not far from the 'basic apprehension' or the 'unexpected disclosure' of God of which others have spoken.[1] MacIntyre finds, having reached this point, that all he can do is to turn to some authority to explicate its content, to ask the authority for a definition of the worshipful. And he feels that this is really the only course open to him. He can get no help from traditional metaphysics or natural theology. Nor, to put it the

---

[1] In the present book, the reader will find this theme of 'intuition' or 'disclosure' given varying measures of prominence in Chs. V, VI, VII, IX, X and XII.—Ed.

other way round, would these ever lead him to that point of discovery of the worshipful. In other words, he wants to eliminate any metaphysical intermediary between the unexpected desire to worship and systematic theology. There are, as I pointed out, fairly obvious reasons why this is an attractive thing to do. There is something mysterious about the step from any religious experience, so-called, to the theology in which it is finally placed and articulated. It is perhaps natural to the religious man to be suspicious of anything which claims to be a perfectly rational account of revelation. The religious man is always disposed to say not that he found God—rationally or otherwise—but that God found him, that the content of revelation forced itself upon him. And this disposition is not unrelated to his frequent appearance of hostility towards metaphysics. 'What has Athens to do with Jerusalem?' In some moods we all speak like Tertullian.

But we cannot, I should submit, remain here. (The biography of Tertullian is a cautionary tale.) For in other moods we find it necessary to insist that there are genuine reasons for belief which are more than descriptions of the content of a particular theology. Such reasons are of various types; they do not fit neatly together into any unified system. They may be moral or aesthetic, or even scientific. We elaborate them sometimes for apologetic purposes, sometimes simply to satisfy our own minds that our particular theology deserves continued belief.

What then of metaphysics and religion? It may not be of much help, but I should like to say something like this. If we continue to say that there are reasons for accepting one set of beliefs rather than another, we are that far committed to something which I should call metaphysics. But it will have to be a metaphysics which can somehow do justice not only to our desire for a Natural Theology but also to our religiously inspired distrust of Natural Theology. Just what it would look like is very much worth finding out.

V

NINIAN SMART

REVELATION,
REASON AND RELIGIONS

Natural theology is the Sick Man of Europe. In view of the subtle and exhaustive objections adduced by Hume, Kant and modern empiricists against the traditional arguments for God's existence, it is no longer reasonable to rely upon these particular supports for theistic belief. But the alternative is not irrationalism, for this can give us no guidance as to what we should choose: why be Christian rather than Hindu, or religious rather than atheistical? But if we can rely neither on metaphysical reasoning nor on unreasoning, we might feel tempted to write off religion altogether. Yet its truth-suggesting fascination in daily life and the testimony of many profound and holy men is not lightly to be disregarded. It is not my present task, however, to produce the theologian's stone, the long-searched-for argument that will convince the outsider. Rather I wish to consider whether there is a middle way between traditional natural theology and some simple appeal to revelation (or to any other authority). I wish, in effect, to adumbrate the religious reasons for holding doctrines. For I believe on the one hand, with the revelationists, that one cannot excogitate religious truth: one has to judge what is given, in the form of revelations and teachings—since ordinary philosophers and theologians are neither prophets nor Buddhas. But I believe on the other hand, with the rationalistically inclined, that one can still detect considerations favouring one position rather than another.

But first a word about philosophical analysis. I take it that the job of the philosopher here is to elucidate, as far as possible, the manner in which religious propositions[1] have meaning. This involves connecting up doctrines and experience. Now of course there is no special reason for philosophers to confine themselves to Christian doctrines and life; indeed, to be fair it is necessary to consider other luminous teachings, such as those of Buddhism. Nor can it be pretended that all the great religions are saying the same thing—even if sometimes their doctrines overlap. But in a way this is fortunate, since contrasts help us to see the reasons for them, and in the comparative study of religions one is not merely enabled to view religious teachings (especially one's own) afresh, but one is also offered the chance to gain some further insight into the relation between beliefs and experiences. In brief, if one regards philosophical analysis here as a rather specialized branch of the comparative study of religion, one can acquire a little more clarity about the religious reasons implicit in revelation. But so far, the philosopher is being a neutral in the conflict of faiths. There is no absolute taboo, however, upon his descending into the dusty arena of general apologetic. I propose here to illustrate what can be done in this way in general defence of Christian doctrine. Admittedly, this need not be the job for a philosopher. But on the other hand, the purism of thinking that philosophical analysis is the only proper employment for philosophers is excessive. Intellectual compartmentalization, though often good at the start, may be sterile at the finish.

Thus, one job a philosopher may do is general apologetic. And so the above remarks can be placed in a different context. One way of refurbishing traditional metaphysics is to claim that it expresses, or even evokes, intuitions or disclosures of the divine Being. Now an appeal to such notions must lead in the direction along which I have already pointed. For if the intuition is utterly bare, it can guarantee nothing which can be formulated in words, and is therefore of no use in supporting doctrines. It must at least lead more naturally to one's saying certain things rather than others, and must therefore (albeit in a weak sense) be expressible. On the other hand, it is scarcely realistic to suppose that such an intuition bears a label containing a detailed and legible inscription.

[1] I use the word 'proposition' here as a generic term to cover statements, commands, etc.

F

If it did, intuitionism would be with difficulty distinguished from, and hardly more plausible than, fundamentalism. It seems, then, to follow that if there are such intuitions, they are dimly suggestive of certain doctrines rather than others; but only *dimly* suggestive. But further, if we appeal to metaphysical intuitions and disclosures we are already indulging in phenomenology; and there seems to be no good reason for confining ourselves to certain intuitions which may or may not arise in certain intellectual (or allegedly intellectual)[1] contexts, but rather ought to contemplate the whole field of religious phenomenology. If, for instance, we are speaking about God, it is reasonable to consider those experiences or disclosures which occur in specifically religious contexts, and which, though considerably ineffable, are dim pointers to certain forms of divine discourse rather than to others.

It might be objected that phenomenology involves merely the description of the psychological content of states of mind, whereas the whole point about an intuition is that it is cognitive, and thus cannot be considered merely as a psychological item. Consequently, it may be argued, an appeal to intuitions does not involve indulging in phenomenology (just as, when we are judging the report of an eyewitness, we are not dragged into a discussion of the psychology of perception). Nevertheless, the contrast seems unrealistic, in the present instance, for a number of reasons. First, to say that an intuition is cognitive is to say that one knows (or claims to know) something in virtue of it; but the same would be true of many numinous experiences (although it must be confessed that more needs to be done to make the notion of 'knowing' in religious contexts perspicuous). Second, intuitions of God only become plausible if they chime in with what is yielded in revelations and disclosures of God (for otherwise why talk of them as 'of God'?); but this already suggests at least some resemblance between revelations and intuitions. Third, even though one can draw a contrast between epistemology and the psychology of perception, the facts pertaining to the latter are by

[1] It may be wondered whether an intuition arising through an argument (such as one of the Five Ways) which can no longer be treated as valid in any straightforward way can properly be described as intellectual; but in any case, it is rather artificial to distinguish between different faculties of the mind.

no means irrelevant to the former. Fourth, where rules of reasoning are not clear (and they are not clear in religion) the distinction
between what is to count as cognitive and what counts as merely
an item in psychology (or social history, etc.) becomes quite
blurred. Fifth, it seems more in accord with common sense to
discuss religious truth not merely in the context of supposed
intuitions but also in the milieu of those experiences and activities
which give religion its living power. I therefore turn to consider
specifically religious experiences and disclosures.

For example, the numinous experience analysed by Otto,
though hardly definitive in its pronouncements, nevertheless
provides the impulse to speak about gods or God. And again,
rather differently, mystical experience (by which I mean the
interior and imageless visions of the great Western mystics, the
samādhi attained by the *yogin*, and so on, and which must be
distinguished from those experiences mainly discussed by Otto),[1]
though various in its flavours and interpretations, does have
certain formal characteristics which suggest certain ways of
speaking about that which is realized. In the ensuing, I am
necessarily crude in my phenomenology, for this kind of task as I
have set myself here cannot too well be attempted in so brief a
compass.[2]

There is one further preliminary point before I proceed, namely
that a defence of religion by appeal to intuitions or disclosures
(the merits of different terms here have to be canvassed) need not
entail that *all* people have such experiences. I am inclined to feel
that there may be some intimation of divinity which every man
may have; but such intimations *may* not occur to all, and in any
case may well be of less evidential value than certain profounder
revelations to the comparatively few.

Christianity presents an ideologically significant picture of the
world which is not derivable from scientific investigations. The
elaboration, systematization and general defence of this view of
the world can not unreasonably be called an exercise in meta-

[1] For a discussion of Otto's term 'numinous' and the distinct characters of the numinous
and the mystical, see my 'Numen, Nirvana and the Definition of Religion' in *Church
Quarterly Review*, April-June 1959, pp. 216–25.

[2] At least, however, I have the excuse of having treated these matters more fully in my
Reasons and Faiths (London, 1958).

physics. There does not appear to me to be any clear line between theology and speculation: for both are concerned with the kind of cosmos we live in. And at least it makes for explicitness to count Christian metaphysics as not an essay in the exercise of pure reason (which happens to be on the side of the angels), but a defence of a position which cannot be worked out by reason alone. Moreover, this is (in a broad, very broad, sense) an empirical approach, since we consider what is given rather than legislate for reality.

Christianity claims to be monotheistic. Of course, the doctrine of the Trinity seems at first sight to belie this fact, and it is a common accusation by Muslims that the belief in the Incarnation, by identifying God with a visible person, is setting up another God beside God. However, we shall return to this *prima facie* blasphemous and polytheistic character of Christianity in a moment. Meanwhile let us consider the reasons for preferring monotheism to polytheism. People may simply say, of course, that the truth just is that there is one God and that polytheists are heathens. But bad names get us nowhere. Perhaps certain intimations or intuitions tell men that there is something divine which glimmers in the world. But why one divine Being rather than many?

Can we not gain some insight into this matter? Perhaps the following considerations may help. First, monotheism gives us a more exalted view of the divine. But what if the divine is not that much exalted? All we can say here, maybe, is that the more profound and tremendous experiences of the numinous point in this direction. For the notion of discrete divinities, often clashing, hardly matches up to the overwhelming character of certain theophanies. Second, monotheism is simpler, and other things being equal we prefer the simpler hypothesis. Third, polytheism is more attached to local legend and therefore is less adaptable to those living outside the magic circle; and it is hard to believe that the experiences on which beliefs in the gods are based are so various in such distinct detail. Fourth, whether or not primeval religion was monotheistic, early religion is polytheistic, but shows a tendency to evolve towards monotheism or monism. Fifth, monotheism integrates better with moral insights (universal in nature) than does fragmentary polytheism, especially as the chaotic legends clustering around the gods may be far from edifying. Sixth, the mysterious and overwhelming presence can be linked aesthetically to the cosmological unease, the sense of the aweful contingency of the world. Seventh, monotheism, as we shall observe, chimes in, to some degree, with mystical experience.

It will be apparent that these comments on the religions of worship are somewhat aesthetic in character—rather formal explications of considerations which can be employed to back judgement. But if anything is to count as the adducing of reasons in religion, this is, I think, where we have to start.

But what of pantheism or monism? Do not all the above arguments favour such views as much as they do monotheism? And certainly the dividing line between pantheism and monotheism is shadowy. For example, how do we distinguish sharply between a picture of the divine Being concealed *within* all things and that of the divine Being as *beyond* them? It is not a matter simply of whether you have a three- or two-dimensional model (both admittedly not literal)? All, I think, that can be said is that again the monotheistic picture is more intensely numinous. It expresses more strongly and vividly the gulf fixed between worshipper and the object of worship, and thus gives more intense expression to that which is met with in theophany. Again, the astonishment incorporated in the cosmological argument, namely that it is not the case that nothing exists, fits in better with a monotheistic picture than with the pantheistic; for divine fiat links with contingency, whereas emanation hints at necessity.

Yet all these points might well pass the Buddhist by. For in Theravāda Buddhism (not to mention the original teachings of Gautama) there is no doctrine of a divine Creator, no worship of a Supreme Being. Instead there is the interior mystical quest culminating in the attainment of *nirvāna*. Mystical quest, you may say? But is not mysticism a union with God? But that is looking at the matter theistically. And assuredly this is not the Buddhist notion, that there is a union between persons. Nevertheless, there are certain loose resemblances between the mystical goal (even in Buddhism) and the object of worship. These resemblances, while

not necessitating a theistic interpretation, make it in some degree
plausible. For in the mystical state, even on an agnostic interpretation, there is a timelessness reminiscent of divine immortality,
a transcendence over mundane experience reminiscent of the
otherness of the Supreme Being, a bliss which links up with the
fascination of the numinous and with the notion of a divine
summum bonum, a lack of ordinary perceptions which hints at the
invisibility of the Creator, a power suggestive of grace—and so
on. It is true that the lack of distinction between subject and object
in the mystical state leads to doctrines of deification and union
with God which may be thought to be blasphemous by the
ordinary worshipper. And not unconnectedly, pantheism chimes
in with the mystical quest: for if God be within all things, it is
not absurd to look within ourselves. Still, though there are such
difficulties, certainly mysticism can be suggestively interpreted by
the theist as a kind of vision of God (and incidentally is less
amenable to a polytheistic interpretation, since the comparatively
'this-wordly' aspect of the gods is less in accord with the imper-
ceptibility and transcendence of the mystical goal, etc.).

Nevertheless, the Theravāda is splendid in its doctrinal
simplicity. It eschews metaphysical speculations about Creation
and immortality, but concentrates almost exclusively upon inner
insight and peace and is not complicated by divine ritual. If we
praise monotheism for its simplicity, why not praise this form of
Buddhism likewise? Why not indeed? Let us do so. But the later
history of Buddhism is instructive. The austere simplicity is
replaced in the Mahāyāna by the proliferation of a doctrinally
complex faith—one where many of the concepts of theism show
themselves: the worship of Avalokiteśvara, doctrines of grace (or
the transfer of merit), the Three-Body doctrine (so reminiscent
of Christianity), and so on. The intimations of the numinous were
perhaps not to be denied. If the Lesser Vehicle, like early Islām
in a different way, is glorious in its single-mindedness, it is thereby
less rich. The Advaita Vedānta, Ṣūfism and mystical Christianity,
as well as the Mahāyāna, are, though complex in welding together
different religious insights, more accommodating. Maybe this will
be thought to be no great gain. But we can only judge from the
experience of spiritual men; and at least in these teachings there is

a fairly convincing weaving together of diverse strands of religious language and experience. The outer God who is concealed from our gaze by the visible cosmos reappears at the depths of the soul. The unspeakably majestic object of worship is found in the ineffability of interior insight. Where directions are not literal, we may perchance attain the same place by transcending the world outwards and inwards.

Admittedly it is hard to argue against such a doctrine as that of the Advaita, where the picture of God is relegated firmly to second place, and where the Godhead is described somewhat impersonally in accordance, *prima facie*, with the insights of the mystical vision. (Not for nothing was Sankara called a crypto-Buddhist.) Here the picture of the personal Lord is itself implicated in the grand illusion of *māyā*. And one must note that this kind of illusionist idealism is naturally generated by mystical withdrawal. The Christian apologist can appeal merely to three points here. First, the strength and vividness of numinous experience may not warrant the relegation of the personal picture of the Lord to second place. Second, realism about the cosmos fits in better with moral insight; for the promptings of conscience and the sentiments of justice and love fade somewhat where all things are illusory. And third, transcendence of the unreal has less merit than transcendence of the real.[1]

So far, then, I have adduced what may be called religious reasons for a monotheism which can, so to speak, accommodate the mystical vision. Thereby two main insights of religion are blended appropriately.

But theism generates a problem. For the exalted view of the divine holiness is reflected in reverse among the devotees. Who can confront this almighty splendour without feeling the converse of holiness? The worshipper so confronted repents in self-debasement. He recognizes not merely holiness in God, but unholiness in himself. The purity of the Godhead reveals the sinfulness of men. And this the more so because in theism morals and religion come together in a most intimate manner, so that religious impurity and moral defect coalesce. Thus the very glory of theism is liable to bring in its train a particular view of man, as

[1] I owe this point to Mr T. S. Gregory, in discussion.

sinful and removed from God's face by a great gulf fixed. How to bridge it?

Men have tried sacrifice, and even a broken spirit. But is it in accord with the supreme blinding majesty of God that puny men should pretend to proffer an adequate expiation, whether by good works or otherwise? The worshipper here must feel that salvation or holiness can only come from the supreme source of holiness. Only God is holy, and so only God can bring holiness. So Allah is said, for all his terror, to be merciful; and here is a deep insight. But is it enough that men should merely live in hope of the divine compassion? Man still feels that it is he that must make expiation for his sins; while on the other hand he supposes that only God can bridge the gulf.

Theism thus brings a religious problem. Yet this is, so to speak, solved by Christianity. For Christ by being both man and God can achieve, through his solidarity with mankind, the expiation for mankind, and, through his Godhood, bridge the gulf. The two requirements are met. Hence too the reaction of the Church against docetism. For though doctrines such as the latter seem to preserve monotheism better they destroy the whole point of Christianity.

But Gāndhi said that the uniqueness of the Incarnation was a great stumbling-block to his acceptance of Christ. Why only one Incarnation? Why the scandal of particularity? First, the Christian doctrine, though it involves a seeming blasphemy, is the simplest of its kind. It is hard, perhaps, for the monotheist to accept what at first sight seems an abrogation of his belief; and it would be blasphemous to do it lightly. Second, multiple incarnations, as in Vaiṣṇavism, seem ill in accord with the majesty of God, especially where animal manifestations are produced through legend. Third, they tend in the direction of docetism, for a person who appears in many forms cannot be thought to *be* one of those forms in the full sense: they are likely to be regarded more as appearances than as realities. Thus the need for atonement will not easily be met by multiple incarnations. Fourth, historical data may be relevant, though I do not propose to examine these directly here.

But history reminds us of a problem. Even supposing that the doctrine of Incarnation strikes a deep chord, how do we recognize the divine human? What are the grounds, for instance, for calling Jesus God? True, we would only here be being wise after the event; but there are certain suggestive things to which we can point. Miracle-working is an intimation of omnipotence; signs of sinlessness correspond to the purity of the Holy One; the actions of an apparent Saviour chime in with the thought that only God can save; and the claim to divinity supervenes rather startlingly on all these. Not only so but, looking further afield, the pattern of history fits in with the Messianic life.

Moreover, just as monotheism itself harmonizes more easily with the moral insights of men than does polytheism, so the Incarnation has a moral significance but dimly adumbrated in pure monotheism of the Jewish or Muslim variety: for Christ in making himself a sacrifice not merely fulfils, as it were, a profound religious function, but illuminates the field of morality by his example. The Suffering Servant helps us to understand the significance of love blended with humility. This is not to deny that elsewhere there are similar conceptions, as in Buddhist compassion; but it may well be claimed that in Christianity there is a striking tragic realism which weaves together the insights of numinous religion, mysticism and morality.

Perhaps all this balancing of insights is precarious and indeed flavoured with subjective preferences. I concede that the basic points, namely the superior richness of Christianity, the emphasis on theism and the religion of worship, the need for atonement and the attractiveness of *agapē*, constitute no knockdown arguments. And there are certainly counter-arguments, such as the imperilling of pure monotheism in Christianity and, perhaps, its Judaic dogmatism whereby little credit is given to the intuitions of the polytheist. Nevertheless, a sympathetic Buddhist or Hindu would, I suggest, regard the arguments as at least relevant. Maybe one can gain no more certainty in such matters than in, say, literary or artistic criticism. But one would not for this reason deny that there are relevant insights (or reasons) in regard to revelations. In any event, it is incumbent upon us to try to give such reasons, for they make explicit our religious value-judgements. The trouble about a great deal of comparative apologetic is that it is not thus explicit.

So much, albeit briefly, for what I mean by religious reasons. There are, however, other tasks for the apologist. Revelations, for various reasons, give different pictures of this world. And some of these apply more easily than others. Or at any rate there are problems about their application which must concern us. I use the term 'application' here for the following reason. On the view here presented, certain revelations or revelatory experiences are basically what are appealed to in defence of a religious position. I do not myself believe that one can gain a knowledge of God simply by observing the physical world. Nevertheless the doctrines themselves present a picture of the cosmos which has to square with reality. That is, we do not see that a daffodil is divine (save perhaps in peculiar contemplations) and thus come to believe in God. But our belief gives us the notion that the daffodil has a divine flavour. (A like remark applies to morality too.) Regarding problems of application, the purposive view of history, for example, implicit in Christianity can be contrasted with the cyclical and repetitive picture provided in Indian religion. More importantly, cosmology poses difficulties of application.

We find that there are billions of stars in countless galaxies. Some of these stars are suns; and some of these will perhaps have planets like ours. The theory of evolution and the possibility of the synthesis of organic from inorganic matter may suggest that it is not incredible (and perhaps even probable) that there is life elsewhere in the universe and that there are in other places reasoning organisms. Such speculations would create acute difficulties about the scandal of particularity: the scandal might indeed seem an outrage. Hinduism and Buddhism, with their florid imaginings of beings of all sorts in all kinds of worlds, find the task of applying themselves to this vast universe less difficult. For the Trinity Doctrine, as a final expression of truth about the Godhead, may suffer if there are men elsewhere to be saved through Incarnation. Agreed, all this is highly speculative, but it is a matter for the philosopher, *qua* metaphysical apologist, to discuss.

Again, there are certain more traditional metaphysical problems concerned with the application of doctrines to the world which ought to be discussed. Notably, there is the problem of free will, which links up with the truth or otherwise of scientific materialism. More precisely, it connects not only with the conceptual problem of whether one could adapt language in such a way as to remove the dualistic ontology which seems implicit in current usage, but also with informed speculation as to the possibility of a unified scientific theory of human behaviour. To this latter recent advances in cybernetics, brain physiology and so forth are obviously relevant.

What then is the situation? First, there is philosophical analysis, which helps to illuminate the structure and epistemology of doctrines, East and West. As such it is best regarded as a peculiar way of doing the comparative study of religions. Then there is general apologetics, the giving (in the present instance) of religious reasons for a certain view of the cosmos; and this might as well be done by the sympathetic philosopher as by anyone else. Here historical facts may enter in, but these already have to be interpreted by reference to certain religious insights. Then there arise questions of a general nature, which though not pure exercises in the *a priori* nevertheless ought to engage philosophers' attention, regarding the application of doctrines to the cosmos as we know it. And all this, save neutral philosophical analysis, can be termed 'metaphysics'. Or it is a sort of natural theology—it is natural, since it does not merely expound revelation but attempts to give reasons on behalf of a revelation; and it is theology because it involves religious beliefs and ways of speaking. But perhaps I am here being a Pickwick, for this is not natural theology in the old sense. It is a soft, rather than the old hard, variety.

Yet what of the glimmering abstractions of yesteryear? What of the Five Ways and the superb claims of reason? Here, I can only feel that the hard metaphysics of the old days, where Aristotle and others conspire with faith, has to be left on one side. It is true that there are uneasinesses about the cosmos which the traditional arguments for God's existence enshrine—in particular the cosmological worry of why anything exists at all. But the rules of argument in this connexion are so debatable that it is absurd to pretend that we have either strong inductions or deductions here. In short, traditional natural theology can supply hunches which perhaps reinforce the insights of religious phenomenology, but it cannot stand on its own.[1]

The main point of this paper may be put in another way by saying that any appeal to religious experience (whether intuitive or otherwise) must inevitably lead to a consideration of the experience not merely of Christians but of Buddhists and others, and thereby to an examination of the way experience is linked to different sorts of doctrines. Through this investigation one is bound to ask what the criteria are for choosing between different formulations of religious belief. And from the apologetic point of view it is necessary to give reasons for accepting one's own faith rather than some other. Since natural theology in the old form appears to me to be gravely suspect, and since an irrationalist appeal to revelation alone (whether fundamentalist or not) is utterly self-defeating, our only choice is to work with the notion of religious reasons of the kind which I have sketched.

All this may seem somewhat programmatic. But even programmes are sometimes useful, and I have tried to illustrate part of the programme of Christian metaphysics. I said at the outset that natural theology is the Sick Man of Europe. I do not profess to have cured him. But at least I have tried to give advice on how to live with one's coronary.

---

[1] This same point about the traditional proofs is made with a rather different emphasis in Ch. X, pp. 172–3.—Ed.

VI

HILARY ARMSTRONG

PLATONISM

It is really rather doubtful whether a historian of philosophy of a narrowly specialist sort ought to thrust himself into the conversation of professional philosophers, even if he is addicted, as many historians of ideas are, to unprofessional reflections on the subject of his study. However, I was invited to take part in this conference and I accepted the invitation, so the question whether I ought to have done so has merely academic interest. It seems only honest, though, to expose to you shortly both my qualifications, or lack of qualifications, and the reasons which have led me to allow myself to be intruded into this eminently respectable party, in spite of the fact that I am a member of the philosophical *demi-monde*, a person addicted to the almost unmentionable vice (in contemporary Christian intellectual circles) of Neoplatonism, and the inadequate interpreter of a philosopher who can legitimately be called a 'mystic', that deadliest term of abuse in the current philosophical vocabulary.

To begin with, then, I am a historian of philosophy, and one who received his first training in that discipline at Cambridge. This accounts for some peculiarities in my outlook, in particular for my conviction that if you talk about a philosopher, and still more if you attack him, you ought to get your facts right and show some solid evidence that you have read and understood him. This conviction does not seem to be universally shared by English philosophers. In *The Times* report of the meeting of English and French philosophers at Royaumont[1] I find this sentence: 'There was some criticism of the English sense of scholarly responsibility, when an Oxford philosopher, who was corrected on his mistaken account of Husserl, replied cheerfully: "What I said about

[1] May 17, 1958.

Husserl was intended as a caricature. I don't care if it's true or false".' I have come across a good deal of this sort of thing in my desultory and severely limited reading of what contemporary philosophers write. Some English Thomists in particular seem unable to refrain from casual remarks about Platonism or Neoplatonism which are only too often stupid caricatures or at best wildly inaccurate generalizations; and this seems to me an immorally irresponsible way of going on. Truth, after all, does matter, and the only way of finding out the truth about a philosophy is to study it with scholarly care, and, if it is a philosophy of a remote time, place, or culture, with all the help which specialist scholars and historians can give you. If you don't want to know or tell the truth about a philosophy it would be much better not to mention it. So one of the reasons which has led me to appear before you is not to tell you the whole truth about Platonism, which would require an enormous and elaborate book in many volumes, most of which I am not qualified to write, but to indicate at least a little of the wide range, depth and variety of that philosophy and of its contributions to Christian thinking, and to show how inadequate and inaccurate some common generalizations about it are.

Another reason which has led me to come here is that it seems to me a good thing that professional philosophers should sometimes hear something about what unprofessional philosophers are thinking, and in particular, perhaps, that Christian professional philosophers should give some attention to the views of Christians who are certainly not professional philosophers but who do spend a good deal of time thinking seriously about their religion. People of this kind, of course, vary even more in their ways of thinking than professional or academic philosophers, and I make no claim to be a representative or typical specimen, though I think my sort of mentality is not uncommon among Christians in this country. It is marked by a considerable distrust of logic and doubt of the power of discursive argument to establish anything very much or very firmly.[1] As a historian of philosophy I know that

---

[1] This should not be pressed to mean more than it says. It does not imply any desire to banish logic or discursive argument from philosophy, but only a lack of confidence in attempts to establish the truth of metaphysical statements, especially about God, by purely discursive or inferential processes.

there are no more fragile, dusty and unmistakably defunct
specimens in my museum than the great knock-down arguments
and universally valid proofs of the past. Myths, symbols and metaphors show much greater vitality. Platonism can provide plenty
of these last; and though Platonists have often shown themselves
extremely vigorous and competent logicians and arguers, they
have never relied exclusively on logical proof or canonized one
particular method of argument in the way in which other philosophies have done. Intellectual certainty for Platonists is a matter
of directly seeing or experiencing something: the whole process of
philosophical discourse is only a way of preparing the mind for
that flash of intuition, that 'light kindled from a leaping fire', of
which Plato speaks in the Seventh Letter (341D) when he is
introducing the great philosophical digression which perhaps
tells us more clearly than anything else he wrote how he thought
one ought to philosophize, and what sort of person an aspirant to
philosophy ought to be. And Platonists have generally thought of
these intuitions, which alone are true knowledge, as so rare and so
difficult even for good men of great natural powers to attain, that
they are not prepared to exclude any kind of discourse that
experience has shown may help to prepare the mind for them. So
they will argue, they will preach, they will compose poetic
incantations, they will appeal to ancient tradition and any divine
revelation which may be available to them, they will call to
witness not only the ordinary experiences of the common man
but the rare experiences of men of exceptional wisdom and
holiness; they will use all the resources of human language, and
not confine themselves to one particular kind of language labelled
'philosophical'. So they have a great deal more to offer than most
other philosophers to an unprofessional, unsystematic, undis-
cursive religious person like myself. Again, Platonists (above all
Neoplatonists) have, of course, produced a number of philosophical systems, more or less coherent structures of interlinked
dogmas, and have often presented their own particular one as the
only authentic version of Plato's thought. But for various
reasons, of which the baffling lack of system in Plato's own
writings is one of the most important, no one system or set of
philosophical dogmas has ever quite succeeded in imposing itself

as the only genuine Platonism, and the Platonic tradition has always remained the most open of all the great philosophies to ideas from outside, not only from other philosophies but from science and theology. In particular the succession of great theologians who are rather loosely classed as Christian Platonists, who have generally been Christians first and Platonists very much second, have freely and vigorously remodelled Platonism to suit the Christian doctrines as they personally received and understood them. This openness is an obvious result of the way of thinking about philosophical discourse which I have just outlined, and the result of it is that a Platonist can be uncommitted, vague, tentative and agnostic about particular philosophical dogmas to a degree unusual among metaphysical philosophers, and highly satisfactory to unsystematic religious thinkers. For instance, I find myself able to accept Dom Illtyd Trethowan's criticism of the concept of potency[1] without feeling that I have in any way abandoned my Platonism, in spite of the fact that the Aristotelian conception has been accepted by the great majority of Platonists (though not by all of them) for a great many centuries. Nor do I think that Platonists are as thoroughly committed to particular epistemological and psychological theories as is sometimes supposed. And even a doctrine which in one form or another is held by everyone who can reasonably be described as a Platonist, the doctrine of transcendent Forms or Ideas, has undergone some very remarkable transformations in the course of its history, as we shall see.

The openness of thought, the distrust of complete closed metaphysical systems, which make people like myself find Platonism attractive, is the characteristic of our curious minds which I particularly want to commend to the attention of Christian professional philosophers. I certainly believe that Catholic Christianity implies certain metaphysical assertions, of a kind which can be made by Platonists, Thomists, and a great many people who are neither. But I am also convinced that it does not and cannot imply a complete closed metaphysical system. Cannot, because it claims to be a universal religion, for all men and at all times. And if the history of philosophy teaches us anything it is

---

[1] *Meaning of Existence*, pp. 117ff.

that closed metaphysical systems are not at all universal; they never appear convincing and satisfactory to more than a comparatively few people for a comparatively limited time. As R. C. Zaehner has argued convincingly in his admirable book *At Sundry Times*, 'Since Christianity claims to be a universal faith, it can only survive by showing that it can assimilate not only what is digestible to the Christian constitution in Plato and Aristotle, but also whatever in Oriental religion seems to point the way to Christ'.[1] To me it seems that an open-minded and unsystematic Christian Platonism offers the best help at present available in our Western tradition for doing this, and also for dealing with those currents of thought in the West, vague and hard to describe but sometimes very powerful, which have some affinities with Oriental religion and cannot, as far as I can see, be effectively understood or controlled by either Thomism or contemporary English philosophy. The future of Thomism, as far as I can see, depends upon its being able to transform itself from the closed system which it appears to most people to be at present into an open philosophy admitting non-deductive ways of thinking and dogmatic variations on important points; many Thomists, I know, are working in this direction. They will, however, probably have to go much further than most of them are prepared to at present in reducing the Aristotelian element in their thought; for the influence of Aristotle always seems to lead to attempts at closed and exclusive systematization, and to a lack of sympathy or understanding for other ways of thinking, which is most noticeable in Aristotle's criticism of Plato. If Thomism does not succeed in opening itself in this way it will remain what, as far as I can see, it is at present, on the whole more of an intellectual encumbrance than a help to the Catholic Church and one of the most effective means of dissuading people from accepting her claims to universality.

What I have said about the undesirability of trying to commit Christianity to a closed metaphysical system applies even more strongly, in my opinion, to exclusive anti-metaphysical ways of thinking, whether of the kind still current among professional English philosophers or that odd, abstract Hebraic-revival

---

[1] p. 166.

G

dogmatism which is sometimes called 'Biblical'.[1] The use of contemporary analytic techniques can, I am sure, be valuable, and study of the Bible is of course essential to a Christian philosopher. It is only when these activities lead to negative dogmatisms that I object to the result. The most monstrous and grotesquely narrow-minded effects of all are produced when some Thomist, anxious to be up-to-date, tries to go all analytic or Biblical or both while still remaining a Thomist, and reaches a quite remarkable degree of intellectual sectarianism and exclusiveness by combining these distinct kinds of narrowness.

It will probably seem to you more than time that I should try to give some sort of a description of this Platonism about which I have been talking so vaguely. But a good deal of this rambling introduction was necessary in order to explain why I find it extremely difficult to do so. After what I have said I can hardly be expected to pick out one of the innumerable interpretations of Plato's own thought, or one of the later Platonic systems, and present it as the one authentic Platonism. And I find it almost impossible to formulate a set of generalizations which will apply to the whole of this vast and complex movement of thought and will not be in some ways seriously misleading. After all, one of my main purposes in coming here was to discourage the habit of writing-off Platonism in a few neat generalizations based on a one-sided view of part only of the Platonic tradition—thinking, for instance, that you have disposed of Platonism if you have repeated Aristotle's criticism of the Theory of Forms or refuted one version of Augustinian illumination. (It is perhaps worth remarking in passing, in case anyone does not know it already, that the progress of scholarship and the growth of intelligent popularization in recent years has made it quite inexcusable for anyone who wishes to make statements about Platonism to be really badly informed about Middle-Platonism, Neoplatonism, or the thought of the Christian Fathers.)

---

[1] This impolite description is certainly not intended to apply to all Biblical theology. It is meant only for those Biblical theologians, Catholic or Protestant, who try to impose the acceptance of what seem to me highly abstract concepts of time or history or person or existence on all Christian thinkers; who try to insist that all true Christians must think as modern Biblical scholars think that ancient Jews thought: or who regard mysticism or metaphysics, or both, as incompatible with Christianity.

The least unsatisfactory thing that I can find to do in these circumstances is to try to show something of what Platonism is like and how it has developed by concentrating on one particular topic, the doctrine of Ideas or Forms. I have chosen this because it is distinctively Platonic if anything is, and also because it has, as I think, been very much misunderstood and many important features of its development ignored. The doctrine of Forms is not, of course, by any means the whole of Platonism. A very great deal more of traditional Christian natural theology than is sometimes realized is Platonic in origin. But Platonic topics like the transcendence and incomprehensibility of God, or the immortality of our souls, will certainly be discussed on other occasions during this meeting and will fit in better there. I am inclined to think that discussion of the Forms has often been led on to the wrong track both by Aristotle's criticism and by the early medieval discussions about universals, which, as Leff points out in his Pelican book *Medieval Thought*,[1] were not really about the existence or non-existence of divine Ideas; they were discussions about the grouping of things into genera and species carried on in terms of logic and epistemology. As a result of these distorting influences the doctrine of Forms tends to be considered almost exclusively from a theory-of-knowledge point of view and to be stated as if it meant belief in the existence of a set of abstract universal eternal objects of knowledge. Now in fact it has always been at least as important to those who profess the doctrine that the Ideas are causes or givers of being, in some sense, to the things of this world as that they are causes of true knowledge in our minds. There have in fact been Greek Christian Platonists who denied, at least by implication, that we could have any knowledge of the Ideas in God because they are identical with God's transcendent and incomprehensible nature; to this we shall have to return. And the Ideas, so I believe, are not thought of by Plato, still less by later Platonists, as abstract in the Aristotelian sense, and in the later and Christian Platonists they are not necessarily universal and are not in any ordinary sense of the word objective.

These statements about the Ideas will not, I think, appear so very surprising to anyone who knows the original texts and the

[1] pp. 104ff.

best scholarly work which has been done on them in recent years. It would be impossible to provide sufficient documentation and demonstration to convince those who do not within the limits of this paper; and besides, the first point (that the Ideas are not abstract Aristotelian universals existing 'by themselves'—a perfectly preposterous and to me inconceivable sort of entities) requires a good deal of technical logical discussion which I am not qualified to attempt. However, on this question of Ideas, abstraction and universals, two admirable discussions are available in English to which I will without more ado refer anyone who is interested. They are Cornford's contrast between Plato's dialectic and Aristotle's logic in his commentary on the *Sophist*,[1] and A. C. Lloyd's superbly competent study 'Neoplatonic Logic and Aristotelian Logic' which appeared in the first two numbers of *Phronesis*.[2] (I call Professor Lloyd as a witness, of course, only on this particular point: he would, I am sure, heartily disagree with a great deal else that I am trying to say.) Abstract thinking, in fact, in the derogatory sense of the word, thinking, that is, which operates with large generalizations rather out of touch with reality about, for instance, 'man', or 'the human mind', seems to me more characteristic of Aristotelian (though perhaps bad Aristotelian) thinking than of Platonic. The Platonist, after all, is not primarily concerned with the question 'What general and universally valid conclusions can I draw from ordinary everyday experience?'—to which the answer, in my private opinion, is 'Precious few, if any'. He is concerned with the question 'How can I come to know God and to be like him, as far as possible?'—and neither 'I' nor 'God' in that question are abstract general terms.

As for the other statements I have made about the Ideas, that they are not thought of as necessarily universal is true from the time of Plotinus onwards (the question of whether there were Ideas of individuals was already being discussed in the second century A.D., but most Platonists then rejected them.[3] Plotinus is

[1] *Plato's Theory of Knowledge*, pp. 268–73.

[2] *Phronesis*, Vol. I, Nos. 1 and 2, November 1955 and May 1956. I should make it clear that these articles are not a demonstration of the difference between Neoplatonic and Aristotelian universals, though they do show this difference clearly in the course of a complex and subtle discussion which it would be unwise for a non-logician to attempt to summarize, but which is of the greatest interest to all historians of logic.

[3] cp. Albinus, Ch. 9.

the first Platonist whom we know to have accepted Ideas of individuals. They appear, of course, in the fully developed scholastic doctrine of Ideas in St Bonaventure and St Thomas; but there is nothing distinctively Christian in accepting them.) The doctrine that there are Ideas or Forms of individuals does not, of course, involve any absurd assertion that there are universals of individuals. It rather denies to the universal any sort of metaphysical privilege or superior reality, takes the Forms right out of the logical and epistemological discussion about the status of universals, and leaves the Platonist who accepts the doctrine and sees these obvious implications[1] free to take any view about any particular group of universals or alleged universals that seems to him to be supported by reason and evidence. If biologists, for instance, want to think of biological genera and species in an extremely nominalist way there seems no reason why a Christian Neoplatonist should feel bound by his philosophical loyalties to disagree with them. Nor will he rest his belief in natural law and universal moral obligations on some alleged discernment of moral universals *in re*, but will rather hold that when we are aware of a moral law or obligation as binding without exception or possibility of dispensation some knowledge of the eternal archetypes is somehow being communicated to us. As we are to have a proper, professionally conducted, discussion on the autonomy of ethics later I will not discuss here at length any points of similarity and difference between this doctrine and Platonism. I suppose that its upholders would agree with me that you cannot derive moral obligations from descriptions of human behaviour by any process of abstraction, conceptualization and deduction; but that most of them would not agree that our awareness of moral obligations is due to the influence on our minds of a reality in which 'is' and 'ought' coincide, in which our selves as they ought to be and the whole pattern of relationships which ought to exist between them are eternally known and willed.[2] If I was challenged to say what a

---

[1] I see no reason to suppose that Plotinus *did* see the implications.

[2] I should perhaps explain that for me the primary moral obligation is to be a good man rather than to perform or refrain from performing particular actions. Goodness is for me primarily a quality of persons, not actions. And I cannot, in thinking about God, separate moral and ontological goodness as sharply as Dr Ewing would perhaps wish. A single good which is both seems to me to be given in the primary metaphysical awareness.

wide moral Form, 'justice' or 'righteousness' (*dikaiosunē*), let us say, becomes in the individualized intelligible world of later Platonism I think I should reply that it is something like the totality of all the right relationships which exist there and ought to exist here between all actual or possible persons, including both what is common to all and what are peculiar though recognizably kindred features of each.

My statement that in later and Christian Platonism the Ideas are not in any ordinary sense of the word objective requires rather more explanation. It depends on the doctrine accepted by all Platonists from the first century B.C. onwards that the Forms or Ideas are in the divine mind. I am not myself completely convinced by the efforts of a number of distinguished scholars to show that Plato himself held this doctrine; if I were, it would make my task of explaining what Platonism is very much easier. But I do not think at present that our evidence is sufficient for us to be able to come to any clear and definitive conclusion about how Plato thought of the relationship between divine mind and the Forms. But there is no doubt whatever about the prevalence of the doctrine in later and Christian Platonism. (I presume that there is no one here who is so ill informed that he needs to be shown that there is nothing distinctively Jewish or Christian about this development.) And with the coming together in the second century A.D. of the simple idea that the Forms are in the divine mind with the Aristotelian idea of divine *noesis noeseōs* there appears the classical form of the doctrine, magnificently developed by Plotinus, in which the World of Forms and the divine intellect are identical; the Forms are just the divine mind looked at from the point of view of the content of its eternal self-knowledge which is itself, a knowledge which is creative, the cause of everything else, including all other minds and their knowledge, because it is the primary and originative everything. If you begin to understand what this means it becomes obvious that the mind which is the Forms is not just an object, sitting there augustly self-thinking for us to look at or think about. Possibly Aristotelian divine minds, the forty-seven or fifty-five cosmic motors, are like that. The Platonic divine mind never is. It is a power working most intimately in or on our minds as their source, working whether we are conscious of it or not, and if we have any knowledge of the Forms it is because the divine mind is raising us as far as possible to its own level, thinking in us and setting off our own thinking. This, I think, is the sort of way in which we have to understand Augustine's extremely imprecise statements about 'illumination'.

This, I think, is the right point to draw attention to the fact that it is good Neoplatonic doctrine to say that this way of talking about the divine mind which is the Forms cannot be taken as an adequate or satisfactory description of God. For Plotinus, of course, the One or Good, who is for him what we mean by God, transcends, and is the source or cause of, the intellect which is the world of Forms, the second hypostasis in his descending hierarchical order. It is perhaps worth mentioning that it is not, first and foremost, the plurality of the Forms which Plotinus thinks of as incompatible with the divine simplicity (though it *is* of course incompatible with it in his thought) but the duality implied in even the highest conception which we can form of thinking. Critical reflection on what Aristotle and his followers had to say about divine thinking seems to have played an important part in his working out of his own doctrine. After Nicaea orthodox Christians could no longer arrange the persons of the Trinity in descending order as Origen had done, with the Father corresponding to the One and the *Logos* to the divine intellect. They could not, therefore, follow Plotinus's too short and easy way to asserting divine unity and simplicity. They did, however, find a great deal of what Plotinus said about the divine intellect-world of Forms better applicable to created being than to God. They apply a good deal of it to our own minds at their highest, and for the Greek Fathers the *kosmos noetos*, the intelligible world, is the world of the angels; a similar way of speaking of the angelic city or world in Plotinian terms is to be found in Augustine.[1] Their intelligible world, in fact, is the spiritual creation, the highest and most perfect created image of God, and

[1] A great deal has been written about this development: the best starting-point is von Balthasar's admirable short summary of it [pp. xviiff. of the introduction to his book on Gregory of Nyssa, *Présence et Pensée* (Paris, 1942)]. A short account, with some further references, will be found in Ch. III of R. A. Markus's and my book *The Great Dialogue*. (Darton, Longman and Todd 1960.)

not God himself. But they continue to assert that the Ideas or Forms which are the eternal creative archetypes of things are (in some way beyond our understanding) in God, and particularly in the *Logos*, the Uncreated Image of the Father, by whom all things were made. The Greeks think that we cannot, strictly speaking, know God and therefore, by implication, not the Ideas in so far as they are identical with the divine essence. The highest level at which we can still speak of knowledge, even supernatural knowledge, is the intelligible or angelic world, and we must pass beyond knowledge to find God. (I am not competent to deal with the Palamite distinction of essence and energies, which probably ought to be brought in here.) Augustine, as is well known, is a good deal less consistent and definite, and does seem to assert that we are aware of the divine Ideas in some way. Whether we follow him or the Greeks depends very much on the conclusions we come to about our knowledge of God and about where negative theology leads us: and as we are to have a proper discussion about this later I will not confuse the issue here. I will only say that I have personally no sympathy with what Dom Illtyd Trethowan has called 'Christian Atheism', and that I do not believe that either Plotinus or the Greek Fathers really meant to assert that we can know nothing whatever about God. Negative or apophatic theology for them certainly does not lead to complete ignorance but to an awareness of the inadequacy of our concepts and language to comprehend or express the reality to which they are none the less really pointing us on—it is always used in close conjunction with positive and affirmative ways of speaking about God. And though *ekstasis* carries us beyond the negative theology, which is after all still an intellectual activity, yet it does not seem to me that Neoplatonist or 'Dionysian' mystics regard the goal of their aspiration as nothing but nothing, an unknown and unknowable negation, or that they ever seriously maintain that everything they have thought or said about God is shown by the experience of mystical union to be simply untrue.

I am going to end my paper by trying to explain why it still seems to me worth while to use the language of the Platonic Forms or Ideas in speaking about God and the world. First of all, though, I should like to make clear that I do not at all mind if other people prefer to say the same things in a different language, as long as I am reasonably sure that they are saying the same things. As I have tried to say already, I have a deep distrust of generalizations about 'the human mind', and consequently about 'philosophy', 'philosophical language', or 'philosophical method'. It seems to me that there are rather a large number of human minds and that they can arrive at substantially the same conclusions by a variety of different routes, and consequently express them in a variety of different terms. Thomists seem to want everybody to be Thomist. I do not want everybody to be Platonist. I do not particularly mind some people being Thomists as long as they do not make foolish remarks about Platonism or claim, against all the historical evidence, that their particular version of Christian-Hellenic philosophy is in some unique way universal and perennial.

But why do I personally still want to use this language, if only in the queer, reserved, stammering way in which my Neoplatonist and Christian Platonist masters have taught me that it must be used about God? It is not easy to arrive at one's real reasons for doing or believing anything—some philosophers, so it seems to me, do not even try very hard to do so. But I think that I can detect two such reasons in the recesses of my mind, which I extract and put forward, not as proofs but as inadequate discursive expressions of personal pressures that are probably operating much deeper down. First, the doctrine of divine Ideas expresses for me in the clearest and strongest way possible my conviction that God is not arbitrary. It is my defence against believing in the horrible deity of Ockham, the God of *potentia absoluta*—a belief to which religious persons are often tempted in their madder or more perplexed moments, but which, I am convinced, deeply degrades the minds of those who succumb to the temptation. It is when contemporary Biblical theology seems to be reinforcing belief in this sort of God, for whom right and wrong are mere matters of arbitrary command, that it becomes for me something dangerous and sinister. Belief in the Ideas means to me that when I think of God commanding or prohibiting, making me aware of a personal obligation or a universal moral law, I do not think of his commands as expressions of an absolute, all-powerful will which could command what is now sin and prohibit what is now virtue if it chose. I think of the obligations laid upon me as expressions of his absolute wisdom and goodness which knows what is really best for me and for all mankind because in knowing himself he knows our eternal archetypes which are more truly our selves than ourselves, and wills in his goodness that we should be as perfectly conformed to them, that is to himself, as possible. 'Let us give back to the Image[1] that which is according to the image': that saying of St Gregory Nazianzen, quoted on the title-page of the *Atlas of the Early Christian World*, seems to me to sum up the morality of Christian Platonism: and I think that here, as at so many other points, St Thomas is still in the Christian Platonist tradition. It should be noted that this Christian Platonist belief in God's wisdom and goodness does not necessarily imply any claim that we know the divine Ideas, but only a faith that God knows them and acts by them. I may continue to find his dealings with men extremely mysterious, even if I am convinced that they are not arbitrary. What this conviction would rest on if one became sure that one could have no sort of awareness at all of the divine Ideas is rather difficult to say. The Greeks, I think, would appeal to revelation and say that the doctrine of Ideas or Forms and the way of thinking about God's wisdom and goodness which it implies is part of the doctrine of the *Logos* rightly and traditionally understood. They are theologians, and in no way concerned to construct a philosophy in the scholastic or modern sense. Christian Platonists in general, I think, are less concerned about keeping philosophy and theology separate than Thomists. But a proper discussion of how we can know that God is not arbitrary, and in general how we can know what he is like, belongs to the enquiry about our knowledge of God, which I must not anticipate.

The other reason is the very deep conviction that I have that this world is an image-world, a visible and changing expression of the invisible and eternal. Here we are at the very heart of Platonism, and it goes far too deep for me to express it properly; and to give any sort of even approximately adequate idea of what it has meant to Platonists would mean putting in as evidence,

---

[1] That is, the Uncreated Image, the *Logos*.

besides a vast mass of philosophical, theological and liturgical texts, a very great many European works of art, Byzantine, medieval, Renaissance and baroque. I think, by the way, that the very small part which it has played in recent centuries in Western scholastic thinking is one of the reasons (though by no means the only one) why that thinking seems so repellent to Eastern Orthodox theologians and philosophers; people to whom we always ought to have paid much more attention than we have been in the habit of doing and to whom we certainly ought to attend now in view of the great and growing concern for Christian unity. It is, at any rate, in the Byzantine Liturgy (and the Liturgy is centrally important for Orthodox thinking in a way in which it is not for ours) that I myself have found the sense of the presence of the eternal in and beyond the temporal and the visible as sign of the invisible most vividly expressed.

The nearest I can get at present to explaining what I mean by this 'iconic' view of the world is to say that in it things are neither valuable 'in themselves' nor valueless 'in themselves' but carry, simply by being what they are, a worth and significance which is given to them from something which is other, but not alien, which is their own proper perfection, and more, and which remains for ever when they pass away. In this way of thinking God is seen in relation to the world first and foremost as the creator of forms or essences. I have always been puzzled and dissatisfied by the sharp distinction some Thomists make between 'essentialist' and 'existentialist' thinking. I cannot in my own mind so separate essence and existence, *what* a thing is and *that* it is, that I can think of either by itself. The 'concept of being' is to me an empty abstraction, perhaps a pseudo-concept, as A. L. Peck thinks it was for Plato.[1] And if I could cut out of my thought about God all consideration of him as giver of forms and concentrate exclusively on him as giver of being it would be only a pseudo-deity, a contentless abstraction, that I should have in mind. I cannot really believe that it would make no important difference to my knowledge about God if all he had created, besides myself

---

[1] "Plato and the ΜΕΓΙΣΤΑ ΓΕΝΗ of the *Sophist*", *C.Q.N.S*, II, 1–2, January-April 1952: cp. especially p. 53. Plotinus, *Enn.* V. 5[32]6, clearly states the inseparability of form-essence and existence, and makes 'being' a collective term for the totality of real beings.

as knower, was some sort of second-rate toadstool—undoubtedly a contingent being—instead of the splendid cosmos of images which he has in fact made to mirror his perfection.

It is important, if you are to understand Platonism at all, to understand that it *is* by being themselves that things image their archetypes. There is sometimes some confusion, I think, on this point, and when Platonists speak of the world as a world of signs and images of eternal reality they are sometimes thought to be carrying on the delightful (and sometimes valuable) activity of finding symbolic correspondences in the universe, to which they are admittedly much addicted, with such an intolerable degree of seriousness as to lose all grasp of reality. But for the Platonist a pelican is not, first and foremost, a symbol of Christ's piety. It is a symbol of Christ's pelicanity, of that in the Eternal World which can only be expressed in creation as a pelican. So the Platonist has not any quarrel with the poet or painter who insists that his poem or painting means nothing else but itself, and is not symbolizing Profane Love or the Virtue of Critical Circumspection or telling a story which could quite as well have been told in plain prose— if, that is, he is a Platonist who follows Plotinus rather than Plato in his understanding of artistic activity, and holds that the artist has some sort of direct access to the Forms or their *logoi* in created minds and is not a mere copyist of sense-reality.

Another misunderstanding which needs to be guarded against is about the nature of Platonic 'other-worldliness'. To regard this world as an image-world is compatible with a wide range of attitudes towards it, from the ultra-Puritanical to the near-idolatrous, and a Platonist will often change with remarkable speed from one to another—Plotinus is a notable example. But there are two ways of looking at the world which are absolutely incompatible with Platonism. You cannot take the world of ordinary experience as just being as it happens to be and able to afford you all the satisfaction you can reasonably want just as it is: and you cannot hate and despise the world. You may be impatient with images, always wanting to get beyond them to the reality, and may try, not always successfully, to use them as little as possible in your thought; or you may love and venerate them to the extreme point which is possible while still remembering that they are images. But you cannot, if you are a Platonist, forget that they are images and that they are holy images, made by God out of his goodness, which they represent in varied forms. Plotinus, in his great treatise *Against the Gnostics* has said the last word, from the Platonic point of view, about the absurdity of a merely negative, world-hating other-worldliness: 'But they do not honour this creation or this earth, and say that a new earth has come into existence for them, to which, say they, they will go away from this one: and that this is the rational form [*logos*] of the universe. And yet why do they feel the need to be there, in the archetype of the universe which they hate?'[1] Platonism has often helped people to love this world with a peculiar intensity, as Plotinus helped the novelist Elizabeth Myers, whose intense love for the goodness of the worst people and the beauty of the commonest things is the one thing that again and again lifts her writing from below mediocrity to something very like genius. As any good history of European science or art will show it has again and again attracted and inspired scientists and artists—its influence on both science and the arts has been, I should have thought, far more positive and beneficial than that of any kind of Aristotelianism. Platonists, of course, have a very vivid, and in my opinion realistic, sense of the troubles and frustrations of our human condition here below and are intensely aware of the precarious instability of things, the continual imminence of change and death. But because their other world is not far off in space or time, because the eternal and intelligible is present to them in its images here and now, their Platonic faith does, sometimes at least, greatly deepen their love for the fleeting goods and beauties they encounter, because they see in them the flash of an eternal excellence, and leads them to the hope that all good and beauty that has passed them and gone is kept safe in God and may, if he wills, be given back to them again when they come to join their fellow-citizens in their true country.

[1] II. 9[33]5.23–27, trans. Armstrong.

RETROSPECT

The discussion of this paper showed me one or two points at which I ought to have made myself clearer—there are no doubt many others. First, what I said against Thomism, though justified by the sort of language still used by some Thomists and the sort of teaching still given in too many places to Catholic clerical students, was never intended to apply to all philosophers who call themselves Thomists. In particular, it was not directed against Dr Daly or Canon D. J. B. Hawkins. Canon Hawkins's writings, especially his recent book *Some Crucial Problems in Modern Philosophy*, are sufficient evidence that he does not deserve the sort of criticisms which I have made. I am in almost complete agreement with what he says about 'perennial philosophy' in the last chapter of that book. It will not, of course, escape the notice of any intelligent Thomist who reads my paper that in spite of my dislike of conventional Thomism I have not succeeded in putting forward any *positive* philosophical doctrine which is not to be found somewhere in St Thomas.

I also want to make clearer than it appears to be in the paper that the only form of the doctrine of Ideas which I consider tenable is that in which they are identified with God's knowledge as the exemplary cause of all things (i.e. the fully developed Neoplatonic doctrine with its medieval refinements). I do not want to use the language of Ideas or Forms except as a difficult but, as it seems to me, necessary way of talking about God. So questions about our knowledge of the Ideas become a special sort of questions about our knowledge of God, and questions about their eternity, perfection, etc., a special sort of questions about God's eternity, perfection, etc. The doctrine of Ideas as universals *ante rem* existing 'by themselves', which certainly seems to have been held by Plato at least at one period of his life, is not one which I hold or wish to defend. But to think that you have disposed of Platonism when you have refuted it seems to me rather like supposing that you have disposed of Greek Christian theology when you have refuted some of the odder opinions of Origen, or of Latin Christian theology when you have rejected the extremer positions of Augustine.

VII

D. J. B. HAWKINS

TOWARDS THE
RESTORATION OF METAPHYSICS

I

It is no longer necessary, perhaps, to meet objections of principle against metaphysics, since anti-metaphysical principles, like that of verification, have a way of turning out to be themselves metaphysical. But a rather stubborn passive resistance to metaphysics remains characteristic of a great deal of contemporary British philosophy. The tactic of the anti-metaphysician—and it is by no means ineffective—is to stay mum and to defy the metaphysician to break through his guard. If metaphysical statements can be dismissed one by one as linguistic muddles, the result is the same in the end as if they had been disqualified in the name of some universal maxim.

In some circles, however, it is no longer a solecism to talk of metaphysics. Yet, even here, it is not very clear what is being done under that title. Perhaps it amounts only to assigning a special logical status to entities like God and the soul. If we seek to give metaphysics a wider scope and a more definite status, we need not expect an easy passage.

In the first place, then, what is meant by metaphysics? Many people, as we have just remarked, take it to mean the discussion of what they would describe as metaphysical or non-empirical entities such as God and the soul. For my part I should wish to say that the soul, in so far as it refers to our conscious life of thinking and striving, is a thoroughly empirical entity, but it might be rash to begin with so direct a challenge. Let us first recall the kind of difficulty which many philosophers since Hume have felt about such matters.

When we say that something is yellow or sweet or noisy or hard, we can point to certain definite types of experience to which we refer by these words. If you are a Frenchman and do not know the meaning of the English word *yellow*, and I have forgotten that the French for *yellow* is *jaune*, I can always point, for instance, to a buttercup and say that this is of the colour that I mean. But to what, people ask, can we point to identify God or the soul? It is when we find this question disconcerting that we tend to adopt the position of Hume.

We may pursue the difficulty in respect of the soul. When we examine the language in which we speak of the soul, it seems to be derived from our experience of material things. By way of a rather gross example, we talk of the villain's soul as black and filthy and of the hero's as pure and white and shining. These expressions are, perhaps, evidently metaphorical, but can we escape less obvious metaphors when we try to talk about the life of mind? We talk about analysing or cutting up our ideas and of synthesizing or putting them together again just as if we were dealing with a sort of jigsaw puzzle. Our ideas are said to influence our actions. What is this mysterious fluid which flows out of our minds into our bodies and is thought to affect the material world? No chemist or physicist has ever discovered it.

But the whole point about the soul is that it is supposed to be other than material things. If we can only describe it in terms derived from our experience of the material world, are we not deceiving ourselves and constructing a pseudo-entity which has no real description at all? Of course there must be some reason for our doing so, but, if we are to translate the language of unsophisticated common sense into more appropriate terms, we may suppose that we are really talking about some rather odd characteristics of bodily activities in complex organisms such as our own. Instead of the awkward duality of body and mind we shall now think of mental facts as adverbial to bodily activities. Thus we may think that we get rid of one bit of bad metaphysics and at the same time dispose of the embarrassing metaphysical problem of the relation of body and mind.

When we consider the language which we use about God, a still more radical difficulty presents itself. God is absolute and infinite, but all our concepts are derived from contingent and finite things. How, then, can we attribute anything positive to God? No doubt we could talk about God in negative terms, calling him absolute or uncaused, infinite or unlimited, but a wholly negative description is no description at all. Yet positive terms, like wise or good, are derived from finite experience and would need, so to say, to be stretched to infinity to become applicable to God. But that might seem to be impossible. Must we not say, therefore, that, in trying to think about God, we are not really thinking anything at all? We might put it in Kantian language and say that we have no genuine concept of God but are merely projecting an ideal beyond the horizons of any possible exact thinking.

If, then, we seek to vindicate the significance of talk about God and the soul, we have to ask a more general question about our language and thinking. Does our language contain any terms which can be used significantly in a new kind of situation? Have we notions which are susceptible of new force in a new field of application? This is fundamentally the question that we ask when we inquire whether we have notions which are not merely univocal or tied down to a determinate range of application but are analogously applicable outside the type of situation in which they were originally verified.

The notion about whose applications we might make the widest claims is evidently the notion of being. Ultimately, then, the question about the possibility of metaphysical discourse turns out to be the question whether we can significantly discuss being and the *passiones entis*, the notions whose generality transcends the distinction between mind and matter. Can there be a systematic ontology as a special branch, or, to be more exact, as the central stem, of philosophy? That is what we have to ask.

II

The contemporary philosopher is inclined to hand over the word *being* to the logician. If it were true that the logician could say all that needed saying about it, there would be no room for metaphysics. What we have to try to show is that the logic of being

H

is not the same as ontology and wherein the transition lies from one to the other.

In any case it should be remarked that the notion of existence is a trifle embarrassing to the logician as such. The pure logician seems to be happiest when he is considering the implicative relations of propositions without having to bother whether the propositions are true or not. Even when adverting to the truth or falsity of propositions, he is most interested in general propositions which may or may not have an application to fact. Nevertheless, even the purest of logicians has to admit that existential propositions are a special class of proposition which exhibit a distinctive grammatical form and that he ought to be able to say something about them.

From the logician's point of view the most obvious thing to say about existence is that it signifies instantiation. If you are referring to a real singular known as such, then by definition it belongs to the real world and you are adding nothing by saying that it exists. But it makes sense to ask of a description whether it is verified or instantiated in fact. Are there black swans? Are there unicorns? Even, in the way in which an ostensible proper name may be part of a description, was there someone bearing the name of Mr Pickwick and behaving as Dickens describes Mr Pickwick as having behaved?

In all such cases we are seeking to pass from concept to fact, asking whether some description or other is instantiated in fact. Hence we are admittedly seeking to pass beyond the sphere of pure logic, but such a passage must sometimes be possible if logic is to be of any use. If nothing existed at all, there would be nothing to which logic could be applied and no logician to apply it. If the logician finds that at this stage he has to change his style and become a metaphysician, so much the better for him.

For, when we know that something exists and say that it exists, we are not saying nothing. When it is presupposed that the subject is a real singular, the statement that it exists is indeed certainly true. It may be a contingent thing, but, given that it exists and is such and such, there is a conditional logical necessity, as Aristotle already recognized, in attributing its actual predicates to it. But, in saying that it exists, we are pointing out something which it has in common with everything else in the real world. If *existence* had no distinctive meaning but was merely a portmanteau word signifying *A* or *B* or *C* or *D* or any other of the innumerable things which we have come across in experience, *nothing* would simply mean something other than *A* or *B* or *C* or *D*, etc. But *nothing* does not mean this. *Nothing* means 'nothing', and, when we reflect on the distinctive meaning of *nothing* and on the fact that *nothing* is the negation of *being*, we see clearly that *being* must have a distinctive meaning too.

Now there is something odd about the notion of being, which Kant expresses by saying that it is not a predicate. What does he mean by this? After all, existence is a perfectly acceptable logical or grammatical predicate. We may ask whether descriptions are instantiated and state that such things exist or not without any impropriety or fear of misunderstanding. The statement that being is not a predicate makes sense only as a metaphysical state-ment. It is only when we transcend the order of the logical passage from concept to fact and try to look at the structure of fact itself that we see, as Kant saw, that being is presupposed to every other aspect of things. To negate being is, ontologically, to negate everything.

Hence, in addition to the logical use of existence as a predicate signifying the instantiation in fact of a concept or description, there is a distinctive ontological or metaphysical way of thinking about existence. From this point of view the existential pro-position has, so to say, to be turned on its head. Being becomes more like an ultimate subject, or subject beyond all subjects, and things are determinate variants of the fundamental energy of being.

III

If we now turn to the Middle Ages, which were a period of con-structive metaphysics, we find a similar distinction of ways of thinking about existence. But the intellectual temptation of the Middle Ages was not to reduce metaphysics to logic but to suppose that logic could go unaltered into metaphysics.

At the back of one meaning of the celebrated distinction between essence and existence we find Avicenna's recognition that existence is predicated *per accidens* of created things. This is a point of view from which essence, or what a thing is, comes first in the order of reflection and, consequently, is equivalent to the concept of a thing. In this perspective existence signifies the instantiation of a concept in fact. But the medievals, unlike our contemporaries, were not inclined to draw the moral that the discussion of being belonged to the province of the logician. The medieval tendency was rather to translate this relationship straight into metaphysics and to say that created being involved the distinction and composition of the two partial factors of essence and existence in the sense, respectively, of what a thing is and the fact that it is.

Such was the distinction of essence and existence emphatically asserted by Giles of Rome (Aegidius Romanus) in the generation after Aquinas, and the distinction has since been asserted in this sense by many Thomists. At first sight it has a pleasing straightforwardness, but on reflection it reveals a serious difficulty. For, if actual things are essences with existence, it would seem to follow that merely possible things are essences without existence. The universe seems to be no longer the sum of real things but rather the sum of all possible things, of which a number really exist while the others do not. But what sort of reality attaches to an essence without existence? It would be easy to devise a label, like *subsistence* as attributed to propositions by a few thinkers in modern times, but the question is whether such a label would have a meaning.

It is only too evident, I will venture to say without further argument, that it would have no meaning. Logically, no doubt, possibility is a halfway house between being and not-being, but ontologically or metaphysically there is no such halfway house. The ontological analysis of possibility has to be somewhat more complicated. Hence the distinction of essence and existence, understood in the sense described, is a piece of logic masquerading as metaphysics. In the ontological order it is unacceptable. This objection, it should be observed, corresponds with what Kant meant when he said that existence was not a predicate.

If, then, we still want to develop a metaphysic in which essence comes first in the order of reflection, we are compelled to absorb existence into essence. This seems to be more or less what Duns Scotus did. For Scotus there is no distinction of essence and existence, but to every logical distinction in the articulation of concepts corresponds a formal distinction in fact. There is no longer any problem about the transition from the logical to the ontological order, for, as far as first-order concepts are concerned, there is complete identity. One oddity, however, remains. All our concepts appear to be, at least potentially, universal. Hence we are forced to acknowledge in the real world a specific factor of individuality or thisness (*haecceitas*). But can we be content to suppose that real things can be adequately analysed as bundles of universals tied together by thisness? Already at first sight this seems extremely queer. Nevertheless it is the result of an attractively simple view of the relationship between thinking and fact, and those later scholastic philosophers who have denied the distinction of essence and existence can be said in a general way, whatever their other specific doctrines were, to have philosophized in the spirit of Scotus.

St Thomas Aquinas is rather more complex. That he asserts an important distinction of essence and existence is clear enough, but it is not so obvious in what sense he intends it. That he is often content to talk in the manner of Avicenna is certainly to be admitted, but there is still a question whether this language is ultimately appropriate to what he means. For, like Kant, he was a firm opponent of St Anselm's ontological argument for the existence of God. But it is difficult to see what objection could be made to the ontological argument from the point of view of Avicennian metaphysics. If essences already have a certain status by themselves, apart from existence, so that it is reasonable to argue from essence to existence, then the divine essence, as all-perfect, is precisely the essence which demands existence and, therefore, necessarily exists. St Thomas, of course, objects that we have not a sufficiently clear notion of the divine essence, but at least, on Avicennian principles, we could see that it involved necessary existence. A more fundamental objection is required if St Thomas's denial is to be upheld.

This more fundamental objection is evidently that to argue from essence to existence is to reverse the ontological order. That

Aquinas thought in this way becomes clearer when he develops the notion of God as being itself, *ipsum esse*. He cannot possibly mean that God is existence itself, for the phrase is nonsensical; existence is always the existence of something. What he means is revealed when he says that being itself involves the whole fullness of perfection of being. Here being can only refer to the whole positivity of things, contrasted in finite things with a limiting factor which makes them this kind of thing and this particular thing, but pure and unlimited in God. Thus the distinction of existence and essence for St Thomas becomes a distinction of positive being and limitation which deserves a special name, such as the distinction of being and quiddity, to discriminate it from the Avicennian distinction of essence and existence, which belongs to the logical rather than the metaphysical order.

Hence one would like to think that, when Aquinas says that the first object of the intellect is being (*ens*), he means that thought begins with an awareness of existent concrete fact and that the most primitive form of judgement is the existential judgement. But the semi-Platonic Aristotelian theory of knowledge which St Thomas inherited stood in the way of such an affirmation. Thought was supposed to be concerned primarily with the universal, and it became a somewhat embarrassing problem how and in what sense we could be said to know the particular at all. We may be led to conclude that Thomism was still in the making when St Thomas died prematurely at Fossanova in 1274. Certainly, for my part, I should like to replace a conventional picture of Aquinas as one whose system was virtually complete as early as the *De Ente et Essentia*, and who had only to go on applying it in this field and in that, by a rather more interesting Aquinas who was still trying to make his fundamental notions clearer when he felt his strength ebbing away and, in the imminence of eternity, was overwhelmed by the incompleteness of what he had managed to do.

A straightforward empirical approach, in which thought begins with an awareness of the singular and the first judgement is, therefore, an existential judgement, is usually associated with William of Ockham, although it was plainly enunciated a generation earlier by that contentious but unjustly neglected thinker, Durandus a Sancto Porciano. Ockham, however, is a disappointing thinker. He seems to leave his brightest ideas undeveloped while plunging once again into the technicalities of formal logic which alone appear to have given him real enjoyment. He was not an anti-metaphysician like some who are regarded as his disciples, but he does not seem to have realized what a worthy job awaited him in the development of a positive metaphysic on a genuinely empirical basis. He shows no sign of understanding what St Thomas wanted to mean by being and, although in many respects a fierce critic of Scotus, denies the distinction of essence and existence precisely as Scotus did.

IV

All these confusions are intended to explain what is unsatisfying in traditional metaphysics and to suggest what sort of reformulation is necessary in order to arrive at a satisfactory systematic ontology. Gilson has done more than anyone else to show the way, but the responsibility for the following concluding remarks is my own.

We must not be bogged down in a thought-world tenanted by universals rather than by things. Otherwise we shall be tempted to suppose that the *being* with which ontology deals is a portmanteau-term covering the real, the merely possible and the merely logical. There is no such unitary concept; there are only the analogies by which we are led to think of the merely possible and the merely logical through their relationship to the real. The primary object of the metaphysician, as it is the primary object of thought in general, is the real in the sense of the existent singular.

Reflection on the existential judgement both gives rise to metaphysics and reveals the contrast between metaphysics and logic. The logician is concerned with concepts and, indirectly, with their possible instantiation; the metaphysician is concerned with being and the forms which it takes, or the limitations under which it is manifested, in this or that thing. A distinction of concepts does not necessarily involve a distinction in fact; there is real distinction and real relation only where there is a difference of being and not merely of aspects of the same real factor.

The job of the metaphysician is to examine the structure of fact in critical relation to the structure of thinking. He has to ask what precisely subsists of notions like potential and actual, substance and attribute, cause and effect, when they are reduced to onto-logical objectivity. That is why it is impossible to become an anti-metaphysician without doing metaphysics. The difference between the anti-metaphysician and the metaphysician is that, while both ask metaphysical questions, the former proposes negative answers. Hume and Kant could no more avoid asking metaphysical questions than Aristotle or Aquinas.

In comparison with these general considerations departmental difficulties seem of small account. That we largely use language derived from the material world in talking about mind can scarcely be regarded as inevitable, for we have a distinctive and immediate experience of mental activity. It is rather a testimony to our primitive extrovert tendency, which gives to concepts derived from the outside world a greater degree of vividness. But, of course, we could not apply such language to mind unless there were genuine analogies between mental and physical activities.

In speaking of God, on the other hand, our language is of necessity analogous. We can talk of absolute and infinite being only by examining what notions derived from experience do not necessarily connote limitation and by attributing their positive content in a fullness beyond our grasp. What has given natural theology a bad name is the impression produced by scholiasts that, when they have said that God is wise or that God is good, they have said something perfectly clear and comprehensible. The meta-physician has to prevent us not only from underrating but also from overrating the range of the philosophical knowledge of God.

The fundamental task, however, is to recall philosophy to attempting a systematic account of the problems of being on a clear empirical foundation. I have tried to suggest that the history of philosophy provides a stimulus towards this and much of the material for it. I would like also to suggest in conclusion that the anti-metaphysical tendencies in modern philosophy have not been a protest of experience in its purity against the vagaries of the a priori but the result of an undue impoverishment of the scope and power of human experience and thinking.

VIII

MARK PONTIFEX

THE QUESTION OF EVIL

When we discuss the argument for God's existence, we have of course first of all to examine the evidence that is proposed, but there is also another side to the question. Even though the evidence may seem convincing we have to ask whether we can reconcile God's existence with certain facts which cannot be doubted. In this paper I am not considering the evidence for God's existence, but the question: granted that the evidence seems convincing, does the fact of evil refute it? It may be felt that nothing very new is likely to be said about this problem, and that in any case it is too vast to discuss in a few pages. Nevertheless I think there are some points that ought to be mentioned however shortly, so that we may have them before our minds at the present time. I am assuming that we mean by God the almighty and all-good Creator.

(1) We must first decide what exactly is implied by calling God almighty. Manifestly it does not mean that God could make an infinitely perfect creature, for that which is perfect in every way and from every point of view is not a creature, but only God himself. Nor does it mean that God could do anything else which is contradictory, for instance combining incompatible qualities in a thing, for such a suggestion is meaningless. A creature must necessarily be limited, that is, confined to its particular nature, and cut off from all that is incompatible with that nature. There are many possible creatures, and each one is limited because it is distinct from others, and also because it is distinct from God. Every creature is limited, even though the limitations may be capable of progressive reduction to an indefinite extent. Hence, when we speak of God as almighty, we cannot mean that there is no limit to what he can do in the perfecting of his creatures.

But why, it will be asked, if this is so, do you call God almighty? What meaning is left to omnipotence if God's power to create must necessarily be limited? I suppose we should have to answer as follows. A creature's power is limited because it does not possess powers that other creatures have; God's power is unlimited because, being the Creator, he possesses not only all the powers that any and every creature possesses, or that any conceivable creature could possess, but even more than this. Thus God is almighty in the sense that he is the source of all power and can do everything that is possible, though at the same time what can be done in the created universe is necessarily limited, since the creature is less than God.

Such, then, being the limitations of God's creative power it follows that there is a corresponding limitation in what he wills to do, in the good he desires. To say that he creates is the same as to say that he wills the good of creatures, since God's purpose for a creature must be that the powers given it should, so far as possible, be realized. But there are limits to what is possible.

(2) Now how does this help us to see whether evil can be reconciled with the existence of God?

First, as to the meaning of evil. A thing is evil, I suppose, when it lacks some perfection required for its due development, or, in other words, for the realization of its natural powers. Thus, in so far as we can speak of evil in itself, it is negative. Since, however, evil means a defect occurring in some positive power, there is a sense in which evil is positive, because the thing which is evil is positive, and evil cannot exist apart from a positive thing. The difference between a good thing and an evil thing is that the good thing is tending towards the maintenance or increase of perfection in itself or something else, while the evil thing is tending towards a decrease of perfection. Hence, where there is evil there is frustration, and where there is consciousness of frustration there is pain. Moral evil seems to consist of the free choice of action which leads to evil and pain, whether this is suffered by the agent or someone else.

The question, therefore, is: Why should God ever will frustration of the powers he has given to creatures? Does not this contradict the fact that he has given them? How indeed can there be even the possibility of evil when God is absolutely good, or how can the idea of evil ever have occurred to anyone? Now this last question perhaps suggests the lines on which we can give an answer. The reason why evil can ever be a conceivable idea is surely because there are creatures who are distinct from God. What I mean is this. It is inconceivable that there should be evil in God himself, because God is by definition absolutely and eternally perfect. On the other hand the creature is by definition other than God, and dependent on God for its perfection. But, since the creature's perfection does not come from itself, conceivably it may lack its perfection in some degree. Hence the very idea of a creature carries with it the possibility of frustration, just because it is a creature and not God.

This, however, is only the first step, and we have to ask, even granted that evil is necessarily conceivable in the creature, why God should ever will that this possibility should be realized. It seems to me that we can only answer that God would never will that evil should occur, unless this were the only means to obtain some good which outweighs the evil. In short the only reason can be that evil is inevitable if a particular good is to be obtained. But how, it will be asked, can evil be an unavoidable condition for good?

Perhaps the following may suggest a possible answer to this. Only God is utterly simple, and it seems that there must be succession and also some kind of complexity in the make-up of every creature. But, if this is so, the ultimate and highest good of the whole may involve evil in some part or for some period before the final end is reached. We can see that this is conceivable. The very nature of a particular created beauty or happiness may be such that frustration in the process is necessary, if the final perfection is to be realized. Some limited and passing pain may well be worth while in order that a particular creature may in the end enjoy its appropriate beauty and happiness.

But I must explain why I think every creature is necessarily subject to succession. There are strong reasons, it seems to me, for holding that every creature must be built up gradually from imperfection to perfection, starting in imperfection and advancing through a process of time, or at least of some kind of duration or succession. For the creature is of its very nature entirely dependent on God, possessing in itself no power to maintain its being. Unless, then, its life is in some sense a process, with a before and after, how can this be so? If there is no before and after in its life, if there is only an indivisible present, the creature could not conceivably come to an end, and, if it could not come to an end, it could not be dependent on God. Thus God alone can in the strict sense be eternal. It seems to follow that every creature must have a life subject to succession, while the highest kind of creature must also have the power to progress in perfection. God, being infinite, can create beings who are capable of further perfection without end, and, therefore, the highest kind of creature must be such that its perfection can continue to increase indefinitely. Hence succession and change seem necessary in the highest creatures.

It should be noticed that, if the creature's life is successive, the evil it suffers may be passing, and the happiness it gains in the end may far outweigh the evil. A passing evil at the earlier stages of the creature's progress may be of small consequence in comparison with the good eventually to be gained, and the evil which we experience in this life may be of this kind.

I need add little to show that the creature must in some sense be complex, since it follows from the fact that God alone is absolutely simple. If a creature is a complex unity, a one-in-many, it may contain parts of different value. Now the purpose of the whole must be to realize the highest value, and the realization of this highest value may be more important than the frustration of lesser parts. This appears to be the situation in the world around us. Man stands at the head of the visible creation because, with his powers of mind and body, there is no limit to the knowledge and perfection he may ultimately acquire. Lesser things, capable of only a lesser perfection, seem designed to serve the purpose of man. Hence, when we speak of the good of a created thing, we must remember that we refer to its highest good, which alone is its true good. It may be inevitable that lesser goods, which ought to serve the purpose of the greater good, should at least temporarily be sacrificed. It may be better that the lives of plants and animals should be frustrated than that man should never have the chance of reaching his end.

What, then, does this argument amount to? In short it comes to this. Every creature must be limited, and it is reasonable to suppose that a creature's perfection may be unattainable unless some frustration occurs in the earlier stages of its career. This may be due to the particular nature of a given creature. We can see that life, as we know it, could not go on in the world around us unless living things preyed on one another, and, again, that man's social nature with its capacity for good involves the possibility of things going wrong and of the innocent suffering, if an individual sins. The possibility of evil is, I suggest, inherent in creation, because the life of the highest creatures must be successive and progressive, and because what is not yet perfect may never become perfect. Yet, if evil is passing and good in the end prevails, and if the evil is less than the ultimate good, and inevitable if the good is to be gained, this eases very much the problem we are discussing.

(3) So far I have been speaking of that kind of evil which results from the nature and circumstances of a particular creature, that is to say, which comes about in accordance with God's plan. But I have not yet spoken of that kind of evil which comes about in violation of God's plan, as a result of the creature's free choice. To deny the possibility of free choice and of sin cuts at the root of religion and morality, but how can such evil as this be explained so as to avoid contradicting God's existence?

The first point I should like to make is this. I think there are good reasons for thinking that the possibility of free choice is inevitable, at least in many cases, for those creatures who are capable of supreme perfection, that is to say, of enjoying ultimately the Beatific Vision. The reasons are these. The highest kind of creature possesses the fullest personality, and this implies consciousness of the purpose of its actions, and control over them. Moreover the creature who is capable of the highest perfection will have an awareness of the infinite Creator who alone is able to satisfy its desires.

Now the possibility of choice, and therefore of a wrong use of choice, seems to follow as a consequence of this. I have already argued that creatures must be subject to succession, that a creature's perfection must be brought about by a process, however short, involving the succession of one event after another. Before the creature enjoys the Beatific Vision it is aware only obscurely of the attractive power of the infinite good, but it is aware in a direct way of the attractive power of finite goods. Hence comes a conflict of desires.

This is man's state in the present life. He is aware of God's sovereignty, but not immediately or overwhelmingly, and he is also aware of his own powers and of his own value. On the one hand he sees, though obscurely, the sovereignty of God and the supreme happiness of union with him, and also a certain frustration at the moment if he is to gain this, because he must subject immediate good to ultimate good. On the other hand he sees the immediate satisfaction he can gain by treating finite good as the ultimate end, and also the frustration to which this finally leads. He is faced with attractions and repulsions whichever way he looks. This situation makes choice possible. I am suggesting it is conceivable that such a state with the need for choice cannot normally be avoided if there is to be the possibility of supreme ultimate perfection.

If, however, this is so, it follows that moral evil is an unavoidable possibility, provided that there are to be creatures of the highest powers. And further it follows that the various evils which moral evil brings in its train are also an unavoidable possibility.

Moreover this point should be noticed. If the need for choice is inevitable for some creatures, and if this means, as surely it does, that there must be a conflict of desires (since a motive must exist both for the good and the bad courses of action between which there is a choice), some degree of pain seems inevitable even before any choice of evil has taken place. For choice lies between satisfying one desire and frustrating another, when both are felt as attractive. Therefore some kind of frustration or pain seems inevitable.

If this reasoning is sound it seems, then, possible to reconcile the evil we find in the world with belief in God. Some evil may be in accordance with God's plan—inevitable if in the end the beauty and happiness for which the universe has been created is to be realized. Some evil may be contrary to God's plan—due to a wrong use of free choice, and permitted by God, because free choice is inevitable if creatures are to exist who are capable of supreme perfection. In short the reason for evil may be that it is inevitable if there is to be the highest good.

(4) Here, however, with the mention of free choice as an explanation of evil we come against a very familiar, but a very difficult problem. Is free choice on the part of the creature compatible with the existence of God? Does not the power to choose freely, to be responsible for one's conduct, imply the power to initiate activity, and can this be possible if God is the first cause of everything? We have to reconcile two assertions which at first sight at least seem contradictory, namely, that every act is entirely caused by God, and yet that the creature can act in a way not caused by God, because he can act in opposition to God's plan.

Now we cannot leave this problem aside, since it is vital for the proposed theory about evil. It seems worth while, then, for me to make some suggestions about it. If free choice means that the creature can initiate positive activity, the problem appears insoluble; this appears directly to contradict God's existence as the source of all that exists, and therefore to contradict God's infinity. I think there is only one direction in which we can look for a solution. It may be possible to avoid contradiction if we argue that free choice only means that the creature can initiate failure, but is not the ultimate source of positive action. I will put the case in favour of this theory.

I suggest that, when there is choice, it lies between a greater and a lesser good. When we choose we choose between conflicting desires, which lead to different ends. Unless the goods differ in value it is hard to see how there can be a choice between them. But desires may shade down from desire for ultimate satisfaction of the highest kind for all creatures to desire for personal satisfaction of the lowest kind at the present moment. Thus desires may be related to one another as greater to less, since they may seek a wider and more permanent or a narrower and more passing satisfaction.

But how does this help to explain choice? It helps in this way. From different points of view either the greater or the lesser good may be regarded as more attractive. The greater good has greater value in the end, but it may be more remote, and may involve trouble or suffering at the present time. The lesser good has less value in the end, but it may give more immediate pleasure at the moment. In so far as a man expands his field of vision to its fullest extent he desires the highest good; in so far as he lets his vision contract, and his attention focus on his personal and immediate interest, he desires the lowest good.

But why does he either expand or contract his attention; what is it which makes him choose one or the other? The answer is straightforward if he chooses the greater good. Then he expands his attention to the fullest extent, and does so because he has the power for this, and causes have acted upon him and enabled him to realize his power. But if he chooses the lesser good there is no need to look for a cause beyond the man himself, since a failure as such is negative and requires no cause. Of course there is a positive cause and a sufficient motive for his taking the lesser good in so far as it has positive value, but there is no cause, only a lack of cause, for his taking the lesser good instead of the greater good. The lesser good is positive in itself, but negative in so far as it is less than the greater good.

Here it will be said: is not the cause of his failure the lack of activity on the part of the causes which have affected him? Now it is undoubtedly true that, if a purely material thing fails, its failure is due to a corresponding lack of activity in the cause which affects it; we can trace the failure beyond the thing itself. A human being, however, is conscious of himself and of other objects, of his own powers, and of the purpose and results of his action, thereby controlling his conduct in a way quite different from that of a merely material thing. Every independent thing is in some sense a source of activity, but man in a very special sense. Therefore it seems reasonable to claim that, although failure in a piece of metal can always be traced to failure in its causes, nevertheless failure in a human being may originate in the human being himself. There is certainly no contradiction in this.

So far I have been speaking of choice between a greater and a lesser good, and I must apply what has been said to choice between good and evil. If the choice lies between good and evil, this means that it lies (as does all choice) between a greater good and a lesser good, but in this case between a greater good which leads to satisfaction and a lesser good which leads to frustration. Of course when evil is chosen there is a positive reason and motive for the choice, but the positive good is such as to lead to evil. If the choice lies between honesty and dishonesty, it lies between the desire for the general good and desire for a personal good involving another man's loss and ultimately our own loss.

The answer I propose to the problem follows from what has been said. A failure to act, being as such merely negative, requires no cause, and can therefore originate in the creature who fails, without our needing to trace it further. When the creature chooses an evil course he chooses a positive good, but one which will lead in the end to frustration. In so far as he chooses a positive good his action is caused by God; in so far as he chooses less good than was possible and a course that leads to frustration his action is due to himself alone. Hence God is always the cause of good, but the creature alone is responsible for evil.

(5) Many objections will at once spring to the mind against this theory, but perhaps the following goes to the heart of the matter. Is not every creature completely in the hands of God? Does not God, as the first cause, entirely dominate the creature's activity, so that, if the creature fails, the failure is due to a lack of causality on God's part, for which God is responsible?

Now, when we consider this objection, we should remember in the first place that we are dealing with the kind of causality which keeps in being an intellectual and spiritual person, conscious of himself and of others, and this must be a kind of causality very different from that which man himself can exercise. A man may make changes in the things around him, but he cannot create these things; he cannot maintain in being a material thing much less a living person. It may be asked: how can a living person, in some sense master of his own acts, be entirely dependent in this way on God? I should reply that nothing can be shown to be contradictory in the notion of such dependence, provided we do not say that the dependent person can be the ultimate cause of a positive act. There would be contradiction in asserting this, because it would imply a finite first cause, a first cause yet not a first cause.

The objector may persist: if the creature fails, must not the

I

failure be due to God, because God has given less causation than was needed? Even though a man can fail without this being due to a lack of causation in the world around him, yet surely his failure must be due to a lack of causation on God's part?

Here we come to a very important point, and my suggestion is this. Of course the failure must be due to lack of causation on God's part, but this in its turn is due to the creature. The creature is able to exercise a negative priority—logical, and not temporal—over God's causal action upon him, so that God's causality is modified as a result of the creature's failure, and not vice versa. Unless, indeed, we agree to this, there seems no conceivable answer to the objection. Unless the creature can initiate failure, failure must be due to God, and then God is responsible for sin. We are saying that God is not God.

But can we agree to this negative priority on the part of the creature, and still hold that God is the first cause? It seems to me that we can. Whatever happens to the creature, and whatever the creature does, cannot affect God in himself. The creature's failure cannot produce any effect on God, but only on the creature who fails, and perhaps other creatures. Therefore, if the creature has a negative priority in the determination of God's causality upon him, this does not imply that it has any power over God. There is no additional act when God creates, additional, that is, to his one unchanging essential act; the only new act is the act of the creature who is created. Hence, if the creature is responsible for its own failure, this does not imply any failure or change in God, but only a change in the creature. If the very existence of the creature can cause no change in God, far less can any failure in the creature's conduct. Negative priority on the creature's part would, therefore, imply no passivity in God, no power over God, and if this is so, how can it contradict God's supremacy?

Is this, however, a complete answer to the question? Would not the proposed theory mean that the creature was to some extent outside God's control, if it could modify God's causality? Does not God determine his causality from eternity, and how can this be so if the creature has any priority, even a negative priority?

The creature would undoubtedly be outside God's control in the sense that it could act in opposition to God's plan: the very notion of sin implies this, in whatever precise way we interpret it. But, even though negative priority would imply this in a special sense, it would not contradict God's power to bring creation to its appointed end. God permits (I am suggesting) the creature to have a negative priority, because this is inevitable if the creature is to be capable of supreme perfection. But there is no question of God's waiting to see if the creature will fail. God sees from eternity exactly what failure occurs through the creature's fault, and permits it from eternity in order that the ultimate end may be realized. Just as God sees the limitations of the creature's nature, so he sees the limitations of the creature's conduct when failure occurs; he sees all this from eternity, and limits his creative act accordingly.

Perhaps it may help to explain what I mean if I put it like this. It would certainly be contradictory to say that there could be any priority on the creature's part capable of preventing God from creating it. But, once the creature has begun to exist, there seems no contradiction in saying that it can limit God's act of causality over the rest of its life. Although on God's part creation is decreed from eternity, God causes a creature to exist whose life has a beginning and gradually develops through a succession of events. God sees the creature's whole career from eternity, but what he sees from eternity is successive. For this reason once the creature has begun to exist it can lessen God's further causation, even though God sees it all from eternity. We must remember again that creation involves no new act in God, but only the coming into being of the creature.

(6) This suggestion of a negative priority on the part of the creature will, it must be admitted, be opposed by many theologians. St Thomas's words may be quoted against it: 'But why [God] chose some for glory, and rejected others, has no reason but the divine will' (*S.T.I.Q.*, xxiii, Art. 5, ad 3). Nevertheless the problem remains: if God's causality is not modified by a negative priority on the part of the creature, how can we avoid the contradictory conclusion that God is responsible for sin?

It may be thought that the answer lies in St Thomas's distinction between God's antecedent and consequent will, and this point needs to be considered. St Thomas tells us that God's will is always fulfilled (*S.T.I.Q.*, xix, Art. 6). He brings up the objection that God wills all men to be saved although all are not saved, and answers by making a distinction between God's antecedent and consequent will. God's antecedent will is concerned with a situation apart from its particular circumstances, while his consequent will takes the particular circumstances into account. St Thomas gives the example of a judge who wills that a man should be hanged, though, so far as the criminal is a man and apart from his crimes, he wills that he should live. So too God, by his antecedent will wills that all shall be saved, while by his consequent will he wills that some, in view of their sins, shall be damned: 'whatever God wills simply, takes place, though what he wills antecedently does not'.

How does this apply to the creature's sinful act? We shall have to say that the sin opposes God's antecedent, but not his consequent, will. But how can God will the sinful act even by his consequent will? We shall have to say that God wills to permit it, rather than directly wills it. St Thomas tells us: 'It is also a part of divine providence that [God] should permit some to fail to reach their end, and this is to reject them' (*S.T.I.Q.*, xxiii, Art. 3, c).

Now here we come to a point which should be noticed carefully. What is involved in saying that God 'permits' sin? Sin is not a necessary evil which God permits as inevitable, as part of his plan, in order that good shall be achieved. If God permits sin, this must mean that he permits a cause to operate which he does not cause himself, since it opposes his plan. If God permits sin, he does not prevent it, and if he does not prevent it, there must be a cause operating which he does not prevent, and which is, therefore, other than himself. But there cannot be any positive action which God does not cause, and so it must be the failure, the not-action, which originates in the creature. Hence I may claim that by implication St Thomas does not oppose, but supports, the theory of the creature's negative priority.

(7) It may be objected that this theory would itself make God the cause of sin. Is not the sinful act a positive act, and is not every positive act caused by God? How can God cause an act of cruelty, for instance?

I must emphasize again that it is a question of God's causing the acts of a conscious person, not of a mere puppet; the acts are those of a person kept in being by God, but not God's acts. Although God is partly the cause of the act of cruelty, he is not wholly its cause. His causal act is modified by the failure of the creature, which has a negative priority over his causal act. Thus we must make a distinction when the question is asked whether God causes an act of cruelty. We cannot simply say either that God causes it or that he does not. The act has both a positive and a negative aspect, and God causes the one but not the other. Of the act of cruelty as a whole we can only say that God permits it, because the nature of the act is wholly due to the creature's failure, and is contrary to God's will. God's causality is deflected, so to speak, by the failure initiated by the creature.

(8) An objection of a different kind must be mentioned. The theory I am defending explains free choice as granted to the creature, because this is inevitable if he is to reach his end. The power of choice is not given because it is valuable in itself, but rather is permitted, in spite of the danger it involves, for the sake of the good. Now the objection may be raised: is it not precisely virtue freely chosen which gives value to conduct, and does not this imply that the creature must be able to initiate positively its choice of good?

Against such an objection I should begin by arguing that it would be contradictory to hold that the creature could initiate a positive act. If so, the creature would not be a creature but God, since God alone is the source of all perfection. I should, therefore, maintain that it cannot be free choice which gives value to human conduct, because all that is valuable comes from God, while free choice is partly due to the creature.

Perhaps the reason why the valuable element in conduct is thought to be virtue self-originated is that self-originated conduct is assumed to be the same as fully human conduct. But is this so? Everyone agrees that conduct cannot have its full value unless there is full knowledge and deliberation, together with a clear realization of the purpose in view. Yet all this seems quite compatible with full dependence on God.

The really important element in conduct must surely be, not

choice, nor even self-consciousness (though this must be present), but the love of God, the desire and will for good; it is from this that every other virtue is derived. To be convinced of this we have only to reflect that ultimate perfection consists in union with God, and that love of God must be the source of such union. Now, when the creature is united with God, he has all that he can desire, and there can be no conflict of desires, such as is required for choice. When the creature is united with God its conduct is of supreme value, and yet there is no room for choice. Choice cannot, therefore, be the valuable element in conduct.

The reply may be made that what is meant is that the love of God is only practised in this life, or at least only practised to its fullest extent, when there are difficulties to be surmounted, and that it is precisely in the choice of good when we are tempted towards evil, that the love of God is shown. If this is what is meant plainly there is much truth in it. No one can deny that, under the conditions of life in this world, the will for good usually becomes more deliberate, more a personal act, the more it involves a struggle. Yet this only proves that under the conditions of this life the love of God and choice usually go together, not that they are necessarily connected, or that choice is the valuable element in conduct or that the creature can initiate positive action.

Certainly there does not seem any reason to suppose that we can only make a fully personal act, that is to say, an act fully deliberate and fully our own, when we have to choose. As I have already said the condition which makes choice possible is a conflict of desires. But why should we not be able to act with conscious deliberation, committing ourselves with the whole will, when we have no desire except for a single end?

(9) There is one more difficulty I shall mention before summing up and concluding. I have argued that God permits the creature to choose because this is inevitable if creatures are to exist with the highest capacities. But how, it may be asked, if choice is inevitable, can God with certainty bring creation to a happy end? Is it thinkable that every rational creature might choose evil, that all creation might come to disaster, and evil and not good triumph in the end. Does not St Augustine say that

God, being utterly good, would not allow evil in his creation unless out of evil he could bring good?

Now the argument proposed does not imply that every creature capable of the highest perfection must necessarily have to choose: all it shows is that sometimes and for some creatures it may be inevitable. It is still open to us to hold that in certain circumstances God can give so strong a desire for good that right conduct will undoubtedly result, and hence that some creatures may attain the highest perfection without having to choose. For this reason it cannot be made an objection against what I have said that some children die too young to be responsible for their conduct. Perhaps they never make a choice, or perhaps they have to choose at the moment of death.

However this may be, it seems quite reasonable to say that choice is normally inevitable without saying that it must always be so. If this is true, we can see how God can bring good out of evil even though choice must usually be permitted. If in some circumstances God can, without spoiling his plan, give enough help to the creature to ensure right conduct, then we may suppose he can do so often enough to bring good out of evil for creation as a whole.

It may be felt: if God can on occasion do this, surely he can always strengthen the desire for right action to such an extent that wrong desires will in fact never prevail, even though their presence may be unavoidable? To this it is only possible to reply that in this life we see a very small part of God's design for creation. The design is presumably highly complex, and the parts interconnected in a way that we cannot follow. There may be reasons, therefore, unknown to us which make it inconceivable in many circumstances that God should strengthen a creature's desire for good so much that it will not in fact choose evil. In other circumstances there may be reasons which make it possible.

(10) I should like to sum up what I have been saying, so that it can be seen as a whole. The question has been: does the presence of evil in the world contradict belief in the existence of God, who is almighty and all-good? I have argued that God is almighty in the sense that he can do all that is conceivable, yet that only limited perfection is conceivable for the creature. So too with

God's goodness. Now one kind of limitation may well be that, if God is to bring to perfection certain forms of beauty and happiness, some frustration and pain are inevitable before the design is achieved.

There remains the far more difficult problem of evil due to free choice, that is, to sin. I have suggested that, if there are to be creatures capable of enjoying the Beatific Vision, they must reach their end by a gradual process, during which they are liable to a conflict of desires. The infinite good which alone can satisfy them is not directly perceived, while finite goods are immediately at hand. Thus the argument is that it may be inconceivable under certain conditions that God should bring a creature to supreme perfection and happiness, unless he permits it to choose freely before the end is reached.

If, then, the question is asked: 'how did the first sin occur, when God's plan was quite unspoiled?', I should answer that even then a conflict of desires and the possibility of choice may have been inevitable. Unless indeed it was inevitable why should God have ever allowed the first evil desire to be felt? Moreover, as I have said, if a conflict of desires was inevitable, so too was some degree of pain.

This leaves the problem of reconciling the creature's free choice with God's supreme control. Failure alone, I have suggested, is due to the creature, while success is due to God. Choice is possible because the creature's desire for the greater good may conflict with his desire for the lesser good. Hence, if he lets his attention focus on the lesser, but more immediate, good, he fails, and the cause lies in himself. God allows the creature to have a negative priority over his own act of causality; God modifies his causality in accordance with the creature's failure. This does not mean that the creature is outside God's control in any contradictory sense, since God sees and permits the failure from eternity for the sake of the ultimate good.

I am saying, then, that evil or the possibility of evil is unavoidable, an unfortunate necessity. But how can evil be a necessity? We must remember that there can be no possibility of evil in God himself, while it must be present in creation, simply because it is creation and not God. Creation is a becoming, a gradual process in which there is a stage of imperfection before perfection is reached. But, where there is imperfection, frustration is possible, and under certain circumstances it may be unavoidable.

It should be noticed that all I am trying to do is to show that there is a possible explanation of evil which reconciles its presence in creation with the existence of God; I am not trying to show that the proposed explanation is certainly the true one. For if there is a possible explanation, this is sufficient to show that no contradiction with God's existence can be alleged, and, if no contradiction can be alleged, the fact of evil cannot be claimed to refute belief in God.

IX

ILLTYD TRETHOWAN

PROFESSOR AYER ON CERTAINTY

It is often impossible to say all that one would wish to say in reviewing a philosophical book; criticism must be summary and cannot be justified in full. Even such an important book as Professor A. J. Ayer's *The Problem of Knowledge* is unlikely to receive, in print, the detailed examination which it deserves, unless the examination takes the form of a book. In the absence of this, it may be useful to subject the first two chapters to a close scrutiny[1] with a view to discovering whether or not Professor Ayer has succeeded in his attempt to meet 'the sceptical arguments'. It will shortly emerge that my own point of view about knowledge and certainty is one which is unfashionable and, in some quarters, discredited. I shall say something in justification of it, but the discussion which follows will not, I hope, be without interest even for those who are out of sympathy with it.

Professor Ayer begins his book with an explanation of what philosophy is, and this takes the form of referring to some of the questions which philosophers raise. Towards the end of this first section, after pointing out that it is 'possible to believe what is in fact true without knowing it', Professor Ayer continues:

'Is knowledge then to be distinguished by the fact that if one knows that something is so, one cannot be mistaken? And in that case does it follow that what is known is necessarily true, or in some other way indubitable? But, if this does follow, it will lead in its turn to the conclusion that we commonly claim to know much more than we really do; perhaps even to the paradox that

---

[1] Since this was written an article by Professor H. H. Price has appeared (*Mind*, October 1958, pp. 433–64) on the last three chapters of the book, with only a brief summary of the first two.

we do not know anything at all: for it may be contended that there is no statement whatsoever that is not in itself susceptible to doubt. Yet surely there must be something wrong with an argument that would make knowledge unattainable. Surely some of our claims to knowledge must be capable of being justified. But in what ways can we justify them? In what would the process of justifying them consist?'[1]

I have quoted this passage because it seems to indicate very plainly what are the chief questions which should engage the reader of Professor Ayer's first two chapters. It is true that he warns us against supposing that he considers all the questions listed to be clear or even coherent; they are only 'instances of the sort of question that philosophers ask'. Nevertheless he adds: 'The next step is to see how one would try to answer them', and we are surely entitled to see in the passage quoted the central subject-matter of chapters entitled 'Philosophy and Knowledge' and 'Scepticism and Certainty'. I propose, then, to confine myself to enquiring just how Professor Ayer does try to answer the questions which that passage contains.

In the second section of this first chapter Professor Ayer begins to raise the question whether the various sorts of knowing have as a common feature a mental state or act. 'We must allow', he writes, 'that what we call knowing facts may sometimes be just a matter of being disposed to behave in certain appropriate ways.'[2] Perhaps so, but it remains possible to hold that, when a dog is said to 'know' its master (the case which Professor Ayer has been considering), although the speaker does not believe that dogs are capable of 'mental states or acts', the word is naturally used because the animal behaves *as if* it 'knew' in that sense; in other words, that there is always some reference to 'mental states or acts' when the word is used. Professor Ayer goes on to accept Professor Ryle's contention in *The Concept of Mind* (Ch. 2) that, in cases of 'knowing how', 'the display of intelligence lies in the manner of the performance, rather than in its being accompanied

---

[1] pp. 4–5 (p. 10). The references throughout are to the Library edition of *The Problem of Knowledge* published by Macmillan (1956) and (following in brackets) to the Penguin edition.   [2] p. 7 (p. 12).

or preceded by any conscious recognition of the relevant facts'. Here again it is easy to reply that, in the case of human performers, intelligence is attributed to them as a matter of fact in virtue of 'mental acts' which are supposed to have occurred in the past, even though habit may have made it unnecessary for them to occur during the performance. The fact that Professor Ayer does not mention these available answers leaves the discussion, although still in the air, with an apparent tendency in the direction of behaviourism. And it is to be observed that, in this passage, although we are (rightly) said to 'recognize objects without troubling to describe them, even to ourselves', this recognition is nowhere described as a 'mental act'. (Professor Ayer does not, however, go the whole way with Professor Ryle, whose paradoxical contention that 'seeing' is not an experience at all is most properly rejected in the third chapter on 'Perception'.)

The next section gets down to business in real earnest, and will require longer treatment. Professor Ayer now considers 'cases in which knowing something is straightforwardly a matter of knowing something to be true'. 'Is it', he asks, 'a necessary condition for having this sort of knowledge, not only that what one is said to know should in fact be true, but also that one should be in some special state of mind, or that one should be performing some special mental act? . . . Some philosophers have maintained not only that there are such cognitive states, or acts, but that they are infallible.'[1] I do maintain that. I maintain that I am not the only member of the human race, and that I know this with *absolute* certainty—that is, I know that I *cannot* be wrong about it. I *may* also describe myself as 'knowing' that something will be the case, when it has always been the case in the past and there is no ground for supposing the extraordinary—but I should have to admit that the extraordinary might occur. I 'feel no doubt', yet I do not enjoy certainty. I *may* further describe myself as 'knowing', when I have made what is in fact only a well-grounded guess and prove to be right. These different uses are well known and hotly debated. I cannot present the full case for them here. What I am concerned to point out is that Professor Ayer at this point simply dismisses

[1] p. 9 (p. 14).

the distinction which I would make between a mere absence of doubt and an *absolute* conviction. He brushes it aside with the remark that 'it may very well happen that even when people's beliefs are false they are as fully convinced of their truth as they are of the truth of what they know', preceded by another appeal to Professor Ryle's 'reductionism',[1] which requires special note.

The appeal is a very curious one, because the claim to absolute certainty which Professor Ayer is disallowing does not involve the denial that 'to know' can be *sometimes* reduced to the status of a 'capacity' verb. I have had occasion to remark already that an acknowledgement of this status is not inconsistent with the claim that 'know' always refers, directly or indirectly, to a 'mental event'. Professor Ayer, having invoked the dispositional use of 'know', now makes a further incidental movement in the direction of behaviourism by denying outright that the capacities some-times referred to by 'know' need *ever* be actualized 'through the existence of a special mental state'. 'What', he asks, 'is this state of mind supposed to be? The reply to this may be that it is unique in character, so that it cannot be analysed in terms of anything else. But what then is the evidence for its existence?' This question brings the ultimate issue clearly before us, for it implies a refusal *a priori* to accept cognitive experience as self-guaranteeing. We may therefore pause to take stock of the position.

One would not expect Professor Ayer to have any use for 'intuition' in his account of knowledge, but it is surprising that he should seem so blandly unaware of other people's views. There are, to speak very roughly, two main attitudes which may be adopted in a discussion of this sort. One is to presuppose that no results are worth having in philosophy unless they follow logically from something else. The other is to entertain all the available evidence without prejudice, to see where it leads us, not only by means of logical analysis, but also by *reflection*. Professor Ayer seems to adopt the first attitude: the second (admittedly much commoner abroad than in this island) was well illustrated in Professor I. W. Alexander's critical study of Lavelle which

[1] pp. 10–12 (pp. 15–16).

appeared in *The Philosophical Quarterly* of April 1958. What it all boils down to in the end is the question whether we are going to admit that a 'metaphysical dimension' is contained in human experience. It would be absurd to embark at this point on any discussion of the most momentous of all philosophical questions. But I do want to insist that Professor Ayer dodges it, and says nothing to the purpose about the objections which can be made to his own attitude. For example, what sort of certainty does he possess, and expect his readers to possess, about the validity of logical consequences? Can he ever be finally satisfied that he has refuted an argument? If he can, and if the sceptic continues to ask why he may not be mistaken, he can only reply that he just *knows* or *sees* that he isn't. And this is an acceptance of cognitive experience and of absolute certainty. The alternative is to play straight into the sceptic's hands by acknowledging universal doubt. This is very well-worn ground, which makes it all the more remarkable that Professor Ayer should appear at this point to ignore its very existence. As we shall see later, he does purport to avoid scepticism in his second chapter, but I shall contend that in fact he never escapes from the dilemma in which he has now placed himself.

We may now continue the examination of Professor Ayer's third section.[1] After his flirtation with behaviourism, he pulls himself up with the admission that 'to be convinced of something is, in a sense, to be in a particular state of mind', but promptly adds that 'it is rather a matter of accepting the fact in question and of not being at all disposed to doubt it than of contemplating it with a conscious feeling of conviction'. He is obliged to admit that such feelings of conviction do occur, but gets rid of the subject for the present as best he can with the comment that 'it would seem that a conscious feeling of complete conviction may co-exist with an unconscious feeling of doubt'. I do not understand how I can be said to entertain a doubt of which I am not in any way aware. But in any case it is obvious that Professor Ayer is continuing to reject in a cavalier fashion the sense which I have claimed for 'being certain' (or 'sure'), because he goes on to argue

[1] pp. 12–15 (pp. 16–19.)

that one can 'be sure' without a 'feeling of conviction' as though the matter could be settled by an appeal to usage without any need of analysis. Furthermore usage does distinguish 'to feel sure' and 'to be sure'. Certainty is an intellectual experience, and it is misleading to call it a 'feeling' unless this is recognized.

The next paragraph in this section which requires our attention must be quoted from at some length:

'There cannot be a mental state which, being as it were directed towards a fact, is such that it guarantees that the fact is so. And here I am not saying merely that such states never do occur, or even that it is causally impossible that they ever should occur, but rather that it is logically impossible. My point is that from the fact that someone is convinced that something is true, however firm his conviction may be, it never follows logically that it is true. If he is a reliable witness and if he is in a good position to assess the truth of whatever statement is in question, then his being convinced of its truth may provide us with a strong reason for accepting it; but it cannot be a conclusive reason. There will not be a formal contradiction in saying both that the man's state of mind is such that he is absolutely sure that a given statement is true, and that the statement is false.'

Professor Ayer adds in a footnote that there are some rare cases in which the truth of something is logically implied by its being believed, and he instances belief in one's own existence—you cannot have a belief in your own existence without being there to do the believing. But, as will later appear, he does not regard such a case as of any particular importance. The conclusion remains, as he puts it, that 'the statement is true if, and only if, what it states is so. . . . And whether the situation really is as it is described is not to be decided merely by examining the attitude which anyone who considers the statement has towards it, not even if the person who considers it knows it to be true.'

There are a good many points to notice about these passages. By way of preliminary it may be remarked that a claim to certainty is here described as a claim to know that a given statement is true, whereas in fact the commonest and most fundamental certainties are not normally articulated at all. But the most important mistake is the supposition that a logical demonstration has anything to do with the matter. I should have thought that Aristotle had settled that. Everything has to start with some kind of experience, and obviously *that* cannot follow from something else. *After* that you may conduct logical processes, but even so you will have to see, to *experience* in that sense, the consequence of a syllogism, the emergence of a conclusion from premisses. If your experience, then, is not, in the last analysis, your guarantee, there is no guarantee. Your experience does not make the truth to be what it is—on p. 18 (p. 22) Professor Ayer suggests that, according to his opponents, a statement is made valid by our seeing that it is—but it does show you that you have discovered what it is. Your experience does not *prove* to you that something is so—it puts you in touch with it. Such statements, I know, will be abhorrent to those who reject 'direct experience'. The question, however, is: can such people avoid the sceptic's clutches?

Finally we must notice that Professor Ayer is still simply dismissing the claim to absolute certainty. The claim is that in some circumstances we *cannot* be mistaken. This is a matter of fact which must be accepted or rejected according to whether we *see* it or do not see it. To say that the claim is not in formal contradiction with the falsity of the statement claimed to be true is entirely irrelevant.

It is only in the second half of this (third) section that Professor Ayer allows the reader (it must be remembered that he is writing for the general reader) to hear something of the other side, and even so the passage is introduced by a further misleading account of the claim to absolute certainty which represents it as describing knowledge 'only as a condition of mind'.[1] Such a mistake has no doubt been made, but the claim which Professor Ayer ought to be considering is the claim that certainty is the self-guaranteeing *awareness of an object*. Thus when he mentions the objection that 'there must be some statements of empirical fact which are directly verified',[1] it is with the air of one conducting mopping-up operations after a decisive victory in the field. In the next paragraph he admits that 'we do just have to see that certain proofs

[1] p. 16 (p. 20).

are valid, and it is through having some experience that we discover the truth or falsehood of any statement of empirical fact'. But he adds that what verifies the statement is 'the existence of the experience, not the confidence that we may have in some description of it'. The general reader may pass this because it has not been made clear to him that certainty is claimed, by some of Professor Ayer's opponents, for *experience or awareness as such*. According to them, awareness is not one thing and a 'feeling of confidence' another; in so far as we are directly aware of something, we *are* certain of it, though we may not experience any 'feeling' in the sense of an affective state. We just *know* that we are hearing a noise, let us say, and the possibility that we may be mistaken is no less definitely excluded because we do not need explicitly to envisage it.

After what has been said Professor Ayer's next words should reveal plainly enough, I think, an *ignoratio elenchi*:

'To take a simple example, what verifies the statement that I have a headache is my feeling a headache, not my having a feeling of confidence that the statement that I have a headache is true. Of course if I do have a headache and also understand the statement, I shall undoubtedly accept it as being true. This is the ground for saying that if I have such an experience, I know that I am having it. But, in this sense, my knowing that I am having the experience is just my having it and being able to identify it. I know that I am having it inasmuch as I correctly take it as verifying the statement which describes it. But my justification for accepting the statement is not that I have a cognitive, or any other attitude towards it: it is simply that I am having the experience. To say that the experience itself is cognitive is correct, though perhaps misleading, if it is merely a way of saying that it is a conscious experience. It may still be correct if it is a way of saying that the experience is recognized for what it is by the person who is having it, though, as we shall see later on, such recognition can be mistaken. It is not correct if it is taken as implying that the experience either consists in or includes a process of infallibly apprehending some statement to be true.'[1]

[1] pp. 17–18 (p. 21).

K

Omitting, then, any further comments on misleading opposi-
tions, I shall draw attention only to a few sentences in this passage.
In the remark 'my knowing that I am having the experience is
just my having it and being able to identify it' Professor Ayer
seems to be giving the game away but for the last six words. These
prove to imply that I cannot properly be said to know that I have
a headache unless I understand a statement to that effect. But it is
surely the case that one *can* know that one has a headache (or
simply *can have* a headache, for it is the same thing) without
necessarily understanding statements about it. 'Knowing' does
not necessarily involve identification in this sense or 'recognition'.
One must be aware of everything for the first time. And the
characters of our awareness vary with the characters of our objects
without any need even of naming them (that statement may be
controverted, but I do not see how it can be disproved). Certainty
does not consist, fundamentally, in 'infallibly apprehending some
statement to be true', although it extends to this. So again we
find that Professor Ayer has rejected absolute certainty ('it must
always remain possible that one is mistaken'),[1] and without understanding, apparently, what some, at least, of its upholders declare
it to be.

In the remainder of this third section (and in the rest of the
chapter) Professor Ayer makes no fresh point relevant to the
present discussion. He warns us in vague general terms against
'assuming that a naïve analysis in terms of act and object yields an
adequate account of knowledge', threatening us with landing
ourselves, if we do, in existentialist or Platonist thickets (this is a
familiar move: see what some metaphysicians have said, and
therefore shun the whole subject), but he does not seem to worry
about the thickets in which we shall be landed if we deny that
there *are* cognitive acts and that they *have* objects.

As we saw at the beginning, the reader will have been encouraged to expect from Professor Ayer a refutation of scepticism. As
the first chapter proceeded, it will have become clear to him that if
scepticism means the rejection of any absolute certainty then
there is no question of Professor Ayer's refuting it, since he is a

[1] p. 18 (p. 22).

sceptic himself. So presumably he means something else by it, and the second chapter will tell us what it is. The first section of this chapter skirmishes on the frontiers of the problem. The conclusion to which the second section comes repeats, in effect, what Professor Ayer has told us already: 'One is conceded the right to be sure when one is judged to have taken every reasonable step towards making sure: but this is still logically consistent with one's being in error. The discovery of the error refutes the claim to knowledge; but it does not prove that the claim was not, in the circumstances, legitimately made.'[1] In other words, we can never be finally satisfied, in any particular case, that we shall not prove to be mistaken, although we are entitled to *say* that we are 'sure' in certain circumstances. So it looks as though the scepticism which is to be refuted is merely the rejection of this not very consoling title.

Here it may be remarked that it is, of course, *possible* to be mistaken about anything in so far as we go beyond actual experience. But it does not follow that we *must* be mistaken at any particular time. The statement is perfectly consistent with the *fact* that we are sometimes right. We *can* avoid mistakes if we take the trouble to do so, and some of us sometimes do. The way in which Professor Ayer continues to harp in this second chapter on the possibility of mistake seems to make it necessary to insist once more on the misleadingness of suggesting that a claim which is based on experience requires a logical demonstration. 'You can't *prove*', Professor Ayer is saying, 'that you aren't making a mistake. So there!' But one is not claiming to *prove* it. One is claiming that an experience proves itself. There is nothing *illogical* about a claim to certainty, because it does not require a logical impossibility of being mistaken but a factual one in particular cases. This has been pointed out, often enough, and it is very surprising that Professor Ayer should continue not to notice it. Instead he continues to put up Aunt Sallies and knock them down. In the present section, for example, he spends a long time pointing out that even if an *a priori* statement is unassailable in itself it does not follow that it is immune from doubt.[2] But who wants to say that it does follow? This makes it even odder that

<hr>

[1] p. 44 (p. 43).   [2] p. 42 (p. 42).

Professor Ayer seems unable to see what does not follow in his own argument, namely (if I may be allowed to say it just once more), that because anyone is *capable* of doubting a certain statement *nobody* is capable of being absolutely sure of it. Professor Ayer may say, relevantly and without illogicality, 'I don't have this experience of absolute certainty, and *you* only think you do'. But he can say no more than this.

In the third section of the second chapter we return to the subject of self-consciousness. It was introduced in the first chapter[1] as one of the difficulties which might have been avoided if philosophers had not been so foolish as to claim 'some infallible state of consciousness'. 'They have perplexed themselves', Professor Ayer there remarked, 'with such questions as what consciousness is in itself and how it is related to the things, or facts, which are its objects. It does not seem to be identical with its objects, yet neither does it seem to be anything apart from them. They are separate, yet nothing separates them. When there is added the further premiss that consciousness is also self-conscious, the problem becomes more complicated still.' Professor Ayer appears to dislike the basic fact of cognitive experience because it is mysterious and unanalysable. But if we are going to talk about it at all, we shall have to use descriptions of that kind. If it is taboo, we shall not expect to get much further.

Nor do we. The *cogito ergo sum*, Professor Ayer now tells us, only proves this: that *if* a man doubts, he must exist; it does not prove that anyone *in fact* knows anything. 'It simply makes the logical point that one sort of statement follows from another . . . this does not show that these statements are in any way sacrosanct, considered in themselves.'[2] Leaving aside all questions about what Descartes thought he was proving or in fact proved, we must notice in this passage Professor Ayer's conclusion that consciousness of one's own existence does not prove, after all, to be a privileged case of certainty. 'It is not clear', he goes on, 'what is claimed when it is said that these things are certain or that one can be certain of them. Perhaps only that I know that they are so, and of course I do.' 'Know' is clearly being used in the weak

---

[1] pp. 19–20 (p. 23).   [2] p. 47 (pp. 46–7).

sense of 'being entitled to say'. The upshot of this section is that 'the consciousness of one's self is not one experience among others, not even, as some have thought, a special experience which accompanies all the others. And this is not a matter of psychology but of logic. It is a question of what self-consciousness is understood to mean.'[1] Professor Ayer is prepared to say that people are self-conscious 'in the sense that they conceive of things as happening to themselves'. But 'the expression "having an experience of one's self" is one for which there is no use'. That, I suppose, is the ground for this further and even more astonishing appeal to 'logic'. Again it is a question of fact. Professor Ayer apparently does not experience himself in his activities. It does not follow that other people don't or that anybody is incapable of doing so if he tries.

Finally, for good measure, Professor Ayer throws in the stock objection to any talk about one's own existence. 'I exist' is, he says, 'a peculiar statement; and not only peculiar but degenerate',[2] on the ground that the verb adds nothing to the meaning of the subject. It is certainly a peculiar verb, but it would take us too far afield to discuss the nature of its peculiarity. I can only point out that it is no justification for declaring meaningless 'having an experience of one's self'. It is not the case that this expression can only be meaningful if we can give a satisfactory account of the expression 'I exist'. On the contrary 'I exist' acquires meaning from the fact of self-consciousness.

The rest of the chapter may be very briefly considered for our purposes. It will be enough to show that no advance is made. We are told that only what is 'expressible in language' can be true or false, certain or doubtful, and that 'experiences themselves are neither certain nor uncertain; they simply occur'.[3] This is again simply to deny that cognitive experience guarantees itself. So we go on to consider statements only. Modern philosophers have made many most ingenious attempts to show that even the simplest-seeming certainties may not be accurate descriptions of

[1] p. 49 (p. 48).   [2] p. 52 (p. 50).
[3] p. 54 (p. 52). In the last paragraph of this section Professor Ayer does say that 'while one is having an experience . . . there is nothing for one to be uncertain or mistaken about', but this cannot be taken as an admission of 'genuine' certainty.

the facts which they are claiming to report. One example will suffice to show that Professor Ayer does not succeed in showing this. He takes our old friend 'I feel a headache'. Suppose, he says, that I do feel one and write this down in my diary. Later on I may come to think that the record does not represent the truth. The obvious answer to this is that we are concerned only with the original experience which I wasn't wrong about. But Professor Ayer says of the sentences 'I feel a headache now' and 'I felt a headache then' that 'it would be wrong to conclude that they expressed different statements: for the state of affairs which makes what is expressed by either of them true is one and the same'.[1] This seems to me quite extraordinarily fallacious. The state of affairs represented in the first instance must include a certainty, unless I am deliberately falsifying the record; the state of affairs represented in the second instance need not. Professor Ayer goes on to argue that when I verify a prediction the statement embodying the prediction is the same as that by which I verify it, although the future tense is used in one case and the present in the other. But the absolute certainty of experience is not claimed for predictions by philosophers who know their business. Thus the state of affairs in the headache story differs on the side of the subject from the state of affairs in the prediction story. Professor Ayer has accused those who uphold absolute certainty of describing the whole situation in terms of the knowing subject. He is now describing claims to knowledge entirely in terms of the object. Certainty, the fundamental cognitive experience, is, I am claiming, a unique relationship between subject and object.

The following sentences are taken from Professor Ayer's last paragraphs on the central topic:[2]

'Statements which do no more than describe the content of a momentary, private experience achieve the greatest security because they run the smallest risk. But they do run some risk, however small. . . . In allowing that the descriptions which people give of their experiences may be factually mistaken, we are dissociating having an experience from knowing that one has it. To know that one is having whatever experience it may be, one must

---

[1] p. 57 (p. 55).   [2] pp. 71–3 (pp. 66–8).

not only have it but also be able to identify it correctly. . . . Once again, this does not mean that we never know, or never really know, what experiences we are having. On the contrary it is exceptional for us not to know. All that is required is that we should be able to give an account of our experiences which is both confident and correct. . . . The upshot of our argument is that the philosopher's ideal of certainty has no application. . . . It would, however, be a mistake to express this conclusion by saying, lugubriously or in triumph, that nothing is really certain. There are a great many statements the truth of which we rightly do not doubt; and it is perfectly correct to say that they are certain. We should not be bullied by the sceptic into renouncing an expression for which we have a legitimate use.'

Mistakes are always possible, that is to say, but this need not worry us because in fact they are infrequent. But what is Professor Ayer's justification for saying that they are infrequent? I suppose he would say that things normally happen as we expect them to happen, although of course we *may* be mistaken in thinking that they do. In fact what it amounts to is that we are encouraged to dismiss the question because in practice we do succeed in rubbing along well enough with things as they are. This is hardly the answer which one would expect to receive from a philosopher. *When* is our account both confident and correct? That is the question which remains unanswered. It can be answered only if, instead of 'dissociating having an experience from knowing that one has it', we recognize that knowledge *is* an experience.

I have quoted passages from Professor Ayer's book only to disagree with them. So I should like to add that it is only where he appears to be dodging metaphysics that I find him so unsatisfactory. What he has to say about induction and about sense-data, in particular, seems to me most valuable. And it is always a pleasure to read him.

There have been some references in this paper to 'metaphysics', and I may be allowed perhaps, in conclusion, to give some further indication, in the briefest way, of my point of view. To the question 'is anything *really* true?' Professor Ayer has answered, as we have seen, that *of course* many things are true, although in any particular case we can never exclude doubt altogether. And this, I have said, is no answer. It seems to involve an 'act of faith' of an unsatisfactory kind in the validity of human knowledge. It might be argued that a metaphysician like Louis Lavelle also requires an 'act of faith' if we are to be absolutely certain. What these metaphysicians really mean, however, is that we are free to accept or to reject the *value* of human knowledge. We have to *recognize* that the fact of knowledge *matters*, that it is our link with a world of supersensible reality, not with abstract essences, but with reality in its relation to its source, and so with that source, with God. This recognition requires a willingness to reflect, and so a choice. (And that involves an 'act of faith' very different from that which Professor Ayer is making.) It requires that we should give metaphysics a fair trial in the form in which it is offered us by contemporary philosophers (not, of course, that this sort of metaphysics is new in itself) who see in it a reflective analysis of experience, leading to a recognition of the conscious, choosing, self and of the ultimate source of the self.

IAN RAMSEY

ON THE
POSSIBILITY AND PURPOSE
OF A
METAPHYSICAL THEOLOGY

I

Here a Mill and there a river
Each a glimpse and gone for ever.

So in *A Child's Garden of Verses* Robert Louis Stevenson epitomizes the transitoriness which characterizes the landscape seen on a railway journey, when we are presented with new scenes and new objects passing before our eyes in rapid succession. It is in such situations that people consult their guide books; love to have land-marks pointed out to them; like to know their bearings. It is in such situations that people display, I would suggest, their metaphysical tendencies. For metaphysics arises from man's desire to know, in a world of change and transitoriness, just where he is journeying; it arises whenever man seeks to map the Universe and to plot his position within it. Kant provides a ready illustration. The three questions by which he expresses his interests:[1] What can I know? What ought I to do? What may I hope? are easily seen as a particular expression of man's metaphysical desire to plot his cosmic position.

Whatever their different starting points and methods, metaphysicians have all shared in the desire to have an outline map of

---

[1] 'All the interests of my reason . . . combine in the three following questions. . . .' I. Kant, *Critique of Pure Reason*, Transcendental Doctrine of Method, II. The Canon of Pure Reason, Section 2, trans. N. Kemp Smith, p. 635.

the Universe, some over-all scheme capable of placing whatever transitoriness brought with it.[1] It is such an outline map that Descartes essays to construct in his *Meditations* and develops somewhat in his *Principles of Philosophy* and *Passions of the Soul*. Alternatively, if we feel helpless against the manifold powers of a threatening world, Spinoza's hope is that his metaphysics will enable us to see our due place in the Universe, replacing bewilderment by a beatific vision, fear by an intellectual love of God, confusion by the Third Kind of Knowledge. Nor do these outline maps exclude the most commonplace and ordinary events. On the contrary, if we feel a pain by eating lobster, Leibniz would show us how these two events occurred together according to a pre-established harmony which resulted from God actualizing what he judged to be the best of all the different worlds that were logically possible. Our lobster-pain takes on a cosmic significance.

So it is that Whitehead can rightly say that 'the true method of philosophical construction is to frame a scheme of ideas, the best that one can, and unflinchingly to explore the interpretation of experience in terms of that scheme. The importance of philosophy lies in its sustained effort to make such schemes explicit and thereby capable of criticism and improvement.'[2] Here is the broad purpose of metaphysics: to elaborate some explicit interpretative scheme, critically suited as far as may be to the whole of experience.

Metaphysicians, then, seek for some kind of language-map by which, in some way, to understand the whole Universe. Now what is the relation of such a map to ordinary language? To answer that question let us first give three examples of maps which while not being in themselves metaphysical, can yet afford clues as to what metaphysics does.

(1) We see a field of cows, and say 'five'. Here is a highly generalized concept associated with the language of arithmetic; a language which can link talk about cows with talk of fingers and toes, talk of balls on a counting-frame, and much else. We may generalize even further. If we see a billiard ball and talk of

[1] Such a scheme, as P. F. Strawson notes in his *Individuals*, p. 9, may be either 'descriptive' or 'revisionary', but we may agree that 'perhaps no actual metaphysician has ever been, both in intention and effect, wholly the one thing or the other'.

[2] *Process and Reality* (Preface).

$x^2 + y^2 + z^2 = C^2$, we link talk about the billiard ball with talk about oranges, about the earth, about an Association (but not a Rugby) football, about tennis balls, squash balls, raindrops and suet dumplings. Again, we look on the waves rising and falling at sea, and when we talk of them in terms such as $\sin \theta$, we use language linking our talk of the sea with talk about wireless and television programmes, about the vibration of bridges and so on. Mathematics in this way provides languages such as arithmetic, algebraical geometry and trigonometrical analysis, which, brought alongside common-sense language, can help to unite what is apparently diverse, can help us to attain wide sweeps of generalization. The same is true, and more so, of such mathematical theory as is used in the sciences, as well as of scientific theory itself which can relate what is, for common sense, utterly diverse. For example, the chemistry of carbon unites soot and diamonds; gravitational theory unites falling apples, the stars and the tides. Some have been so impressed by this generalizing power possessed by mathematics and scientific theory that they have asserted that what could not be talked about in terms of the precision languages of mathematics and science 'is not really there'; that, for instance, the redness of the sunset is no more than the vibrations of certain colourless point particles. But this is plainly a blunder if it means that what falls outside express treatment by mathematics or the sciences 'does not exist'; that there is no 'redness' of the sunset. Mathematics, like the exact sciences, is as such only an ancillary scheme. We shall see that despite many differences metaphysics, too, must be likewise regarded as an ancillary scheme.

(2) Similarly, logic—whether traditional or modern—is a scheme, less or more complex, less or more unified, whose purpose is to illuminate, as and where it can, the connexions between assertions which occur in ordinary discourse. At this point we may usefully quote an illustration which Strawson gives in his *Introduction to Logical Theory*:[1]

'The formal logician now aims at an exact and highly systematic logic, comparable in these respects with mathematics. But he cannot give the exact and systematic logic of expressions of

[1] *loc. cit.*, pp. 57–8.

everyday speech; for these expressions have no exact and systematic logic. What he can and does do, is to devise a set of rules which satisfies his requirements and, at the same time, while not doing full justice to the complexities of ordinary usage, and diverging from it in many ways, does touch ordinary usage at some vital points. The formal logician, in relation to ordinary language, might be compared with a man ostensibly mapping a piece of country of which the main contours are highly irregular and shifting. But the man is passionately addicted to geometry, and insists on using in his drawings only geometrical figures for which rules of construction can be given; and on using as few of such rules as he can. Naturally his maps will never quite fit. But a good many landmarks are identifiable on his drawing, and there is a rough correspondence between some of the main features of the country and some of the main lines of the map. The logician, we may say, manufactures the elements of a language of his own, which, unlike ordinary language, is subject to rigid and systematically connected rules, and some of the symbols of which exhibit logical analogies to familiar expressions of ordinary speech, as those expressions are commonly, though not always, used. And in the process of system-construction he may, and does—if only by contrast—teach us a good deal about the logic of ordinary discourse.'

What the logician does, then, is 'to devise a set of rules which satisfies his [formal] requirements and, at the same time, while not doing full justice to the complexities of ordinary usage, and diverging from it in many ways, does touch ordinary usage at some vital points'. The metaphysician is guided by other 'requirements', but he likewise is concerned to devise a system which touches ordinary usage at vital points.

(3) Thirdly, we take an example from elementary physics. Crossing a footbridge over a stream, we put our stick in the water, and say 'It looks bent'. We then kneel on the bridge, run our finger along the stick, and say 'Yet, it's straight'. So far we are using ordinary language: but ordinary language is now puzzling. For how can we talk of this stick being bent and straight *at the same time?*

And now along comes the physicist with his Theory of Refraction. We hear talk of light being some kind of wave motion; with its speed different in different media; that therefore light 'rays' are bent in passing from air to water. Geometrical diagrams are now produced to show why sticks look bent in water, ponds look shallower than they are, and so on.

Now what exactly does this Theory of Refraction do? Has the physicist got some super-microscopic insight which sees light actually changing its speed in the water, as a ship or a swimmer might do? Nothing as simple and straightforward as that. Rather has the physicist resolved our perplexity, and released our tongues (and done much else with which we need not now concern ourselves) by bringing alongside the puzzle a rather complex map—the Theory of Refraction. Look at it like this, he says: and then he entertains us with talk of light rays, their speed in different media, refraction at the boundary between two media, and so on. If we are willing to buy his wares, then our tongues become loosed. His 'theory' makes it possible for us with justification to use 'bent' and 'straight' of the stick at one and the same time by saying 'The stick is *really* straight: it only appears (or seems) bent'.

In this way, the physicist, by bringing his theory alongside ordinary language, provides us with language links of such a kind that the problematical character of our original assertion disappears. The theory enables us to make logical connexions which hitherto we found impossible to forge; and we declare our acceptance of the theory, we acknowledge its illumination in using the word 'really'. This is the option we are taking seriously, in what the preacher calls 'a very real sense'.

With these examples in mind, what suggestions can we make already about the character of metaphysics and its relation to ordinary language? Our reflections suggest that, like logical theory, mathematics or the sciences, metaphysics is an ancillary scheme. That it is a distinctive kind of ancillary scheme we need not for a moment deny. Indeed it will be essential for us to formulate in due course the character of this distinctiveness. But already there arise one or two points about metaphysics that are worth making.

First, we may already understand the better part at least of what might be meant by saying that metaphysics is concerned with 'Reality'. For we have seen that an option for some particular ancillary scheme is often expressed in terms of the 'really—seem' distinction. Words such as these—'really', 'seem'—are (as in the case of the 'bent stick' example) hints that we have brought a supplementary language map alongside ordinary language to illuminate it. Now those metaphysicians who have been traditionally concerned with Reality and Appearance have been concerned, at least in part, with opting for some large-scale map by which to illuminate and organize the diverse assertions of ordinary language. For instance when a metaphysician says 'Evil is really only good misperceived', he need not deny any common-sense talk about good and evil. He certainly need not deny that for us all there is a perfectly proper use of the word 'evil'. At the same time, by his metaphysical assertion he is expressing his option for some map which while allowing all that, believes talk about good and evil to be most reliably structured, and its logical relations best shown, by a large-scale map which includes no talk about evil at all. Again, if some metaphysician says 'When you look at a daffodil it's *really* the Absolute of which you are aware', he is, at least in part, opting for a map which, allowing ordinary language about daffodils, believes this to be most reliably structured, its connexion with all our other talking best shown, on a scheme which talks of no 'objects' but only of the 'Absolute'. We might make the same kind of point about Bertrand Russell's one-time claim (and I would say near-metaphysical claim) that tables are *really* only groups of sense-data, sensibilia, or what you will. Here is the claim that all talk about tables is most reliably and most illuminatingly mapped in terms of statements about nothing but sense-data. Similar remarks are true of the mathematical metaphysician's claim that physical objects are 'not really red' at all.

As I have said, this is by no means the whole story of what is involved in metaphysics, and not even the whole story about the metaphysical use of 'Reality', but it is a very proper part of it. We can also see the point, as well as the misunderstanding, behind G. E. Moore's remark that when anyone says X is really Y, the one thing of which you can be sure is that it is not. In one sense

Moore was right: X is always X. 'Everything is what it is, and not another thing.'[1] But when someone, and it is most often a metaphysician, says X is *really* Y, he need not be denying that X is X. What he is doing by this remark is rather to commend to us his own option for a large-scale map dominated by Y, as that which not only gives a suitable place to talk about X but also, he would claim, gives the best and most illuminating view of the Universe. Moore's remark blinds us to the character of metaphysics, and confuses metaphysics and ordinary language.

Which leads us to three other interim points:

(1) Metaphysics is no mere extension of ordinary language—a kind of Honours Course in the use of words. It has a different logical character altogether—consistent with being an ancillary scheme illuminative of common-sense assertions as a whole.

(2) Yet, we can, I hope, see the great truth behind the view of philosophy as clarification, the view associated especially with Bertrand Russell and G. E. Moore. In constructing metaphysics in the way we have visualized we would in fact be performing an exercise which brought clarification, because illumination, to the utterances of common-sense. There is also a sense in which we could speak of metaphysics as being, in C. D. Broad's phrase, 'critical common sense'; for it would be concerned, in a critical fashion, to organize common-sense assertions in accordance with some perspective or other. But, on the interpretation given above, there would be no suggestion of *replacing* ordinary language by another sort of language; common sense would still remain as ever it was. Or nearly so. For there is an important qualification to be made here.

(3) While metaphysics, like the precision languages of the sciences, is from a logical standpoint an ancillary language, we must recognize that psychologically there is (as always with ancillary languages) likely to be a mixing of words. Yet, if that mixing is done without an awareness of the additional logical complexity which is thereby brought to ordinary language, we shall only be in even greater muddles at the second move. The remark is relevant to many discussions, e.g. about the 'nature' of

[1] Joseph Butler, *Fifteen Sermons Preached at the Rolls Chapel*, Preface, § 39. Quoted by Moore on the title-page to *Principia Ethica*.

so and so, which are frequently at cross-purposes simply because 'nature', in its metaphysical use, is not distinguished from 'nature' and 'natural' in common-sense talk.

While there may be, then, and for a variety of reasons, as a matter of *psychological* fact, some transfers of words between a metaphysical scheme and ordinary language, this does not at all deny what we have insisted to be the special *logical* status of metaphysics, consistent with its being an ancillary scheme.

Now at this point it may be said that the character of metaphysics, as I have given it, compromises the possibility of any metaphysics distinctive and worthy of the name, and this brings us to the essential and important question we postponed a little while ago. For in arguing that its logical status is importantly similar to that of mathematics and scientific theories, do we not imply (it might be said) that a metaphysics is only some sort of high-grade scientific theory after all? In trying to become clearer about the purpose of metaphysics, have we not made the logical status of metaphysics too close to that of a scientific scheme?

The point may be put like this. We have seen that it is the function of the sciences to provide precision languages by means of which puzzles, discrepancies or problematical phrases can be resolved, and logical links provided where none existed before. We have said that metaphysics is pre-eminently a venture after unity: an endeavour to provide a scheme of maximum interpretative power. Where then does metaphysics differ from a high-grade scientific scheme? Why should not the sciences provide us with the over-all scheme and supply us with such integrator words as we need?

The short answer is that there can be no genuine union of two logically diverse scientific languages[1] by means of words native to either. For any such uniting words would commit type-trespass in the language to which they were not native. For the same reason, no third brand of scientific discourse could unite the two diverse languages: otherwise the same difficulty would be twice repeated. So we look in vain for genuine integration by scientific words: we look in vain for what might be called a scientific meta-

---

[1] I take it as agreed that such logical diversity characterizes what is talked of misleadingly by the one word 'science'.

physics, where even the high-grade integrations are in the last resort cashed in terms of observables.

The consequent cost of a total over-all map, of the kind the metaphysicians seek, is integrator words not native to any of the diverse observational languages of the sciences, yet able to combine with and supplement them: words which, while able in this way to secure a reference to observables by associating with scientific discourse, are not confined within its logical patterns.

We need not deny that a certain amount of integration apparently can be and is done by the sciences. What were traditionally such logically diverse areas as light, heat and magnetism and electricity, for example, have been integrated by concepts such as mass, velocity, energy. But we must recognize that the new integrated language is an alternative to, and does *not* incorporate, the former disintegrated and separate languages. Rather it talks in another kind of way altogether about what hitherto needed two different languages for discussion, and what that was is never given except in terms of the ordinary language from which we started. Indeed, in science, any gain in comprehensiveness seems to be at the expense of particularity. The more generalized the scientific scheme, the further distant does it seem to be logically from the assertions of ordinary language. Every new-born child produced by scientific generalization belongs to yet another logical generation. We need do no more than recall the following kind of sequence: 'red sunset', 'light waves', 'electrons', 'fundamental particles', to see the widening logical gap which such scientific sequences present. At any rate, such increased integration as is provided by scientific generalization leaves many diverse, and in some ways still indispensable, languages strewn about the path of progress. Integration done by the sciences is not at all a matter of integrating diverse languages; rather does it consist of *replacing* diversity by more generalized and less diverse schemes.

It may, however, be that large areas of scientific discourse, and even diverse areas of such discourse, suggest some common highly generalized concept. As illustrations we might mention Matter or Evolution; and the way some phenomena, especially in physics, are co-ordinated has led to their being talked of in terms of something like personal qualities, e.g. the 'attraction' of unlike magnetic poles for each other, the 'repulsion' of similar magnetic poles, the 'cussedness' of Lenz's Law.

Further, such concepts have sometimes become the cornerstone of 'metaphysical' maps—matter and evolution being easily recognized as bold aspirants of a century ago. In this way it might again seem that science could, in principle, provide the integrative concepts that metaphysics needs.

To such a suggestion our reply must be twofold:

(1) There is no reason why, *as a matter of psychological fact*, our metaphysical key-words should not be thrown up and suggested by scientific discourse. It may be, e.g., that the metaphysical concept of substance has been derived by extrapolating from the scientific concept of matter or a particle; it may be that a metaphysical concept such as Process (for Whitehead) or Activity (for Berkeley) could be suggested by reflecting on the scientific concepts of change or interaction, and so on. But if these concepts have no other grounding, and no other anchorage than in scientific phenomena, they will provide us with but pseudo-metaphysics; they will be at best useful jingles which, mnemonic-like, associate diverse scientific languages. They will at best have the curiously uncertain status of Kant's Regulative Ideas.

(2) Contrariwise, even though these concepts are suggested by scientific discourse, and even though they are rightly detected as structuring such discourse, they will only be metaphysical if they are not native to scientific language at all, but have their ground and logical origin elsewhere. They will only be metaphysical if, in that origin, they are to be anchored in situations not limited to the spatio-temporal observables with which scientific discourse is wholly concerned.

By this rather circuitous route we have now reached a point to which we might have passed much earlier, viz: the view that metaphysics, to be genuine metaphysics, must have reference to more than observables, i.e. to the unseen. If our reasoning is reliable, this is in fact our conclusion. For metaphysical integrators, being not native to any scientific language, must have their grounding in what is more than spatio-temporal, i.e. they must be 'meta-physical' in a more obviously traditional sense. For metaphysics is not merely (what I suggested much earlier) the construction of some kind of ancillary map—it is (as we now begin to see) the construction of a map in accordance with a vision of the unseen.

From what we have said, then, about the purpose of metaphysics, whose aim is to construct as complete a map of the Universe as possible, which in particular will link together the various precision languages of the sciences, it follows that the possibility of metaphysics depends on there being words which, not being native to any of the languages of science:

(a) are able to unify these logically diverse languages; and
(b) are given by reference to what is more than spatio-temporal.

If then we are to justify the possibility of metaphysics, we are left with two questions on our hands:

(a) How do distinctively metaphysical words unify?
(b) What empirical grounding or foundation can such integrator words be given?

To answer these questions we may well ask others: Where will such integrator words be found—words which, not being themselves descriptive in their use, can nevertheless be united with words which are descriptive? What indeed is the fact which justifies metaphysics? If it is given in a vision of the unseen, what sort of empirical circumstance does that phrase describe? I propose to answer these questions by taking a specific example of a metaphysics, viz. theism.

The suggestion which I propose to outline in the second part of this paper is that the situation which justifies metaphysics is very like what justifies for each of us our own use of 'I', and that in this word 'I' we have a paradigm for all metaphysical integrators.[1] But we may readily recall one or two other examples whose relation to this one I will not further discuss. 'Being'[2] is sometimes claimed as an integrator word which unifies assertions about all particular existents, and is given by reference to an 'intuition'. Again, 'Absolute' is sometimes offered as an integrator

[1] C. B. Daly approaches a similar point from another direction in Ch. XI.
[2] See Ch. VII.

word belonging to a unified over-all scheme, and is then given by reference to what F. H. Bradley called 'immediate experience', something which breaks in on us when we 'see' the unsatisfactoriness of stories about terms and relations.

I only mention these other examples to show that our concept of metaphysics is by no means restricted to theism, though it is by theism that I shall exemplify it, and it is 'God' which I believe (for reasons which lie outside the present essay) to be the integrator word which provides the most simple, far-reaching and coherent metaphysical map.

II

We left our first section with two questions:

(1) Where can we find words which, not being themselves descriptive (and so native to scientific language), can nevertheless be united with words which are used descriptively? We shall have answered that question when we have provided actual specimens of metaphysical integrators.

(2) How can such words be given by reference to what is more than spatio-temporal? We shall have answered this question when we have shown the kind of situation which justifies any and all systems of metaphysics.

To succeed in answering either question I suggest that we first consider yet another question:

Can human behaviour in principle, and on all occasions, be adequately and satisfactorily treated in terms of observables, in terms of what can be perceptually verified?

Let us admit at the outset that human behaviour would be no more than the observables which characterize it if A's saying 'I did X' *always* meant in principle no more than B's saying of A, 'He did X'. Further, let us readily admit that *sometimes* this is the case. Sometimes I *do* speak of myself as others speak of me, i.e. wholly in terms of observables. Let us take two examples to illustrate this contention. An undergraduate rushes in for some kind of decanal permission. But the Dean is immersed in administration, so he says, to make it clear that he is saying something of official necessity which does not at all harmonize with his personal wishes to be helpful and kind: *'The Dean is busy*; come back in an hour.' Meanwhile, we may note that, if I am the Dean, this assertion does not entail 'I am busy', for 'I' may have what is called 'deep contentment' or 'inward peace' below the rigours of decanal administration.

Again, someone might ask the Bishop 'Who preached the sermon last week?' And he might answer, *'The Bishop preached'*. Very true, because it had been a very official, prelatical, impersonal sermon, so that people said, 'Just like the Bishop's purple self'.

Now the very oddness of the two italicized remarks shows that the circumstances they describe do not normally cover the case, that normally more might and must be said. Sometimes it *may* suffice, but normally it will *not* be enough to talk of my behaviour in terms of the Dean (if I'm the Dean), or the Bishop (if I'm the Bishop). So while we may readily allow that 'I' sometimes functions like 'he', yet we may also argue that this is not the whole account of the logic of 'I'. At this point we are both echoing and rejecting something which Wittgenstein once said.

As Professor J. R. Jones reminded us in a recent paper to the Aristotelian Society,[1] Wittgenstein, according to Moore, 'was quite definite that the word "I" or "any other word which denotes a subject" is used in "two utterly different ways", one in which it is "on a level with other people" and one in which it is not. This difference, he said, was a difference in the grammar of our ordinary language'.[2]

There are thus two uses of 'I'. But Wittgenstein said, let us notice, that this difference is just a difference of 'grammar', and by this I suppose he meant not only that the distinctive use of 'I' is not one which is perceptually verifiable (with which we would agree), but more positively (with which we would not agree) that the difference arises merely and simply because we need somehow to distinguish the speaker from the hearer. I do not deny that we need to make the distinction. *My point is that more needs saying as well.* But what 'more'?

---

[1] 'The two contexts of mental concepts', *P.A.S.* 1958–9, VI, pp. 105–24.
[2] 'Wittgenstein's Lectures in 1930–33', G. E. Moore, *Mind*, January 1953, p. 14. Quoted by J. R. Jones *loc. cit.*, p. 116.

To answer that question consider the three assertions:

(a) 'The Dean shuts the door', said by the Dean or someone else, say *B*, of the Dean.
(b) 'I shut the door', said by the Dean of the Dean.
(c) 'He shut the door', said by *B* of the Dean.

There is no difficulty with (a); everything can be verified equally well by everybody; speaker and hearer are on the same footing. But in (b) does 'I' just 'indicate' the speaker? Certainly it does that; but it surely does more than peg the assertion to this point, this speaker, this chap talking. For it asserts that particular existence which I know to be definitely mine. Now I agree that this 'extra' in (b) is not a perceptually verifiable 'more'. It is not like the 'more' we tell about Tom's uncle by speaking of 'Tom's *rich* uncle'. The 'more' in this assertion (b) is something which can never be enumerated in observational terms. How then can it be secured?

If *per impossibile* we could give our identity descriptively, our individuality would have disappeared. The subject would have been objectified. We would have become, as I have implied elsewhere,[1] so public as to be lost in the crowd. This same reflection occurs at the end of Professor Jones's paper. 'If, through suppression of the sense in which "I" is not replaceable by "he" I am placed in a relation [for instance] to my anger such that, when I make an avowal of anger, *it is as if I were actually saying*, "He is angry", and implying no more by this than *you* mean by it, then, although what is being *said*, namely, that I am angry, is unaffected, my sentence now lies for me in a surrounding in language which is radically decomposed—the surrounding of the grammar of what I am saying. And the consequence is a straining of what I would call my deep sense of the grammar. Something is disturbed which involves my whole ability to use language. This is why, I suggest, the cumulative impression is one of *deep* paradox.'

'The ghosts of occult contents, and processes "stowed away in some peculiar medium", proved exorcizable. But a "ghost" is built into grammar. And it will not be laid.'[2]

---

[1] *Philosophical Quarterly*, Vol. 5 No. 20. July 1955 'The Systematic Elusiveness of "I"' See esp. pp. 197, 199, 203.
[2] *loc. cit.*, p. 124.

But if there is 'more', where the 'more' cannot be perceptually verified, we return to our question above: what is its empirical basis? How do we come to recognize this 'more'? The answer is: In a disclosure, a disclosure in which I come to myself and realize myself as more than the observable behaviour I display. The stock example of such a disclosure is that of David and Nathan, when at Nathan's 'Thou art the man!' David comes to himself, the 'penny drops' and the disclosure occurs. What 'I' distinctively stands for, what I am to myself more than I as he is to you, is something which *a fortiori cannot be described*. It can only be evoked in and for each of us, and that means given (as we have said) in a disclosure that justifies our use of 'I' in the extended sense, the sense which belongs to a situation not restricted to the observables in terms of which other people (as well as I) can talk of it.

Here is a word—'I' for each of us—which is, then, not descriptive, and yet it can be united with any number of descriptive words. We may say 'I'm angry' or 'I'm a neurotic' or 'I'm a malaria case', or 'I'm a wage-earner' or 'I'm busy', and so on.[1] 'I exist' is entailed by assertions such as 'He's a wage-earner'; 'He's a neurotic' in the languages of economics, medicine, psychology; and in so doing it becomes an integrator of these logically diverse areas.[2] Further, what is, in spatio-temporal terms, non-descriptive about 'I exist', is given in a disclosure situation. Here, then, is a paradigm for metaphysics. Here is a metaphysical integrator, given by reference to a disclosure which transcends the spatio-temporal. Here is solipsism as the primitive metaphysics,[3] though I am not pretending that Wittgenstein would have agreed with my present interpretation of that remark.

[1] That some of these may be assertions in ordinary language I neither doubt nor deny; but as such they would not interest us for our present purpose. Further, the possibility of words moving between metaphysics, science and common sense has been explicitly allowed for above.

[2] Or if it be held that, supposing my temperature is 98.4°, then 'I exist' *and* 'His temperature is not 98.4°' are not together self-contradictory, it might be said not so much that 'His temperature is 98.4°' entails 'I exist' as that 'I exist' is a *presupposition* of making this or any other scientific assertion about me; that the scientist in making his assertions *commits* himself to the existential claim. See P. F. Strawson, *Introduction to Logical Theory*, p. 175, for this same point. It is also one which accords with the general thesis of M. Polanyi's *Personal Knowledge*: that scientific understanding presupposes 'personal knowledge'.

[3] Wittgenstein, *Tractatus Logico-philosophicus*, 5.641, cp. 5.64 and 5.62.

(ii) Let us now continue our argument by recalling assertion (c) which we enumerated above, where B says of the Dean 'He shut the door'. This *may* imply for B something of an objective disclosure around that pattern of observable behaviour known as 'The Dean', revealing something corresponding to what we know subjectively in the case of ourselves. In any case we must not suppose that a 'disclosure', a penny dropping, is something utterly and wholly subjective. I become aware of myself as I become aware of an environment transcending observables. Look at it like this, and here I take up again the two uses of 'I'. Can we not all recall a primitive state where we talk of ourselves in terms of proper names such as 'Neeny', where these are wholly restricted to our public behaviour. Even at this stage we are of course aware of ourselves. My point is that at this stage we have no language to fit. We use of ourselves a word 'Neeny' which others can use in precisely the same kind of way. But when we later use 'I' significantly of ourselves, it is because we recognize it as being used as an indicator word by others for themselves, relating to their public behaviour and more, and we recognize that we ourselves want to talk precisely of that, of 'Neeny' and more, and so of 'I'. In short, the use of the word 'I' commits us also to pluralism of persons. It is not likely that we should use 'I' for ourselves, if there were nothing else but ourselves. So we become aware of ourselves as we become aware of an environment transcending observables. But this 'objective' awareness has many recognizable differences. Already we have seen that of the awareness may be *prima facie of* other persons. Now let us see how else it can be characterized. Let us begin with an example which makes another point as well.

I am absent-minded, so before I start on my journey my wife ties string round my finger to remind me to get petrol. I have been travelling oblivious of it for some hours; being bored, relieving the boredom by inventing problems to solve or giving lifts to hitch-hikers and so on. Then, on chancing to feel the string, the 'penny drops', there is a disclosure. I recall my need; look out actively for the next pump, and stop. What has happened? On seeing the string I have ceased to be the bored traveller, the problem-solver, the conversation-maker, and become 'myself'. It is in such cases, in such self-awareness, that I have suggested that there occurs a situation which is more than the observables it contains, but even here we get a little of an objective element. I come to myself on remembering the circumstances in which I left my wife, her words, her directions, and so forth. It is true that my keeping a look out for the petrol station may be no more than a quasi-reflex action, in which case there would be no disclosure at all. Here is the first and extra point which this example makes, and it warns us that there may be cases of alert, integrated behaviour which may be deceptively like that which accompanies what we call disclosures. We may be psychologically alert and integrated without 'coming to ourselves'—we then lack what the existentialists call 'authenticity'. The same point arises again in the second example which follows.

But leaving that on one side let us notice the possible presence even in remembering of an objective element, and let us notice that there would be rather more of such an objective element in a detective ncvel, where, when the penny drops we suddenly 'see' the culprit, when the solution forces itself on us. There would be even more of this objective element in a situation of moral challenge.

This last and very important point can be illustrated by two more examples. We may remember the story of Robin Hood and the Tinker who searches for him with a warrant from the Sheriff of Nottingham. The Tinker unexpectedly meets Robin Hood and the conversation proceeds like this:

Q. Do you know Robin Hood?
A. Oh, very well indeed, I have the closest knowledge of him.
Q. Where is he now, I wonder?
A. I am sure he cannot be very far away.
Q. Is he strong?
A. Fairly so. He had a successful bout with a very skilled wrestler the other day.
Q. How tall is he?
A. Just about my height.
Q. Colour of hair?
A. Brown.
Q. Is he clever?
A. He has misled a lot of folk.

Now supposing Robin Hood had concluded such question-and-answering like this: 'And I'm the man.' What would be added by this claim that 'It is I'? There are two possible answers. Some might say, as I have admitted, that 'I' is purely indicative. It just says: What you see now, this body, this chap talking with you, is of a part with all we have been describing. Nor can this be denied. The leading question is: Is that all? For another answer is possible. When Robin makes his confession, there might be a disclosure. The sequence to date, plus the pattern before the Tinker, then becomes part of a disclosure situation where the Tinker discerns around 'Robin Hood' an objective challenge. We may recall some remarks by Berkeley about 'seeing Alciphron'.[1] If what we mean by 'seeing' is to 'see' the visible surface, the hair, face, skin, etc., then in this sense we never 'see' Alciphron. To see Alciphron is to 'see' more than this. For Berkeley such a disclosure—of what is visible and more—occurred when Alciphron moved or acted. For the Tinker, a similar disclosure occurred as a moral challenge.

This same point can be made by a second example where we might consider someone sweeping up the litter on Hampstead Heath on the day after a Bank Holiday. The brush goes backwards and forwards making always an equal angle with the vertical, and the sweeper proceeds with leisurely tread. Hardly a person, we might be tempted to say. A mechanical sweeper might do the same. Descriptive language would be quite adequate for the situation. Then there appears among the litter a pound note, and the sweeper is (we might say) 'touched off'. Already there is the prospect of another drink or two; already the mouth waters like Pavlov's dog. Still, there need be no disclosure as we have been using the word, though criteria such as surprise and heart-throbbing would be there, and might deceive us. It might be (as we noted above) hardly different from a reflex action. Once again we must be on our guard at supposing that disclosures have occurred when they have not, when the visible circumstances may be deceptively similar. But then among the litter occurs a letter marked 'Confidential', and the writing is that of the sweeper's son to a girl friend, or the sweeper's daughter to a boy friend. Now,

[1] *Alciphron*, Dialogue IV, § 5.

without any doubt, the sweeper comes to himself. He is presented with a moral challenge, indeed with what may be a moral conflict: should he or should he not read this letter? He has ceased to be a mere sweeper, or even a sweeper throbbing for a drink. He has become 'himself' when confronted by a moral challenge. Generalizing the example, we may say that 'I' come to myself most characteristically in relation to a moral challenge which equally—but 'objectively'—goes beyond observables.

So we can see how, besides 'I', there arise other metaphysical words which are grounded in what is 'objectively' revealed in a disclosure. Amongst such words are (as we saw earlier) those which we use of 'other persons'. We have now seen how other metaphysical words or phrases may be grounded in that objective challenge which is talked of in terms of obligation and duty. We see how, e.g., 'Duty' may arise as a metaphysical category.

It may be useful to develop this particular example a little further. We recognize something as an obligation or duty, or more strictly as a *prima facie* obligation and duty, when (as we have said) it presents itself to us within a disclosure situation. But it is notorious that there can be 'conflicts' of duty—the Hampstead Heath sweeper may think he has a duty to exert a protective providence over his son or his daughter; equally well a duty to respect his or her privacy. We then have the prospect of a disclosure presenting us with two challenges which generate conflicting responses. The only way to resolve the difficulty is to develop the empirical details in each case until there arises within the one disclosure a single challenge and response. When men have spoken of Absolute Duty, Absolute Goodness, or Absolute Perfection, they have been searching for an appropriate label to a disclosure situation in which there was no possibility of any other than a single unambiguous, unmistakable response. But it would not seem that this is ever the case with *formulations* of duty. In short (as we shall see presently) a disclosure labelled 'Absolute Duty' or 'Absolute Perfection' is one which closely resembles in its character the disclosure to which theists appeal when they speak of 'God'—for here again it is claimed that we have some kind of guarantee linked with descriptive corrigibility.

Meanwhile, let us notice how contemporary developments in

ethics can be related to this discussion of disclosures. It is pointed
out in another paper[1] how it is being increasingly recognized that
in the language of ethics the descriptive and the evaluative
elements are intertwined. This accords well with what we have
said about disclosures, though I am not pretending that all of those
who recognize the intertwining would agree with my account of
the matter. What I suggest is that those who have attempted, in
whatever diverse ways, to make ethics wholly descriptive are
those who would ignore or deny the kind of transcendence which
what we have called a disclosure demands and provides. Next, to
recognize ethics as being at one and the same time descriptive and
evaluative is, I suggest, to allow for a disclosure which is *both*
spatio-temporal and *more* than spatio-temporal. The language of
ethics which speaks of such a disclosure is, in virtue of the spatio-
temporal elements, *descriptive*; it becomes *evaluative* in so far as it
concerns something which is distinctively my active, personal
response. But to speak of 'response' means that I would now go
further than even an evaluatory theory, and see the language of
ethics as not only descriptive and evaluative, but also responsive,
i.e. responsive to a transcendent challenge whose description
demands metaphysical words like 'Duty'.

But now we return to our concept of metaphysics as a single
all-embracing map of the Universe. Does this not mean that the
various metaphysical words already cast up need themselves to be
organized? The claim of the theist is that they are all of them
organized in relation to the word God.[2] Which brings us to our
third and last sub-section.

(iii) God. Taking up our last point we may say that all the
traditional proofs of God's existence can be regarded, in principle,
as techniques to evoke disclosures, to commend the word 'God'

---

[1] Ch. I, pp. 16–20.

[2] Incidentally, this is also why, if we are asked what a disclosure discloses, several
answers are possible. A first answer might be, in relation to the examples we have given:
'my wife's warning', 'Robin Hood', 'his son's letter'. But for the theist all these phrases
would be brought in relation to the answer which supplements them all, without replacing
any, viz. 'God'. So the theist would speak (for example) of seeing God in a friend, finding
God in literature, family relations and so on. If the theist sponsors any doctrine of
creation, he need not apologize for ultimately relating every disclosure to God, especially
when he recalls that there are many who associate the disclosures evoked by the salt in
their stew, the cream in their coffee, the sugar in their tea and so on with the disclosure
which occurs when they speak of their girl-friend: 'You'—'You are the salt in my stew', etc.

diversely in relation to what is objectively disclosed, and so to approach the one concept 'God' from diverse directions. In short, the traditional proofs may be regarded as a somewhat crude exercise to carry out the programme indicated in the concluding paragraph of (ii).

If there were no other disclosures but those around persons, we might be content with a pluralistic map; if there were no other disclosures but those reached by ethical techniques we might be believers in 'Absolute Values'—ethical humanists like Russell at the present time. But disclosures are more diverse than this, and in outline the justification for theism arises because the word 'God' is such an admirable integrator. Disclosures can occur which do not arise around personal nor moral behaviour but around cosmic events or microscopic phenomena. These can occur when we reflect on causal sequences, when we look at daffodils in a particular way, or penetrate into the secrets of the ocean-bed. In all such disclosures we are aware of some 'other', which cannot be thought to be another 'I'. Such situations as these are *pre-eminently* those which afford the empirical basis for theism. For they connect 'God' with all those features of the world that a metaphysics confined to persons or values would have to ignore. 'God' can now integrate not only talk about persons and values but talk about science and perception.

But how do we then talk about this integrator word 'God'? Despite all we have just said, our *first* move towards an answer must be: model 'God' on 'I'. This means, more broadly, that we shall speak about God by qualifying any and all descriptive language—whether of people, human behaviour, or the Universe —in such a way that it tells a more than descriptive story, in such a way that it evokes a disclosure, and this I suggest is most generally done either by qualifying descriptive language infinitely, or qualifying descriptive language negatively. I have developed this suggestion at great length elsewhere.[1] All I need remark now is that talk about God is certainly *never* apt if it is in terms of plain descriptions alone. To be more positively helpful and reverting to our earlier remark, we might say that the logical behaviour of

[1] See, e.g., my *Religious Language*, especially Ch. II, and *Freedom and Immortality*, especially pp. 113–14.

'I', being grounded in a disclosure and ultimately different from all descriptive language, while nevertheless being associated with it, is always a good first clue to the logical behaviour of 'God'. Further, with reference to the unifying character of metaphysical language, just as 'I' acts (as we saw) as an integrator word for all kinds of scientific and other descriptive assertions about myself, 'I exist' being a sort of contextual presupposition for them all, so also may 'God' be regarded as a contextual presupposition for the Universe. 'I am active' is entailed by all kinds of scientific descriptions and links them together. Likewise, we might say, and certainly as a first move, 'God is active' links any and all descriptive assertions about the Universe, such as science in particular specializes in.

So to a brief recapitulation. The possibility of metaphysics arises (i) because there is at least one integrator word 'I'—hence solipsism is the logical primitive metaphysics; and (ii) because this word 'I' is given in relation to a vision of the unseen, a disclosure situation. The possibility of a metaphysical theology arises when, to talk of the objective constituent of all disclosure situations which go beyond what is seen, to unite the various metaphysical words that are cast up in this way, we use the word 'God'. This word 'God' is modelled on, though it has necessarily important differences from, 'I'.[1] These differences are in fact grounded in the observable features of those various disclosure situations which more aptly lead us to God rather than to ourselves or other people.

Let me now conclude by mentioning three implications.

(1) The language we use about God will always have to be so constructed that it is potentially generative of, evocative of, a disclosure. It must have within it the potentiality to make pennies drop, to evoke a disclosure which contains observables and more, a disclosure of the kind we know when each of us comes to himself.

We can therefore deny the possibility of a metaphysical theology for two reasons. We may do it on *philosophical* grounds when we believe that observables are all that there is. But can we believe that at least of ourselves? What I am saying is that a true

---

[1] The reader will find this same point approached from different directions, and discussed further in Chs. XI and XII.

estimate of personality and a true estimate of religion stand or fall together; there can be devilish parodies of both. Alternatively, we may deny the possibility of a metaphysical theology because as a matter of *psychological* fact we have never known what a disclosure was. That reflection reminds us how much of our culture today is inhibitive of disclosures, and atrophies vision. It is not easy to have vision when there is growing uniformity about our environment and greater standardization of life, when personal relations tend to be overlaid and screened by a rigorous efficiency and so on. Such uniformity, standardization and efficiency may be both inevitable and representative of genuine progress. But we need all the more, and all the more is it difficult to provide for, 'pennies dropping'.

(2) Our reflections can help, I believe, in a question which various papers have raised:[1] the matter of intuitions and what is guaranteed in an intuition. For the same questions of incorrigibility and misdescription arise about myself. We may go back to Professor J. R. Jones's paper. On page 121 he says: ' "He is angry" . . . is an interpretation and, for that reason, corrigible. It is an interpretation of the user's emotion in the light of his behaviour and of his behaviour in the light of the situation in which he is placed. I do not mean that an onlooker can never arrive at the recognition that someone is angry without conscious inference or even some research. Sometimes he has to look for the explanation of the other person's behaviour, sometimes not. My point is simply that logically "He is angry" has the status of an interpretation and is, therefore, always, in principle, corrigible.' With this we cannot disagree. But Professor J. R. Jones has said earlier: 'The avowal "I'm angry" as spoken from within my involvement, is intrinsically "hall-marked" and, therefore, incorrigible.'[2] But is it? Is not all that is incorrigible my existence in

---

[1] See e.g. pp. 78, 81, 141–52 and Ch. XII, especially §§ X, XI, XII.

[2] *loc. cit.* pp. 120–1. On this point Dom Illtyd Trethowan would agree with Professor Jones as against me, and consider that (at least in some cases) 'I'm angry' or 'I'm in pain' was incorrigible—that here were some incorrigible descriptions. While I am naturally very willing (as I indicate in the next paragraph) to allow degrees of corrigibility for descriptions, I cannot see that it will ever reach zero, without a word changing its logical character from a descriptive to a proper name. But Dom Illtyd would no doubt reject this antithesis precisely at this point. At any rate, while our positions are broadly similar, he would plainly give a rather simpler answer than I do to the basic question of what an intuition 'delivers', and so take a less complex view of assertions about God than I do in the paragraphs which follow.

relation to some other? What happens in the case of ourselves is that we know something incorrigibly, to which corrigible descriptions are inevitably applied.

We might perhaps then say that we are as certain of God as we are of ourselves. But any and all description, no matter how attenuated, in both cases is more or less problematical. The furthest we could go might be to say that there would be nothing puzzling about (say) 'I am active' if it were clearly seen that this was on a different logical level from all other phrases, being merely meant to bear witness to that part of a self-disclosure which is an invariant. Even so, the very use of the word 'active' may be going too far, and would go too far if it had any 'descriptive' element. All the same 'I've a pain', for example, affords a better clue to 'I exist' or 'I'm active' than some more complex descriptive phrase such as 'I've fibrositis in my shoulder'.

Thus God is guaranteed to us very much as we are to ourselves. But no description is guaranteed. The basic assertion about God does not stand or fall on one or many particular verifiable assertions. Yet as with ourselves, so with God, intuition and description come together.

What we are claiming indeed is that there is in fact a basic assertion both about ourselves and about God which can neither be rightly regarded as 'absolutely certain' or 'wholly corrigible'. For neither of these phrases is appropriate to the unique status it has. For it combines in one and the same assertion incorrigibility and corrigibility, and if we wish to devise any apt label for it at all (though here again there could be grave misunderstanding) it might be 'probable'. For it would be 'probable' in Butler's sense, a sense which makes a 'probable' utterance completely determinative of one's total behaviour. In our own case, we might display the matter as follows:

I have a headache

= There's a headache .... which is mine.
   (descriptive, corrigible; relating to 'objects')   (incorrigible)

= I exist .... with a headache.
   (incorrigible)   (corrigible)
      |———————— 'probable' ————————|

But if we do so display the argument, we must notice that 'probable' relates to the peculiar logical status of the *total* assertion. It *does not* imply (for example) that the assertion about my own existence is 'probable'. In a similar way, we might wish to regard 'God exists' as formally indicative of the 'incorrigible' element in any total theistic assertion.

(3) A more general conclusion: all and every brand of metaphysics will, as we have seen, plead integrator words with respect to disclosure situations in which we are aware of what is more than observables. We might then judge between different brands of metaphysics as to how successful their integrator concepts were in effecting a unified scheme. That such a task brings immense difficulties is obvious. But one reflection may be permitted at the outset. So far as I can see, no integrator concept will be in principle justifiable which does not begin by being modelled on 'I'. In short, there cannot be a justifiable sub-personal metaphysics. But that is not to say that a metaphysics which was no more than personally structured would be adequate. Theism needs to be much more subtle than that.

C. B. DALY

METAPHYSICS
AND THE
LIMITS OF LANGUAGE

I shall not begin by attempting to define what I mean by metaphysics; it has become clear in recent discussion that most of the difficulty about deciding whether or how metaphysics is possible comes from confusion or uncertainty about how to define metaphysics. In a sense, the whole point of this paper is a request for a definition of metaphysics; the definition cannot come at the beginning, but will, it is hoped, emerge in the course of the paper. I shall begin with some historical considerations.

I. METAPHYSICS IN RECENT BRITISH PHILOSOPHY

The most convenient point at which to begin a survey, which must here be brief and sketchy, of recent discussion on the possibility of metaphysics, is with the belligerent anti-metaphysical doctrine of the Logical Positivists, particularly as formulated in the first edition of Professor Ayer's *Language, Truth and Logic*. In assessing the value of any 'elimination of metaphysics', it is important to find out what precisely is being marked down for elimination, as well as the reasons given for the elimination. A good deal of the discussion about metaphysics in the last twenty years has been vitiated by the unhistorical and question-begging descriptions given of metaphysics, and by the unfortunate habit of condemning metaphysicians on the basis of propositions torn from their context and understood out of all relation to the immediate argument and the ultimate intention of the author. For Ayer, in 1935, metaphysics seems to have been represented mainly by some of the more paradoxical sentences of Bradley or McTaggart and some of the more tortuous and obscure utterances of Heidegger; but it is not evident that he tried very hard to enter into the minds or discover the intentions of these philosophers.

Ayer left his readers in no doubt as to what metaphysics meant for him. It meant one or other of two things: either assertions about 'a reality transcending the world of science and common sense'; or assertions purporting to describe empirical reality and yet not being statements of science or of common sense, and not being amenable to observational tests. Both types of metaphysics are excluded for the same reason, that they fail to conform to the conditions of empirical verification under which alone a factual statement can be meaningful. Philosophical analysis can, he claimed, uncover the grammatical blunders and logical errors which led philosophers into the illusion of metaphysics. But this is a work of supererogation: the verification principle, by itself, deprives metaphysics of all plausibility and all excuse. Whether it claim direct acquaintance with non-empirical 'entities' like moral values, or immortal souls, or God; or whether it claim to know these indirectly by inference from experience; or whether it claim to deduce the nature of reality from rational principles, metaphysics is in all cases a tissue of pseudo-propositions.

This 'elimination of metaphysics' amounts to the claim that only the empirical sciences can know objective reality or discover facts or utter meaningful sentences about facts; and that metaphysics, claiming to describe reality and to state objective truths is, necessarily, literally senseless. That logical positivism was itself a nest of metaphysical assumptions and fallacies is now generally agreed and a matter of history. But it had at least the effect of focusing the attention of philosophers upon the nature of metaphysics and its relationship to science and its claim to meaningfulness and truth. Discussions arising out of the logical positivists' monolithic doctrine of meaning have led philosophers to recognize the endless diversity of languages and of meanings. The monopoly of meaning is denied to 'science and common sense'; and attention is paid to the persuasive, promissory, poetic, ethical and metaphysical uses of language and to their varieties of claim to meaning. The 'Wittgenstein I' slogan, 'The meaning of a proposition is the method of its verification', has been replaced by the 'Wittgenstein II' slogans, 'Don't ask for the meaning, ask for the use', and 'Every kind of statement has its own kind of logic'.

The dogmatic denial of meaning to metaphysics has thus been succeeded, in British philosophy, by a qualified tolerance which is prepared to concede that metaphysics has some sort of meaning and to enquire into what kind of meaning this can be. This marks a definite progress. It is, however, a limited progress. The first qualification of the new tolerance towards metaphysics is that it is still fairly universally assumed that, whatever validity meta-physics may have, it cannot make true statements about Reality. Hence, its validity can consist only in its power to call attention, by paradox, to neglected aspects of experience and to recommend new descriptions of familiar facts. It will be granted today that 'a metaphysical system may have many virtues, such as elegance, simplicity, originality, comprehensiveness, depth, or the power to give psychological satisfaction'; 'but', it is added, 'the claim that any such system is exclusively true or uniquely faithful to Reality, is a claim which sets metaphysics on quite the wrong ground'.[1] Metaphysics is often accorded respect today as a work of inventive or constructive imagination. Its role is acknowledged in breaking the tyranny of established linguistic habits and conventions and thereby stimulating scientific research along new lines. Although its questions cannot be answered, they may challenge and spur science to discover answers to questions that can be answered. Metaphysics may thus turn into science.[2]

In the context of contemporary discussion, it is obvious that a major problem for the metaphysician is to clarify the relationship between metaphysics and the empirical sciences, between meta-physical statements and empirical facts. He must resume Professor Wisdom's reflections (in the paper on 'Gods') as to how meta-physical disputes can be carried on when there is, in one sense,

[1] G. J. Warnock in *The Revolution in Philosophy* (London, Macmillan, 1956), pp. 122–3.

[2] See F. Waismann, 'How I see Philosophy' in *Contemporary British Philosophy*, ed. H. D. Lewis (London, Allen & Unwin, 1956), pp. 463–4, 490; R. von Mises, *Positivism* (Harvard, 1951), p. 9; John Wilson, *Language and the Pursuit of Truth* (Cambridge, 1956), pp. 94–7; cp. J. W. N. Watkins in *The Listener*, November 28, 1957, p. 886.

'agreement about the facts' and, in another sense, 'in part a difference as to what is so and therefore as to the facts'.

The second qualification attaching to the new open-mindedness about metaphysics is the persisting bias against general ideas, against the posing of problems in general terms, or the attempt to find general laws of thought or ultimate justifications of reasoning. It is still widely held that such terms of traditional metaphysics as 'reality', 'being', 'existence', 'universals', are, or are derived from 'systematically misleading expressions'. Thus, there is no such thing as Being; there are beings. There is no such thing as Truth; there are true statements. There is no problem of induction; there are enquiries into the validity of particular inductive arguments. One of the, to my mind, baleful legacies of 'Wittgenstein II' (as he is commonly interpreted) to contemporary philosophy is the convention that philosophical problems are not to be solved but to be dissolved, by the process of translating them from the plane of abstract generality to the plane of concrete particularity. This bias against the generalized problem or the generalizing mind, this convention of 'take-nothing-but-the-concrete-case', is one of the favourite means of escape from metaphysics in contemporary philosophy. The metaphysician must, therefore, show that it is possible and inescapable to pose problems in terms of utmost generality; that there is a problem of existence, of truth, of how science or any knowledge is possible, of the conditions of intelligibility of experience as a whole, of the grounds of existence of the world and of myself.

But it will have to be shown, at the same time, that this does not mean that, in doing metaphysics, the (language-) 'machine is idling', to use the 'Wittgenstein II' terms now so often used to disqualify metaphysics. It must be made clear that the metaphysical problem is posed by experience, arises within experience; that the metaphysical idea is 'gripping' into empirical reality; to put it crudely, that the metaphysical wheel is being turned all the time by empirical cogs.

2.   THE PROBLEM OF THE SELF

This can perhaps be best shown by discussing the problem of the self. This problem, so important for all discussion of the possibility of metaphysics, is one of the most maltreated problems in contemporary British philosophy. Not unnaturally, discussion of this question frequently takes Descartes' *cogito* for its text. I select Professor Ayer's treatment of the *cogito* because I think it is representative of the contemporary approach to the problem. I hope to show that it both misunderstands Descartes and misrepresents the problem of the self.

In *Language, Truth and Logic*,[1] we read: 'What [Descartes] was really trying to do was to base all our knowledge on propositions which it would be self-contradictory to deny. He thought he had found such a proposition in "*cogito*", which must not be here understood in its ordinary sense of "I think" but rather as meaning "there is a thought now". . . . But even if it were true that such a proposition as "there is a thought now" was logically certain, it still would not serve Descartes' purpose. . . . "I exist" does not follow from "there is a thought now". The fact that a thought occurs at a given moment does not entail that any other thought has occurred at any other moment, still less that there has occurred a series of thoughts sufficient to constitute a single self. As Hume conclusively showed, no one event intrinsically points to any other.'

The main defect of this critique of the '*cogito*' is that it sees Descartes as exclusively concerned to make a logical point and uses to refute him a logic which, because of metaphysical preconceptions, excludes the phenomenological or existential point which Descartes regarded as the core of the argument. Ayer's Russellian logic had no symbol for 'I' or for 'exists'. This logic rests on the convention that 'I' is a logical construction out of the objective sense data which alone are before 'my' consciousness. One can give 'I' meaning in this logic only by analysing it into the object-language of 'something', 'some particular perception'. Therefore 'I think' must be translated into 'something thinks', from which all that would follow would be the tautology, 'something is a thinking thing'. Now the important point about this logic is that its epistemological basis is Hume's empiricism. It is a translation into logical syntax of the words: 'When I enter into *myself*, I always stumble on some particular perception or other. . . . I never catch myself at any time without a perception and never can observe anything but the perception. They are the successive perceptions only that constitute the mind.'

In *The Problem of Knowledge* (1956), Ayer's view of Descartes remains unchanged. He argues that the '*cogito*' succeeds only in making the trivial logical point, that, 'if I start with the fact that I am doubting, I can validly draw the conclusion that I think and that I exist. That is to say, if there is such a person as myself, then there is such a person as myself, and if I think, I think.' It is, of course, a fact, he goes on, that I know that I am conscious and that I exist. But these facts are of no logical significance. 'It is conceivable that I should not have been self-conscious, which is to say that I should not know that I existed; but it would not follow that I could not know many other statements to be true . . . my whole conception of knowledge would be impersonal.' Hume's point about the self, he contends, is true, not as a matter of psychological fact, but as a matter of logic. 'There is nothing that would count as having an experience of one's self; the expression, 'having an experience of one's self' is one for which there is no use. . . . The consciousness of one's self is not one experience among others, not even, as some have thought, a special experience which accompanies all the others.' The sentence, 'I exist', is a degenerate statement, one in which the verb is a sleeping partner, all the work being done by the demonstrative. 'It approximates, therefore, to a gesture or to an ejaculation. To say "I exist" . . . is like saying "look!" or pointing without words. . . . To know that one exists is not, in this sense, to know anything about oneself, any more than knowing that *this* exists is knowing anything about *this*.'[1] Professor F. Alquié remarked, in the course of lectures on Descartes at the Sorbonne in 1955, that, so far as he was aware, no one had ever entertained an idea so absurd as that '*cogito*' meant 'I am René Descartes'. He seems to have overlooked Lord Russell and Professor Ayer.[2]

[1] Pelican edition, pp. 44–52. Lord Russell's treatment of the '*cogito*' is very similar. Thus in *History of Western Philosophy* (London, Allen & Unwin, 1946), p. 589, he writes: 'The word "I" is really illegitimate; Descartes ought to state his ultimate premiss in the form, "There are thoughts". The word "I" is grammatically convenient but does not describe a datum.' Compare his essay 'Mind and Matter', in *Portraits from Memory* (London, Allen & Unwin, 1956), pp. 137–8.

[2] See F. Alquié, *Science et métaphysique chez Descartes*, 'Les Cours de Sorbonne', Centre de Documentation Universitaire, Paris, p. 74.

I believe that there are important mistakes in Descartes'
inferences from the *'cogito'* to the nature of the *res cogitans* and
other metaphysical conclusions. But the mistakes are not those
attributed to him by Ayer. Descartes would have thought it
absurd to say 'there is a thought now'. He would have held that it
is not merely psychologically false but logically self-contradictory
to say that if I were not self-conscious, and therefore did not know
that I existed, 'I [sic] could still know many other things'.[1]
Descartes' *'cogito'*-experience is of 'I thinking, "there is a thought
now" '; 'I knowing or doubting that I know many things'; 'I who
doubts, understands, affirms, denies, wills, refuses, imagines,
perceives'; 'I co-existing with and involved in every experience'.
The empiricists are looking for some perceptible thing or object
of experience corresponding to 'I'. Obviously there is no such
'thing' or 'object'. They conclude that there is 'no such thing' as
'I'. Descartes' whole point is that there is an 'I', but it is not an
object of thought but a subject thinking, without which there
could not be any objects of thought.

For Descartes, 'I think, therefore I am' is not a logical truism,
much less an ejaculation or a gesture: it is an act of reflection
which reveals the nature of man and of his situation in the world.
I know that I exist precisely in my knowing that I think about
and seek to understand the world, that I demand certitude but
encounter error and feel doubt, that I think beyond the limits of
my knowledge and grasp the idea of perfection in and with my
recognition of my own imperfection. From the *'cogito'*, Descartes
proceeds to reflect 'on the circumstances that I doubted and that
consequently my being was not wholly perfect' and to enquire
'whence I had learned to think of something more perfect than
myself'. He seeks a reason why he should not have 'the whole
remainder of perfection, of the want of which I was conscious'.
He asks, 'how could I know that I doubt, desire, or that something is wanting to me and that I am not wholly perfect, if I
possessed no idea of a being more perfect than myself, by comparison of which I knew the deficiencies of my own nature?' He
finds in his own lack of being, his own desire and need for being,
his own aspiration after perfection of being, the necessity to

[1] Ayer, *op. cit.*, p. 47.

affirm his dependence for being on a Perfect Being who is God.[1] In other words, Descartes' themes are those of self-knowledge and self-activity, aspiration towards ideals, immanence and transcendence. They are the themes which are central in the philosophy of Europe, past and present, but are too often excluded from contemporary British philosophy because they do not fit in with preconceptions derived from scientific empiricism.

The *'cogito'* of Descartes is not, therefore, a logical, but an existential starting point. The true point of departure of Cartesianism is not *cogito* but *sum*. His question is not the trivial one 'Am I?', but the one which has linked the great metaphysical with the great humanist tradition, the question 'What am I?' Descartes' real significance is to have inspired the humanistic metaphysics of the French spiritualists down to Le Senne and Gabriel Marcel. It is not an accident that philosophies which accuse Descartes' procedure of barrenness and pronounce the notion of the self to be a mistake, tend also to be atheistic philosophies. It would seem that to exclude discussion of the self from philosophy is to exclude discussion of God from philosophy too. Professor Ramsey has called attention to the logical relatedness of 'I' and 'God'.[2] This is surely an aspect of the truth, so familiar to saints and mystics, that God is *intimior intimo meo*. It receives striking negative corroboration in modern positivism, for which both God and self are meaningless.

3. THE PROBLEM OF EXISTENCE

Traditional metaphysics saw itself as concerned with being-in-general. By far the most important single cause of the anti-metaphysical movement in recent British philosophy was Russell's logic, in so far as this forgot its proper character and mistook itself for an ontology. Russell's theory of descriptions was long thought to have disposed of the problem or problems of being which had provided a livelihood for metaphysicians for so long,

---

[1] Meditation II.

[2] *Miracles*, An Exercise in Logical Mapwork (an Inaugural Lecture), Oxford, 1952, pp. 14–17, 20–1. Compare the same author's *Religious Language* (London, S.C.M. Press, 1957), p. 38.

and to have 'cleared up two millennia of muddle-headedness about "existence", beginning with Plato's "Theaetetus" '.[1]

From the metaphysician's point of view, the important implication of all this was the alleged disappearance of 'exists' as any kind of true assertion about any actual thing, and therefore the abolition of 'existence' as an object of philosophical investigation. 'Existence' can be predicated solely of a propositional function or, derivatively, of a class. 'Existence-propositions do not say anything about the actual individual but only about the class or function.' 'When you take any propositional function and assert of it that it is possible, that it is sometimes true, that gives you the fundamental meaning of existence. . . . It means that propositional function is true in at least one instance.' With regard to the 'actual things there are in the world . . . it is a sheer mistake to say that there is anything analogous to existence that you can say about them'. 'Existence in the sense in which it is ascribed to single entities is thus removed altogether from the list of fundamentals.'[2]

It is, however, notable that there is, in contemporary British philosophy, a considerable reaction against the Russellian theory of descriptions and its attendant logical atomism. This is, for example, one of the recurring themes in the representative selection from recent philosophical papers edited by Professor A. Flew and published as *Essays in Conceptual Analysis*.[3] The critics are not, of course, concerned to rehabilitate metaphysics. But the effect of the criticism has been to show that a particularly prevalent sort of anti-metaphysics was based on a logical mistake. The moral is that questions which arise in ordinary language cannot legitimately be pronounced meaningless or be dissolved by appeal to a special logical language. The attack on the theory of descriptions is part of the continuing struggle of British philosophy to free itself from the grip of the 'metaphysics to end all metaphysics' of dogmatic empiricism, and to repudiate the imposition by it on philosophy of monopolistic criteria of meaning

---

[1] Russell, *History of Western Philosophy* (London, Allen & Unwin, 1946), p. 860.
[2] Russell, 'The Philosophy of Logical Atomism' (1918) in *Logic and Knowledge*, ed. Robert C. Marsh (London, Allen & Unwin, 1956), pp. 177–281; see especially pp. 229–34; compare 'Logical Atomism' (1924), *ibid.*, pp. 323–43.
[3] Macmillan, London, 1956.

and truth, taken from mathematics, empirical science and formal logic.

There is no need to do more than cite some of the best-known papers in the above-named collection. P. F. Strawson ('On Referring') has shown that chief among the 'fundamental mistakes' in Russell's theory is his confusion of 'meaning' with 'mentioning' or 'referring'. His 'troublesome mythology' of the logically proper name is due to his mistaken idea that if there are expressions which have a uniquely referring use and if these are logical subjects, then there must *be* the objects which they are used to refer to. But 'meaning' is not 'mentioning' or 'referring to'. 'Meaning' has to do with the directions governing the ways in which expressions have to be actually used to make true or false assertions; and these directions, like these uses, are too endlessly complex and unclassifiable to be reduced to any single formal model. Russell's model was the result of his preoccupation with mathematics and formal logic. 'The constructor of calculuses, not concerned or required to make factual statements, approaches logic with a prejudice. . . . Neither Aristotelian nor Russellian rules give us the exact logic of any expression of ordinary language, for ordinary language has no exact logic.'

G. J. Warnock, in his paper 'Metaphysics in Logic', carries much further the same kind of criticism of the 'logico-ontologists' and makes points which are of some importance for our topic. He is mainly concerned with the abuse of the device of the 'existential quantifier'. This convention assumes that there is a single, univocal meaning of 'exists' or 'does not exist' in ordinary language, corresponding to the meaning of 'expressions allowed to be substituends for bound variables and expressions debarred from such employment' in quantificational logic. But this is to show 'insufficient sense of the perils involved in imposing the neat simplicities of logic upon the troublesome complexities of language'. There is an elasticity and variety about the use of 'is' or 'exists' in ordinary language to which no logical symbolism can do justice. To allow only one meaning to 'exists' is to try to force 'Pegasus', '23', 'intelligence', 'redness', 'republicanism', into a single bag. 'None of these designates a single object, but they fail to do so in ways utterly diverse.' The question, are there or not abstract entities, is not just like the question, is there or not a city called Leeds. 'The expressions supposed to correspond to the existential quantifier . . . are too diverse and intricate in their uses to yield the necessary results.' The existential quantification device blinds logicians' eyes to the differences between phrases such as: There is . . . There is such a thing as . . . exists . . . Some . . . At least one . . . There is something which. . . . All are dealt with by the use of the existential quantifier, and it is thence assumed that they are interchangeable, that they all have the same meaning, even that logic has 'proved' them to be the same. Warnock's conclusion is that the whole apparatus of quantificational logic has little or no application to the ordinary words and idioms in which the problems of ontology are initially expressed. 'These problems arise from and can be settled in ordinary language and cannot be confined to or settled in a special language. If one cannot deal with the philosophical problems of ontology upon the field of discourse in general, one cannot deal with them at all. There are problems which we cannot look to the logician to settle for us, and the old problems of ontology remain among them.' This is a conclusion which, he admits, amounts only to the 'highly-charged platitude' that philosophy is not logic.

A sympathizer with the Thomist tradition in metaphysics will be pardoned for suggesting that what Warnock is really pleading for is a recognition of the analogical character of language. It seems to be in fact a feature of contemporary British philosophy that it has rediscovered, in the return to ordinary language, the traditional doctrine of the analogy of being. For what are Waismann's concepts of 'language strata', 'systematic ambiguity', 'open texture of language'; or Austin's studies of how variously we use the terms, 'I know', 'I promise', etc.; or Urmson's investigation of the 'grading term' 'good'—what are these but reinvestigations in contemporary terms of the old problems of *analogia entis*? When Wittgenstein spoke of 'family likenesses' between linguistic usages and said that 'every statement has its own logic', he was, though not saying the same thing, at least grappling with the same problem, as Aquinas was when he wrote 'Analogous prediction is intermediate between mere equivocation and complete univocity of meaning. Analogous terms are not used with the same meaning, as univocal terms are; nor yet with totally diverse meanings, as equivocal terms are; but when a term is used analogously, the meaning varies in the different uses, but there is a resemblance, different for each case, connecting together the various uses.'[1]

Already it is clear that the purely logical criticism of Russell has removed many obstacles to metaphysics. But there is more to be said by way of showing that the problem of existence is a real problem, and by way of trying to uncover the philosophical meaning of Russell's and Ayer's attempts to exclude it from philosophy. It seems to me that G. E. Moore, in the 1936 Symposium, 'Is Existence a Predicate?',[2] provided a pertinent logical enquiry into the meaning of 'This exists' and unwittingly provided a logical prelude to a metaphysical enquiry into existence. He argued that in all cases in which one can say something like 'This is a tame tiger' one can also say significantly 'This exists'. This is because in all such cases, 'you can clearly say *with truth* of any such object "This *might* not have existed", "It is *logically possible* that this should not have existed".' The statement 'It is logically possible that this should not have existed', seems to mean, 'The sentence "This does not exist" is significant', and if 'This does not exist' is significant, 'This does exist' must be significant too. It is not possible for 'This might not have existed' to be true unless 'This does in fact exist' is true and therefore also significant.

So far, Moore is stating in logical terms what metaphysicians have meant by the contingency of finite being. Heidegger's going-on about Nothing in *What is Metaphysics?* is not due to a blunder about the logic or grammar of the verb 'to be', is not the result of thinking that Nothing is a name for 'something peculiarly mysterious'.[3] It is a phenomenological transcription of Moore's common-place logical observation that of any empirical object we can significantly say 'This might not have existed'; or 'This being might have been Nothing'. There is sound logical sense as well as phenomenological depth in Heidegger's obscurities of

---

[1] *Summa Theologica*, 1.13.5.
[2] *Aristotelian Society Supplementary Volume XV*, pp. 154–88.
[3] As Ayer charged in *Language, Truth and Logic*, p. 44.

utterance: 'Nothing shows itself [in dread] as essentially belonging to what-is while this is slipping away in totality. . . . Only in
the clear light of dread's Nothingness is what-is as such revealed
in all its original overtness: that it "is" and is not Nothing.' It is
because we know that any being *might not* be that 'Nothing ceases
to be the vague opposite of what-is: it now reveals itself as
integral to the Being of what-is'. For Nothing is Heidegger's
name for the fact that we and things are contingent beings, that
we are but *might* not-be. Only when we advert to the Nothing in
us and in things do we really notice the *being* in us and around us.
Existence then appears, not as something we can take for granted,
but as something which should surprise us, awaken us to 'the
utter strangeness of what-is', call forth our wonder and our
thankfulness, arouse our questioning and compel us to try to
understand, 'Why is there any Being at all—why not far rather
Nothing?' And that is the whole meaning of metaphysics.[1]

Moore makes a second and very important point. He asks, what
then becomes of the consecrated doctrine that existence is not an
attribute? He suggests that 'This exists' always forms part of what
is asserted by 'This is a book', 'This is red', etc. Now 'is a book',
'is red', etc., are said to stand for attributes because *part but not the
whole* of what is asserted by any value of '*x* is a book' or '*x* is red',
etc., is 'This exists'. But 'exists' in 'This exists' does not, in that
sense, 'stand for an attribute', because the *whole and not merely a
part* of what it asserts is 'This exists'.

To appreciate the significance of this, it is necessary to recall
that the formula 'existence is not an attribute' was called forth by
and has always been connected with the refutation of the ontological argument, and of the associated doctrines of the priority of
essence over existence and of the possible over the actual. (A great
deal of contemporary anti-metaphysics is based on the erroneous
belief that *all* metaphysics is committed to the ontological argument and its implications.) Against this, it was important to stress
that existence is not 'one of the attributes' or part of the definition
of a thing, and cannot be deduced from the definition or essence

---

[1] See Heidegger, *Existence and Being*, Eng. trans. (London, Vision Press, 1949),
pp. 368–9, 376–80. One may compare here M. B. Foster, who speaks of the necessity of a
'repentance in the sphere of the intellect', as a preliminary to the recognition of God.
[See *Mystery and Philosophy* (London, S.C.M. Press, 1957), p. 46.]

of the thing. But this does not mean that existence cannot be known, affirmed or enquired into. Existence is presupposed to any predication of attributes; it is the *toujours-déjà-là* of all knowledge. It is not that it is the 'Something-I-know-not-what' underlying attributes. It is given with and present in and coaffirmed with all attributes. It is so much everywhere and so much everything that we do not notice it. It is so familiar that we take it for granted. We cannot know anything, say anything, do anything, except in terms of it. But it might not have been there; and we might not have been there to encounter it. Therefore it is meaningful to say 'Things exist'; and it is meaningful to ask 'Why is there anything?' and 'What does being mean?'

When existence is 'removed from the list of fundamentals' and questions as to its meaning and causes are pronounced meaningless, this is because of the improper extension to philosophy and to human thought in general of the criteria of meaning and of truth, the assumptions and the methods which are proper to the empirical sciences. Science puts men and existence in brackets. It takes it for granted that there is a world of things and events, and that man observes it. But it is of no interest to science *that* the world is; only *how* it is. It is of no interest to science as such that science is man-made; it matters only that science go on. It is a condition of the existence of science that man and being be; but science could not be if it called its own conditions in question.[1] Science must take the existence of objects as irreducibly given; and proceed to observe, analyse, measure, correlate them. It must take the fact of knowledge for granted and try to make it as impersonal, objective and anonymous as possible. Its truth-tests, verification and falsification by observations, will never include the person of the observer, but only require that an experience occur or be possible.

The contemporary effort to restore metaphysics is essentially a struggle to prevent man himself from being depersonalized by the methods of impersonal investigation and anonymous verification he has devised for science. Metaphysics is part of the defence of

[1] A. D. Ritchie has written recently: 'Scientific investigation goes most smoothly and easily when nobody enquires into fundamentals.' (*Studies in the History and Methods of the Sciences*, Edinburgh, 1958, p. 192.)

humanism in an age dominated by the concepts and attitudes which are legitimate and necessary for science and technology but which become dangerous when they are thought to be adequate to explain all that man is and all that man seeks and needs to know. Hence Gabriel Marcel presents his metaphysics as the rejection of the omni-competence of the principle of verification, the refusal to leave man and being in brackets, the assertion of the primacy of *being* man over *having* tools and techniques. He writes: 'When I am faced with a [scientific] problem, I work on the data in front of me; but everything proceeds, and quite rightly proceeds, as if I had no need to pay any attention to the "I" who is at work; for the purpose in hand, "I" am only a prerequisite. But when my question bears on being, the position is entirely different. Here the ontological status of the questioner comes into the first place. . . . Here we enter into the realm of the meta-problematic, that is to say of mystery. A "mystery" is a problem which calls its own conditions in question' (and thus puts itself beyond the possibility of solution by the methods of the science in which it arose).[1] 'To pose the ontological problem is to question oneself about the whole of being and about one's own self as a whole.'[2]

Marcel's thought, on this point, is similar to Heidegger's. Heidegger criticizes the imposition on all thinking of the logical categories and the observational and mensurational procedures proper to the sciences. For the sciences, 'any particular thing is only what it "adds up to" and any count ensures the further progress of the counting. . . . The "coming out" of the calculation with the help of what-is (i.e. objects) counts as the explanation of the latter's Being. . . . Calculative thought places itself under compulsion to master everything in the logical terms of its procedure. It has no notion that in calculation everything calculable is already a whole before it starts working out its sums and products, a whole whose unity naturally belongs to the incalculable which, with its mystery, ever eludes the clutches of calculation.'[3] Heidegger criticizes the science-derived correspondence theory of

---

[1] *Être et avoir* (Paris, Aubier, 1935), pp. 144–6, 169ff.

[2] *Positions et approches concrètes du mystère ontologique* (Louvain, Nauwelaerts, 1949), p. 57.

[3] 'What is Metaphysics', in *Existence and Being*, Eng. trans. (London, Vision Press, 1949), p. 388.

truth, as professing to make truth 'independent of the explanation of the essential nature of all that "is", of its very *being*—which explanation always involves a corresponding explanation of the essential nature of man as the vehicle and perfector of the intellectus'.[1]

Both G. Marcel and Heidegger might have had precisely Russell and Ayer in mind in their critique of scientism. The result of the Russell-Ayer brand of empiricistic logic is exactly to eliminate the 'I' and 'being' from philosophy, as they have been eliminated from science—for science is the source of their logic and methodology. (Russell doubted 'whether philosophy as a study distinct from science and possessed of a method of its own is anything more than an unfortunate legacy from theology'.)[2] Ayer, though considerably less brash in the last decade than Russell or his own younger self, has continually been haunted by the idea of nonpersonal or person-neutral knowledge and by the possibility of the elimination of the observer from experience and his reduction to the experienced. In his last book, he still relies on these devices to refute Descartes and to get himself out of the logical holes he falls into in explaining how we know the past and other minds.[3]

G. Marcel and Heidegger insist on bringing the 'I' and 'being' back into philosophy and declare that when 'I' and 'being' meet, metaphysics begins. For metaphysics is the 'I's' quest for the why of being and for the why of the self as the questioner of being. There are no why's in science. But it is almost a definition of man in European philosophy from Socrates to Sartre that he is the being who demands to know the why of his own being and of being.

4. THE METAPHYSICS OF HUMANISM

One does not prove that metaphysics is possible merely by showing that the available anti-metaphysics is mistaken. It would now be pretty generally accepted by philosophers that there are no good reasons for saying that metaphysical questions do not arise, or that they are meaningless or trivial. But there is still much

[1] 'On the Essence of Truth', in *Existence and Being*, pp. 324-5.
[2] In 'Logical Atomism', in *Logic and Knowledge*, p. 325.
[3] See *Problem of Knowledge*, pp. 47, 154-70, 214ff.

N

doubt as to whether they can be meaningfully answered. There
is a fairly general recognition nowadays of what D. F. Pears has
called 'the Protean metaphysical urge to transcend language'.[1] But
it is commonly felt that the urge is bound to fail. For, by
definition, metaphysical answers would go beyond the limits of
reason and of logic and of meaningful utterance.

The problem, therefore, remains of showing that metaphysics
is positively possible. In the end, there is no conclusive way to
show that anything is possible except to produce it. I must therefore try, however sketchily and imperfectly, to produce some
specimens of metaphysics. I hope at least to show that metaphysics is not empirical science; or, to be more precise, show that
the point of metaphysics is that empirical categories are not
adequate to the reality which is given in integral human experience.

(1) *Being as Known by the Self*

Modern phenomenology, returning to scholastic studies of the
intentionality of consciousness, has stressed that the starting point
of knowledge is not consciousness but being. The point of
departure of philosophical or second-order reflection is, therefore,
not knowledge but things-known. The existentialists say that all
reflection is reflection on the preflective presence of being to us
and of us to being. They follow Husserl, who stressed that all
thought is thought of some *thing*. And Husserl re-echoed
Aquinas, who wrote: 'That which is first known by the intellect
and is present in all its knowledge, is being; and all our knowledge has to be expressed in terms of being.'[2] That is why all
pretence to deduce being from thought, to reduce being into
thought, to define being, to analyse being, to put being in
brackets or to explain it away, is futile. Being is always-already-
there before I know it; always-still-there in everything I know
and say. Just as I am always-already-there before I know anything, and always-still-there when I am explaining anything, or
trying to understand myself. Being and the self are not like
anything else I know; they are in my knowing of everything.

This is the source of all the talk about the meta-problematic,

---

[1] See *Logic and Language*, Second Series, ed. A. G. N. Flew (Oxford, Blackwell, 1955),
p. 64.   [2] *De Veritate* q. 1, a. 1.

the mystical, the inexpressible, in modern philosophy. But does it follow that I cannot know or say anything about being and the self because these are the absolute presuppositions of all knowing and of all saying? This metaphysical agnosticism comes, I believe, from two errors. First there is the error of thinking that the 'being' lies *beyond* things. In truth, it is *in* things, it *is* things, only we do not notice it; we see things, not their thingness, not the fact that they *are* and are not Nothing. With this we group the corresponding error of thinking that the self lies *beyond* knowledge. In truth it is *in* knowledge; but we do not notice it, because the self is knowing, not a thing known; is experiencing, not a datum of experience. Empirical psychology, as Bergson pointed out, always misses the *ego*, seeing only mental states. Secondly, there is the error of thinking that all knowledge must be clear, distinct, final, leaving its solved problems behind like milestones in its march to ever new discoveries. But knowing is not all or nothing; it has an 'open texture'. Because not all can be known about everything, it does not follow that reasoning is absurd. It is the unreasonable demand for all-explaining reasons that drove Camus to proclaim absurdity. 'I demand that all should be explained to me or nothing. But reason is powerless before this cry from the heart. . . . To be able to say, just once, "That is clear", then all would be saved. But . . . nothing is clear, all is chaos, and man keeps only his clear-sightedness and the exact awareness of the walls that hem him in.'[1]

But though not all can be known about anything, there is something that can be known about everything that can exist: that it is something, and is not nothing. Here is something that is true of all that is or that could be or that must be.[2] When Alasdair MacIntyre says: 'Our concept of existence is inexorably linked to our talk about spatio-temporal objects',[3] we feel bound to protest that the

---

[1] *Le Mythe de Sisyphe* (Paris, Gallimard, 1942), pp. 44–5.

[2] Compare John Wilson, *Language and Christian Belief* (London, Macmillan, 1958), pp. 13–14: 'God must be real in the same sense as physical objects are real, for the word real has in fact only one sense—either something is real and exists or it is unreal and does not exist. "Real" and "exists" are definitely not ambiguous words, . . . Instead of the Vedantists' "Not this, not this", the Christian must be able to say "At least this, and at least this". . . .'

[3] See 'The Logical Status of Religious Belief', in *Metaphysical Beliefs* (London, S.C.M. Press, 1957), p. 202.

words 'linked to' are ambiguous and their ambiguity can cause a serious misunderstanding. No metaphysician, no theist will deny that there must be empirical linkage, 'empirical anchorage',[1] for all talk about the metempirical. But such concepts as those of 'existence', 'reality', cannot be and are not limited to talk about empirical objects. My self exists, knowing exists, and they are, although involved in all spatio-temporal experience, yet certainly not contained within the limits of 'our talk about spatio-temporal objects'. It is impossible to deny the term existence to that without which spatio-temporal objects could not be known to exist. This is what is meant by scholastic philosophers in saying that knowing is convertible with being. Nothing can be thought of except in terms of being, in relation to being. Nothing can be that is not intelligible, or related to thought. There are as many different kinds of being as there are things. The application of the term *being* cannot be restricted to spatio-temporal objects. It must be allowed to all reality whose existence is involved in or is implied by or is a condition of the being of and our knowing of spatio-temporal objects. Hence there can be no *a priori* logical or linguistic disqualification of metaphysics. There cannot be, in the absolute sense, anything that is Unknowable or Inexpressible. Of the Unknowable, we know at least that it *is*, and the reasons for and implications of its unknowability. Of the Inexpressible we can at least say that it *is* and is different from the empirical things which we do know.

It is not that *un au-delà de la pensée est impensable*; but that *un au-delà de l'être est impossible*. Everything that I know is part of my world, my experience, and all that I can know, all that there can be for me, has the unitary character that it is being-known-by-me, being-for-me. The diversity of beings cannot be absolute. As we have seen in the case of Russell and Ayer, it is only by the logical trick of putting the *ego* in brackets, that absolute pluralism or logical atomism can be made to look plausible. All being is ego-unified. But there is no ego-centric predicament. The unity of being is not just a unity-for-me or a unity-in-my-thought. My thought is of things that are 'there' independently of thought. Unity-for-thought is imposed by unity-in-things. There is at

---

[1] The phrase is Professor Ramsey's: see *Religious Language*, p. 14.

least the minimal unity in all being; that it somehow *is* and is not nothing. There is at least the minimal intelligibility in all that there can be: that it can be known that it is, and that at least some description of it has a reference. There are as many ways of being as there are things, as many uses of 'exists' as there are meaningful sentences. But since all consciousness for me is consciousness of things-in-my-world, it follows that meaning for me is determined by meaning-in-terms-of-my-world. And my world is the world of empirical objects and of I-knowing-them. Hence, all that I can know or meaningfully say to exist is either an object or occurrence in, or a feature or description of, or an implication or condition or presupposition of, my knowledge of empirical objects.

(2) *The Self as Knowing Being*

Hume was right, that 'I can never catch myself at any time without a perception'. Ayer was right, that 'there is nothing that would count as having an experience of one's self'. Merleau-Ponty was right, that 'the true *cogito* is not a *tête-à-tête* of thought with the thought of this thought; they join hands only across the world'.[1] But everything counts as an experience of my self-experiencing-something. The self is in the having of perceptions and the spanning of the world; but it is not describable in terms of the world nor analysable into a bundle of perceptions. That is 'the mystical' of Wittgenstein, which we should rather call the metaphysical. My knowledge of empirical objects cannot be adequately described in terms of empirical objects.

Knowing cannot be defined, classified or understood, any more than being can be defined, classified or understood. You cannot *classify* 'knowing' because the word 'knowing' has the logically baffling quality that, unless what it *means* were the case, it could not exist as a word nor could any other word or thought or thing exist. 'Knowing' is not a 'kind' of a word, as knowing is not a kind of a capacity; just as, and for the same reason that, being is not a kind of a thing. This is what the scholastics meant by saying that being is not a genus but is transcendental, and that knowledge is convertible with it. You cannot, therefore, describe knowing adequately in language, for no term in language can be or have

[1] M. Merleau-Ponty, *Phénoménologie de la perception* (Paris, Gallimard, 1945), p. 344.

meaning unless knowing is already there. Yet we do *know* much about knowing and we are somehow describing it when we say that it is not like any empirical occurrence or object whatever. There is some knowledge of knowing involved in all knowledge of things; but the exploration of knowledge lies beyond our knowledge. As Wittgenstein said, 'The metaphysical subject [is] the limit of the world'.[1]

But is it then just the inexpressible, which shows itself, but of which no word can be said? The use of spatial and chronological metaphor is inescapable in this context, but it can be very misleading. (How much nonsense about Plato has come from taking literally what he says about *pre*-existence and the apartness of the Ideas.) The words 'beyond', 'outside', almost inevitably suggest that the philosophers who use them have believed in a 'place' 'outside the walls' of ordinary experience to which, in virtue of some peculiar super-cognition, they have a privileged access denied to lesser mortals. But philosophers have meant, or should have meant, that there is a mystery *in* all knowing and in all being; that there is a 'beyond-experience' in all experience, an 'outside-language' in all language; and that experience is not adequately described unless this metempirical in it is recognized.[2] When we find that we 'run [our] heads up against the limits of language', we should not say that there is something beyond 'ordinary' language that we could know in 'extraordinary' language or non-linguistically. Nor, on the other hand, should we say that there is 'nothing beyond' ordinary language in the sense that empirical concepts and terms describe without remainder all that there is. What we should say is that there is something *in* ordinary language which is not 'ordinary' and not expressible in empirical terms.

But the metempirical is real. We know it. We *are* it. It is not just the inexpressible, the mystical. We can become progressively more aware of the implications of its inexpressibility. It is much to

---

[1] *Tractatus*, 5. 641. One thinks here of Father Illtyd Trethowan's words: 'If we take knowledge seriously, we cannot help being theists.' *An Essay in Christian Philosophy* (London, Longmans, 1954), p. 87.

[2] Malebranche said: 'No. I will not bring you into a strange country, but I will perhaps teach you that you are a stranger in your own country.' Cited by H. de Lubac, in *Les Chemins de Dieu* (Paris, Aubier, 1956), p. 88.

know that there is that in us which we cannot describe or understand. It is to know something about it when we say that it is not an object or a body, not-material, not-empirical, nor empirically limited. To be aware of limits is to think and to know and to be beyond those limits. Since metaphysical questions arise, metaphysical knowledge is possible. My questions reveal what I know and what I am. If my empirical knowledge forces me to ask questions which *cannot* be answered in empirical terms, then I know that empirical knowledge is not adequate to the reality which I am. But to know that knowledge is inadequate is a valid and a most important kind of knowledge. It is a perpetual invitation to deeper reflection; but also an awareness that reflection will never come to an end of what there is to know.

It is not the metaphysicians who have professed to 'explain' existence, 'decipher the riddle' of life, 'account for' morality, 'solve the problem' of thought, of soul and body, etc. It is scientists, and 'scientific' philosophers, who have professed and do profess to do so.[1] Lord Russell has written: 'In favour of this theory [of Mind and Matter], the most important thing to be said is that it removes a mystery. Mystery is always annoying and is usually due to lack of clear analysis. The relations of mind and matter have puzzled people for a long time, but, if I am right, they need puzzle people no longer.'[2] But what sense could it have to say, 'I have solved the problem of mind and body. . . . Now that that is clear, we shall tomorrow turn to the next problem—we shall construct a machine which will make it clear what thinking and deciding are'? . . . These are not just problems which we solve, but realities which we are. The problem of 'mind and body' is not a problem that could be *solved* by Russell's theory or anyone else's theory. It is something we shall be solving, by living it, realizing it, becoming it, until we die. If we could give a 'scientific explanation' of morality, it would cease to be morality. If we could give a cybernetic account of thinking, what we would

---

[1] M. B. Foster, in *Mystery and Philosophy* (London, S.C.M. Press, 1957), p. 17, writes: 'What is to be questioned is not the practice of analysis but the belief that nothing is really puzzling and that therefore there cannot be anything puzzling that we can legitimately want to say.'

[2] 'Mind and Matter', in *Portraits from Memory* (London, Allen & Unwin, 1956), p. 153.

have explained would not be thinking. Gilbert Ryle, near the end of *The Concept of Mind*, remarks that philosophers may yet come to recognize that man perhaps is, after all, a man. But this is not, as he seems to suggest, the end, but the beginning of philosophy. To resist all pretences to explain man in terms of the non-human; to strive for ever deeper realization of the human; but to know that there is always more to know about man than can be known, that is the task of metaphysics.

The accounts given by metaphysicians about the soul were not intended as 'solutions to problems', as mathematics, formal logic or science understand solutions. Their language was a refusal to put empirical–science limits to man's reality, or formal–logical limits to man's self-awareness and self-discovery and self-fulfilment. The terms 'mind', 'soul', 'spirit', are not clear and distinct and closed ideas which end puzzlement; but 'open' ideas of inexhaustible fertility, which arouse wonder and are permanent invitations to the reflection and effort that will translate our assent to them from notional into real, that will convert them from theory into way of life.

(3) *Truth as Adequacy*

But is metaphysics, then, only emotive or evaluative, not descriptive, factual or true? Does it only express an 'interesting and challenging attitude to life'? Must we conclude, as Susan Stebbing once did, that metaphysical systems 'are great as works of art are great. Hence their spiritual significance. They heighten the joy of living but they do not give knowledge; they are a source of inspiration, but they do not yield understanding'?[1] Platitudinously, but profoundly, it depends on what we mean by 'true'. And philosophers have been content for far too long with concepts and criteria of truth which scientists evolved for quite other reasons than their adequacy to human experience.

Science must, of its nature, be amenable to verification or falsification by observational tests. It is easy to conclude that the truth, perhaps even the meaning, of a scientific hypothesis is the sense-observations had or expected in respect of it. Whence it is

[1] 'The Method of Analysis in Metaphysics', in *Proceedings of the Aristotelian Society*, n.s. XXXIII, 1932–3, p. 94.

easy to generalize that truth, perhaps also meaning, in all cases is the correspondence of a statement with observational or ostensive data, or with empirical objects. This is the source of the correspondence theory of truth, as of the picture theory of language. But neither of these theories is tenable. It has been well said: 'There are no that's in the world. . . . Sentences and facts cannot correspond in any way that suits the needs of a correspondence theory of language.'[1] It is a fundamental misconception of language that it grows out of gestures or is a substitute for pointing. Thinking and talking are not naming.

It is often thought that the Platonic-Aristotelian-Medieval definition of truth is the same as this modern correspondence-theory. Heidegger, who has devoted much labour to refuting the modern theory, finds its prototype in Plato. This is a great misunderstanding. The fact is that Plato's notion of truth is a better statement than Heidegger's own, of what Heidegger, to my mind, wants to say, namely that truth is not a static, closed correspondence of idea to thing, but a greater or less approximation of empirical datum to idea, essence, ideal; in Heidegger's language, a 'revelation of what-is', a 'relationship of open resolve', 'a directive to turn to what-is'.[2] It was the doctrine of Plato which, through Saint Augustine, came to Aquinas as the doctrine of *adaequatio rei et intellectus*; where *adaequatio* is closer in meaning to 'adequacy' than to 'correspondence', and has little if anything in common with modern notions of 'correspondence'.

The fact is that language never fully corresponds to what we know there is, in us and in things, to be described. A concept is never just a record of an observation or a copy of an object; the object always falls short of what it causes us to know.[3] In turn, our concepts and descriptions always fall short of their empirical objects; they can express everything about them except their

[1] Miss E. Daitz, 'The Picture Theory of Meaning', in *Essays in Conceptual Analysis*, ed. A. Flew, pp. 66, 74.

[2] 'On the Essence of Truth', in *Existence and Being*, pp. 322–3, 328, 333–4. Compare A. de Waehlens, *Phénoménologie et Vérité* (Paris, Presses Universitaires de France, 1953), pp. 63ff.

[3] Compare David Pole, *The Later Philosophy of Wittgenstein* (Athlone Press, 1958), p. 83: 'There is always more meaning in an expression than we have given it.' He speaks of language as 'a developing, self-correcting system'. Cp. Brice Parrain, *Recherches sur la nature et les fonctions du langage* (Paris, Gallimard, 1942), pp. 154ff.

being. Existence is not itself conceptualizable, but is the condition of all conceptualizing. That which is co-predicated in all predication is not itself a predicate. Furthermore, no empirical description can comprehend the reality of myself who am making it. The totality of empirical knowledge could not possibly answer my questions about myself and about my knowing and about being. By this, I know that I exceed the totality of empirical things.[1] Wittgenstein said 'The feeling of the world as a limited whole is the mystical feeling'.[2] We should rather say, it is that element within experience which makes metaphysics necessary.

A 'correspondence' or 'verification' theory of truth can be made plausible only by leaving the self and being out. The having of observations, the enumeration, even the ideally complete enumeration, of all the objects or facts or empirical data that there are in the world, would not be an adequate description of reality; it would leave out the describer and the being of the described. No statement about reality as a whole could be empirically verifiable, in the sense of its 'being possible to describe in observational terms two different states of the Universe—one that takes place when the statement is true and another one when it is not'.[3] A statement about reality as a whole *must* be compatible with all states of the Universe, or 'neutral in respect of matters of fact'. It is a commonplace that the principle of verification is such a statement and is not itself empirically verifiable. All metaphysical statements are of this kind. The question remains: how then can they be true?

I suggest that their truth is their adequacy to reality as a whole, or to the totality of experience. This is not to be interpreted as psychological adequacy, or capacity to reassure and inspire. It is a question of allowing fully in one's descriptions and explanations for all that there is in human experience. I do not say 'describing completely' or 'explaining clearly'. I have consistently argued that no language can succeed in doing either. But metaphysical language *can* be adequate to reality as a whole; first of all negatively—by exposing the falsity of claims that empirical des-

[1] Professor Ramsey speaks of 'dissatisfaction with empirical descriptions' as a prerequisite to knowledge of God. See *Religious Language*, pp. 52, 62.
[2] *Tractatus*, 6. 45.   [3] von Mises, *Positivism*, p. 76.

criptions are adequate, the falsity of all 'nothing-buttery'; second, positively, by recognizing the existence of the metempirical within experience and by accepting the duty of making sense of it; third, by recognizing that what goes beyond experience and yet is involved in experience cannot be the infra-rational, the irrational or the absurd. It is this that Gabriel Marcel means by his concept of 'mystery'. 'Mystery' is his name for the presence within experience of an 'I' and 'being' which are not adequately describable in empirical terms. Recognition of this 'mystery' is metaphysics; he calls it 'concrete philosophy' or the philosophy of complete experience, as Bergson had called metaphysics 'integral experience'.

(4) *The Sense of the World*

I spoke of 'the duty of making sense of' the metempirical within experience. But how do we know that the world makes sense? How can we know that the correct attitude is not that of Camus? —'Man finds himself before the irrational. He feels in himself his desire for happiness and for rationality. The absurd is this confrontation of man's demand and the unreasonable silence of the world.[1] . . . To live is to make the absurd live. To make it live is to look it full in the face. . . . One of the only coherent positions there is in philosophy is revolt. Revolt is a perpetual awareness by man of the irrational in his own existence. It is the demand for an impossible transparency.'[2]

Something similar is often being said, though in less dramatic words and with less tragic accent, in contemporary British philosophy. The first thing I should like to say about it is that it seems to suppose that 'the irrational' (i.e. the self and being) somehow confronts reason, or stands opposite to and apart from reason, that reason has 'the irrational' all round its edges. But I have argued that 'the irrational', in the sense defined, is *in* all reasoning and cannot be the opponent or enemy of reasoning or be 'beyond the edges' of reason. My existence as a reasoner cannot be absurd. It is I who recognize and challenge 'absurdity'. Camus was equating the rational with the completely understood; the irrational with all that I cannot completely describe in empirical

[1] *Le Mythe de Sisyphe*, pp. 44–5.   [2] *Ibid.*, pp. 76–7.

terms. His 'absurd' is only a misleading name for the metempirical elements in experience. But even Camus could not consistently regard these as absurd or even as unknowable. He defined man and humanism by them. It was in their name, and the synonymous name of humanism, that he revolted against the rationalism of empirical science. 'Man in revolt' is another name for man-transcending-the-empirical world, or man-the-metaphysical.

Furthermore, metaphysics does not pretend to achieve the 'impossible transparency' which Camus thought reason required. When I say that the metaphysician tries 'to make sense' of the metempirical in the empirical; when I say that the theist posits the existence of God because otherwise the existence of anything would be inexplicable, my statements could be misunderstood. 'To make sense of' is ambiguous, because it suggests that when the metaphysician has done, 'all is now clear'. 'Inexplicable' is ambiguous in so far as its opposite may seem to be 'completely explained'. The theistic metaphysician does not pretend that the existence of God 'makes everything clear' and explains away all problems. He does not make a 'postulate of universal intelligibility' in the sense of demanding that reality shall be positively and exhaustively comprehended by us.[1] He postulates intelligibility only in the minimal sense that being shall not be self-contradictory, or absurd. All proofs for the existence of God are, in one form or another, a *reductio ad absurdum et contradictorium* of the non-existence of God. They try to show that the non-admission of God is the inadequacy of description which amounts to a contradiction: treating part of experience as if it were the whole. Metaphysics begins with the recognition that there is mystery in being and in experience. But it is not merely the recognition of mystery. Metaphysics cannot end until it has rendered such reason of that mystery that it shall not become instead absurdity. The true alternative is not mystery *or* clarity, but mystery *or* absurdity.

The theist will not claim to understand Creation; but just that, without it, the existence of the world is impossible. He will not

---

[1] Hence Ronald W. Hepburn's objection is not merited: 'Can *no* explanations be valuable unless *complete* and *ultimate* explanation is also possible?' [*Christianity and Paradox* (London, Watts, 1958), p. 181].

claim to comprehend God; but just to know that he is real and that his reality 'exceeds by its immensity every concept that our minds can form'.[1] The metaphysician is not dispensed from the need to turn to scientists for information about the 'how-it-is' of the world. He is not dispensed from puzzlement about the 'that-it-is' of the world. But the humility of his little knowledge is of vast importance for man. Aquinas said: 'The least knowledge that can be had about the highest things is more desirable than the most exact knowledge about lesser things.'[2] It is wonder, not curiosity which animates the metaphysician; and wonder is akin to admiration. 'It is an indispensable condition of all true and lasting admiration that its object should be greater than our knowledge of it; and the growth of knowledge, far from touching the limits of the marvellous, should convince us more and more of their inaccessibility.'[3]

[1] St Thomas Aquinas, *Summa contra Gentiles*, I 14.   [2] *Ibid.*, I 5.
[3] Abbot Vonier, *The Personality of Christ*, in *Collected Works*, Vol. I (London, Burns Oates, 1952), p. 107. Compare Camus in *Discours de Suède* (Paris, Gallimard, 1958): 'Admiration is the supreme joy of the intelligence.'

XII

HYWEL D. LEWIS

GOD AND MYSTERY

Beth yw Duw
  Ond enw ar amherffeithrwydd deall dyn?
Ac fel y nos o flaen y wawr, mae Duw
Yn codi ei babell ar ddynesiad dyn,
Yn codi ei babell, ac yn mynd, yn mynd.

What is God
  But a name for the imperfection of man's mind?
And as the night before the dawn, so God
Strikes his tent at the approach of man,
He strikes his tent, and goes, and goes.

BEN BOWEN

I

The idea of God is unique. This has often been said of late, but
not always with the best understanding of why it should be said.
Religious apologists have come to see that much in the arguments
of their opponents is beside the point, and only seemingly
decisive or relevant, because it has failed to take sufficient account
of the radical difference between the idea of God and other notions
we may have to consider. But this has often amounted to little
more than a dim discernment, a hunch, or a move that has become
fashionable and accepted without due apprehension of its force.
There have thus been further travesties of the position the
apologist should be taking up and these have invited new
criticisms, or adaptations of old ones, which seem to be very
devastating and final because they appear to deprive the religious
philosopher of the card by which he thought he would most
surely win his trick. I should like therefore to look again at the
alleged uniqueness of the idea of God and attempt to indicate

some features of it which do not seem to me to have been duly appreciated even by its sponsors.

The point that most needs to be stressed is the quite radical character of the difference between the idea of God and any other idea we may entertain. It is not just that it is non-empirical. Many ideas might be that, mathematics or certain *a priori* principles perhaps, or some non-natural quality in ethics, but we do claim at any rate to be able to indicate fairly satisfactorily what these ideas mean. There may be no strictly factual exemplification of them, and in the case of the alleged non-natural quality of goodness no analysis of any sort may be possible. But there is nonetheless much which may be said; we may indicate what sort of things have a non-natural quality, we may draw contrasts between it and other properties, for example physical ones or mathematical or causal ones. We may make it fairly clear what this property is not, and when we have, in these and kindred ways, induced in others the apprehension of this property, or helped them to realize that they have been apprehending it all the time, we know that it is some one thing or type of thing that they have before their minds, and we do not doubt that they grasp this something in its true nature or as it really is in itself. They may not be able to describe it, except obliquely in terms of its concomitants and so forth. But they know what it is like, and there are certain things at any rate with which there is not the slightest likelihood of their confusing it.

Take again the elusiveness of certain concepts we find in science, in physics perhaps most of all, the ideas of waves of light, of magnetic fields, of atoms or nuclear energy. There may be a sense, though what it is precisely need not be considered now, in which the scientist does not know what any of these are, in the way for instance in which a man knows a colour or some sensible object. But there is at any rate the whole body of determinate, if also intricate and difficult, statements the scientist makes about these concepts. It is possible to talk well or foolishly or quite absurdly about them, they have their intellectual location, and some considerations are relevant, others not, to the soundness of assertions made in such a context. The allegedly mysterious or elusive nature of certain scientific entities, or whatever atoms or electrons may be thought to be, is consistent with discourse about them which is largely intelligible in the way in which experts normally find themselves intelligible to each other. Whether the mystery is as real as it seems and what may be the prospects of reducing it, does not matter now. We know, or at least the scientist does, when we are encountering nuclear energy and when we are not, and what may or may not be done with it. Science consists largely, if not wholly, of such knowledge, and whatever lies beyond this is still some part of finite reality with its determinate character which we distinguish from other things in terms of normally intelligible statements we may properly make about it. The mystery is partial, and in principle there may be no mystery at all; we do not have to step outside what we experience and understand to talk sense about it.

II

Turn now to our knowledge of other minds. This will require closer notice, partly because it is a little more central to my theme and partly because there has been grave confusion in the thought of those who have made our knowledge of one another prominent in their consideration of the mystery of the being of God. That is particularly true of writers who make much of an alleged 'I-Thou relation'.

The notion that there is some mystery in our knowledge of one another is not in fashion at present, the prevailing tendency being to speak of minds entirely in terms of observable behaviour or entities. My mind will thus be my observable behaviour or disposition to behave, or the point of view or context of my body, and the seeming unavoidability of using the first person singular will be, in varyingly ingenious ways, accounted for in these terms. This, I must say boldly, does not convince me at all. The proneness of Professor Ryle's 'ghost' to make a fresh appearance the moment it has been thought to be finally laid, is not, as some suppose, merely because it has been built into the structure of our language or is unavoidable in descriptions of overt behaviour, but because we are directly aware of ourselves as non-material beings,[1] and there is also involved in this a quite irreducible

---

[1] Cp. Chs. X, XI above.—Ed.

difficulty of knowing what it is like or means to be another mind.

The last point may seem to be quite unnecessary heresy, but I should like in fact to stress it. There are, it seems to me, two matters about the nature of mind which need to be noted and carefully distinguished by those who wish to make a sharp opposition of mind and body. The first is the peculiar difficulty of saying what they mean by mind or consciousness. It is this which seems to make them easy prey for their critics. For either they will make statements about mental activities which both sides will recognize, statements of a neutral kind which do not amount in themselves to a hypothesis drawing expressly a distinction between mind and body, or they will speak in terms much too reminiscent of observable matters or draw analogies which must suggest they should be cashed in physical terms. This is one of the difficulties involved in speaking of mind as substance or even as entity, it suggests that the mind is at any rate quasi-material and this at once invites the challenge to show where such realities are made manifest; in short, we play into the hands of our critic by playing his game. We ought, instead, to stand very firmly on the irreducible character of the distinction between mind and body and resist the temptation to think of mental processes as ghostly duplicates of physical ones. That does not preclude making use of analogies or metaphors drawn from the physical world, and the very tantalizing situation of the dualist is that, sooner or later for certain purposes, he is bound to have recourse to figurative terms of just that sort, running the constant danger of misleading himself and his opponents. A crude form of this would be the talk about 'mind-stuff' which had a high vogue at one time. But there are many more subtle ways in which the dualist may give away his position, or seem to lack the courage and consistency of his conviction, by being daunted by the peculiar difficulty of saying just what it is that he holds and what he takes consciousness to be.

In the last resort the dualist must insist that what consciousness in itself is cannot be described. We may contrast different mental activities with one another, but that is not to say what it is for them to be mental. There ought not to be anything radically disconcerting about this except on the assumption, dogmatically

o

accepted in much recent philosophy, that there must be *some* empirical reference to all assertions. On the other hand, and this is what matters most for the purpose of this paper, we must not make too great a mystery of the nature of consciousness. That is just what happens when we speak of mind, or 'the self', as if it were some 'thing in itself' which we did not know at all except as having to be postulated to explain what we do observe or experience in some other way. The Kantian reply to Hume may be sound and important, but I much doubt whether it can be properly and meaningfully advanced without presupposing initially a direct access to mental activity which is *sui generis*; and the point I wish to stress is that we do know quite well what consciousness is in being conscious ourselves, however hard it may be, in view of its distinctiveness, to say what such consciousness is. We cannot of course turn round and look at ourselves being conscious. It was because he thought it was this or nothing that Hume said he could not 'catch himself without perceptions', and it must not be denied that, for such reasons, there is a certain elusiveness about mind which tempts us, most of all in certain philosophical moods, to say that it can be nothing beyond what we observe. But the situation is never that desperate, however much modern philosophers may be tried by it beyond their powers or patience.

Mind, then, is not a mystery in the sense that we do not know at all what it is. We know it in being minds, which is as direct a way as any. It is not occluded from us or known only at some removes. This is one reason why it is not enough to put the point I have been making by saying that the mind or self is only known as a subject, never as an object. For while this is an admirable pointer in the right direction, it must not be allowed to lead us into the false supposition that the self is real only in some formal or highly tenuous way. Rather than that it is much better to speak of mental substances or entities. I know myself as a real being, although what I know here is not primarily body.

A further way of putting the present point would be to say that in knowing other things I am also conscious of myself, although what further this consciousness of myself is cannot be described, it can only be recognized. Consciousness is in this sense always self-consciousness, although self-awareness in the sense of noting or introspecting what sort of persons we are individually or what thoughts and feelings, and so on, we are most prone to, is another matter with difficulties of its own.

III

The second of the matters which I said should be noted about mind is that there is a very profound and important sense in which it is impossible for us to know what it is to be another person. This is a very difficult point to explain, and I am not at all sure that I ought to do more here than note it. We can quite clearly know what other persons are like in one sense, the sense that is relevant in ordinary discourse. We may know that X is pleased or angry, or that he is disposed to be pleased or angry, or whatever it may be, on certain occasions. We have a wealth of knowledge of this sort of each other; human life would not be possible without it, however incomplete and uncertain our understanding of others may also be. Moreover, for X to be pleased means the same as for me to be pleased. There is no great mystery here, whatever the view offered of the way we come to have this knowledge. And yet there is a sense in which I can never know what it is to be another person having these experiences. There is an ultimacy and mystery about self-identity and the distinctness of persons which we cannot reduce at all. It is not that there are some things about other persons which we do not in fact know, nor that we can never be quite certain of our opinions about one another. Both these things are true, and it may in practice be very hard to know some things about other persons or to eliminate the possibility of error and misunderstanding here. But there seems to be no regard in which the kind of knowledge we already appear to have in some respects about other persons is inherently incapable of extension. The difficulty I have in mind now is not that of completing or consolidating our knowledge of one another in the ordinary sense, but the much more radical one of knowing what it would be like to be another person having my present experiences or others similar to them.

To those who do not feel this difficulty there is little that can be said. For, as I have stressed, it is not a question of exhibiting, directly or indirectly, what there is over and above what we know about ourselves or others. Understanding may be induced at this point or evoked in various ways, but not by describing what it is we understand.

One important feature of what I now maintain is that, as the matter presents itself to me, the peculiar and elusive ultimacy which belongs to persons in the way I have been noting compels us to think of the distinctness of persons in a way that precludes their being, or becoming, parts of a universal mind or being merged in some other fashion in each other. There seems to be a barrier beyond which our lives may not flow out into each other, and this is not just something we encounter as a matter of fact, but an ultimate inescapable limit of all finite attainment. Only God can surpass it and know the mind of another truly from within, and what it means for God to encompass this must remain totally obscure for us. To be God, absolute and unlimited, he must achieve it, but in a way which does not at any point make the achievement reciprocal or remove the irreducible ultimacy of the distinctness of persons—and, indeed, it seems to me, of all sentient beings.

This in turn has repercussions of a very far-reaching nature on our personal relations, and the problems to which these give rise. Some of the deeper forms of these problems have their source in a failure to cope adequately with the limitation which prevents us from knowing one another wholly from within. Not apprehending the final character of this limitation we strive obstinately to overcome it or in some other way rebel against it. We expect to know one another as we are known by God. This leads to frustrations and distortions of aim which are most evident in intimate personal relationships, such as those of sex and the family; and about this we have much to learn, I believe, from obscure and unsystematic, but often discerning, writers like recent existentialists. Sartre in particular has much to say about sex in this vein which is not well appreciated outside the circle of his close admirers. A judicious view of sex must counter the tendency for it to become an outstanding form of the desire of human beings to surpass their own limitations respecting their coming to know one another, and thus to appear as a kind of appetite which, instead of taking its place in happy and healthy relationships, becomes wholly and maddeningly insatiable. This is one of the ways in which religion impinges very closely on problems of sex and the family. On the one hand it should induce the humility by which we accept our finite created status and do not attempt to set ourselves up as God; and, on the other, when distorted and idolatrous forms of religion encourage men to aspire to some divine or quasi-divine status, this will inflame perverted forms of sexual aspiration and be inflamed by it. The desire to cause hurt for hurt's sake, and other evil passions, have much to be explained in the same terms and likewise call for the understanding and acceptance of a limited finite lot that sensibility to our own relation to God ensures.

What has to be remembered here, for wisdom in our dealings with each other, is that personal relationships are not impoverished and made less intimate and tender by the limitation in question now and the mediated character of our knowledge of one another. For the mediation that is involved is not obtrusive and allows of such close and dependable and easy understanding as to give us all which properly human relationships require. Where it fails that is also part of the human situation. To pine for more, rather than cope with the situation in which we do find ourselves, is neither secular nor religious wisdom. Richness in living turns on what we learn about one another and the affections and other reactions so engendered, not on the mode of this knowledge.

As ordinary persons, or in ordinary life, we are not in any case much bothered by the mediated character of our interrelationships, since ordinary persons do not reflect upon the problem of 'other minds' any more than they ponder closely the problems of perception. We have been so made, and the world is such, that we enter into the closest relationships without needing to give thought to the way this happens. It is philosophers who worry about having 'inferred friends', and I do not think they need have such a worry at all if they adopt the right attitude to the relationship of sophisticated reflection to normal experience, an achievement on which wisdom in philosophy much depends.

Perhaps it should be added that, with growing sophistication, philosophical reflection may find that, in the present regard as in others, it has more to do than it has had in the past in bringing people generally to a better adjustment of themselves to their world and fellow-creatures. For while it is not given to many, by either aptitude or opportunity, to reflect closely on their lot and station, we have seen that delusions and false expectations do present themselves in subtle ways and lead to mischievous complications and perversions. And the cure for this may in part be found in the spread of proper philosophical understanding.

IV

These and kindred matters have been much bedevilled recently by misleading allusions to an alleged 'I-Thou' relationship. These terms seem to cover many different things and they have been used, even by responsible writers in serious theological or philosophical works, without drawing careful distinctions or noting how precisely the terms are meant. A fairly straightforward and unobjectionable use of the term 'I-Thou relation' would be to indicate those moments when, as we say, we feel very close to one another or are in a state of unusual rapport, when we are very much aware of 'the other', or of the other as a person. A contrast may be drawn in this way between casually noting passers-by in the street, persons who 'mean nothing to me' or whom I take for granted, and sitting with a friend, or an enemy, of whom I am acutely conscious. In the one case we have, as it is sometimes put, an impersonal relationship and, in the other, a personal one. This is not altogether as happy a mode of speech as is thought. For I certainly do not think of the casual passer-by as anything other than a human being. I do not regard him as 'a thing' in the sense in which the lamp-post is 'a thing'. I know that he is a conscious being with a sensitive body and so forth. I should be frozen with horror if a car seemed about to run him down. But normally I have no particular interest in the passer-by, someone quite unknown to me perhaps diving into the Tube at the rush hour. Even if he should be an employee in a firm which I manage, there is no harm, but often much advantage, in my just thinking of him as 'one of the hands'. Human life would be impossible if we could not for certain purposes just take people for granted. We cannot have intimate relationships with everybody or be expressly concerned about anyone who comes casually or incidentally within our ken. Moral wisdom turns much on knowing when and how much to involve ourselves in the lives of others. We may be too unmindful of the fact that persons with whom we are only remotely connected are after all warm sentient human beings and we may not be sufficiently ready to have sympathetic dealings with them as need arises. There is probably much substance in the complaint that modern life and institutions are becoming, or encourage us to become, too impersonal in our dealings with others in this sense. There may also be ways in which it is quixotic, under conditions of life as we know it, to try to enter very closely into the lives of other persons—and an invasion of their privacy and responsibility for their own lives.

Ramifications of these themes could be many, and in their place important. But all I wish to do at the moment is to draw attention to the general distinction which few would wish to query, between the more intimate or 'personal' relations we may have with one another and our more detached or impersonal relations. Within the former we may also distinguish between the general fairly close dealings we have with certain individuals, those within our own circle, our relatives, friends, colleagues and so on, and the moments or occasions when these individuals or someone else not normally important for us come to count for us in some specially vivid manner, when we are more acutely conscious of them as persons than we are normally, as when, in some dramatic situation perhaps, a man looks, in love or anger, in another's eyes. This, of the two possibilities in question, seems to be the one mainly intended by those who make much of the words 'I-Thou'. But they are not as clear on the point as they should be and they confuse these fairly innocuous usages with much more questionable ideas and procedures.

In the first place they usually make the distinction between the 'I-Thou' relationship and our other contacts with persons exceptionally sharp, and sometimes absolute. But it is surely, in the present sense, a matter of degree. I am sometimes more, sometimes less, conscious of others as persons. As already observed one never regards another human being altogether as 'a thing', and there are infinite variations and gradations in the intimacies we may have with one another and the ways in which we may find other persons 'more real' to us.

In addition, and much more serious, the two senses of 'I-Thou' already noted are much confused with a further very questionable one. This is the view that we become peculiarly intimate with one another in some fashion which is no extension of our knowledge about one another. We get as it were behind the scenes or we by-pass the elaborate or uncertain business of observation of any evidence in some direct relation of mind with mind. It is also held that a similar relation may be established with material things. This suggests the distinction familiar to philosophers between 'acquaintance with' and 'knowledge about'. But whatever may be said of this distinction, I do not think it was ever intended that acquaintance, say with sense data, was quite without content and in all ways uninformative. On the contrary 'knowledge about' was largely built up out of the material supplied by acquaintance. But what seems to be intended by those who speak of an 'I-Thou' relation which is not 'knowledge about' is some mysterious union with other minds (or with non-mental entities) which in no way discloses anything specific about these, a bare relation as it were. And I fear that I cannot at all understand what this might be. There are in addition the weighty, to my mind unanswerable, objections usually adduced against the notion of immediate awareness of other minds as advanced by Cook Wilson and his followers—the fact that we may be taken in at the waxworks for instance. I conclude, therefore, that there can be no substance in the belief that there is an 'I-Thou' relation in the present sense, the attractiveness of the idea being due mainly, I suspect, to failure to distinguish carefully between it and the uses of the term 'I-Thou' noted earlier.

But, finally, there is the view, admittedly difficult to present, which I have advanced earlier, namely that there is a very important sense in which an individual is a world to himself and a centre of consciousness which no one may strictly penetrate. In itself this tells expressly against the third form noted of the alleged 'I-Thou' relation. But there are also moments, and highly

important ones for the richest personal relationships, when the
realization that other persons are distinct, in the present sense, is
vivid and lights up the whole of our relationships with them. We
do not, admittedly, learn anything new about them in this way,
or reduce in the slightest the mystery of their being distinct
persons; that *ex hypothesi* is just what we cannot do. But the
apprehension in question has a sobering effect on our relations
with others, and will have much to do also with the excitement
and sweetness of intimate personal relations. Dim apprehension
of these matters has also, I suspect, enhanced the appeal of the
notion of 'I-Thou' relations. But the total result has in that case
been one of greater confusion. For the sense in which a person
may be profoundly and movingly aware of his friend, or enemy,
as 'other' is thoroughly distorted and cover is given at the same
time to the quite unfounded and misleading notion of 'acquaintance' or quasi-acquaintance with other minds. If I am anywhere
near the truth in what I hold, the latter relationship is not a
possible one at all. It is not possible with other finite beings, and
much less is it possible, as it seems so often alleged to be, with
God.

v

The last observation brings me back again to my main topic. My
chief concern hitherto has been to indicate some of the ways in
which we may speak of mystery in our apprehension of the world
and of other persons. I now want to insist that in none of these
cases have we the sort of mystery which must be ascribed to God.
This has already been anticipated in the case of the more elusive
concepts that men have recourse to in science, and in the matter
of our consciousness of ourselves as minds. For it was made plain
that mystery, in these cases, is not of a very ultimate sort. We
know what it is that we talk about, and we know it substantially
as it is. The matter is a little different in respect of the way in
which, as I also went on to show, minds are occluded from each
other just by being other minds; and this needs more careful
note.

The ultimate and irreducible character of the mystery which
attaches to other minds in virtue of being *other* brings it very close

to the mystery involved in the being of God. We are confronted with something of which nothing can be said expressly beyond noting its mysteriousness, and this reflects here a defect in knowledge itself, not in the availability of description. This much enhances the relevance of the problem of 'other minds' in general to the problem of our knowledge of God. But the two cases are nonetheless far from parallel. For when we speak of another mind we really do mean *mind* in the sense in which we know ourselves to be minds. In ascribing thoughts, feelings and decisions to my neighbour I ascribe them to him in precisely the same sense as I have them myself. If I judge that someone is frightened I take this to be the case in exactly the same way as I might be frightened myself in a similar situation. There may be some ways in practice in which I might have to say that I do not know or understand his fear, that is I may well fail to know all there is to know about it or to appreciate the strength or reasonableness of it. But this has nothing to do with understanding in general what sort of thing it is, and that holds of all that we learn about each other. We learn it by being in states not substantially dissimilar ourselves. So that while there is the peculiar and quite irreducible difficulty, and one exceptionally hard to note fairly in discussion, of knowing what it must be to be another mind, there is no radical obscurity about what we take to be the case specifically about one another. It is with beings like ourselves, and intelligible to us in the sense that we are intelligible to ourselves, that we are dealing.

In the case of God the position is quite different. For he is 'other' not merely in the sense in which we are so to each other, but in the sense that we cannot know at all what it is to be God. The mystery is *total*, and the question of intelligent discourse, even to the minimal extent of affirming there to be this mystery, is acute as it is not elsewhere—and quite peculiar in form. That we may, nonetheless, cope with this problem, and indeed make very bold affirmations about God, seems to me also true, as I shall stress again at the close. But I do not think we can make genuine headway with the task, so vital for Christian apologetics, of indicating just how the special claims of religion are made, unless we are first of all quite clear about the sense in which God is also an irreducible mystery to us.

VI

It is this last matter, of course, that agnostic or sceptical critics stress. A total mystery offers no hold to the mind, we can make nothing of it. The traditional arguments and kindred approaches to religion have failed and invited the usual criticisms just because they tried desperately to make something of the mystery in a way in which it is not possible to make anything of it at all. One step in the wrong direction here is fatal, however cautiously and gingerly we take it.

The most obvious examples of this are to be found in the classical and more familiar versions of the traditional arguments. It is very hard to present the cosmological argument, for example, without lapsing at some point into the supposition that the relation of God to the world is some extraordinary form of the relation of cause and effect as we find it in our experience of the world. Once the error is committed the trap closes on us. Our opponent has but to observe that the First Cause, so understood, has to conform to whatever principle of cause and effect we have to assume to begin the regress alleged to be terminated by a First Cause, and must thus be itself a member of a series of caused events in a way which precludes its being a First Cause. Most of the stock objections to the cosmological argument are variations on this theme.

Some critics, for example, observe that 'the natural habitat of "cause" words is the ordering and grouping of our experiences and the manipulating of what is to come'.[1] If 'cause' has no other use than this, or if the apologist can be caught out using 'cause', as applied to God, in the way it appears in its natural habitat, then the position is made ridiculous as the claim that, in all our observations, we have never yet found a Universe without a First Cause. No one, in fact, does make that sort of claim, but the suggestion is that such an absurdity is the only possible result of applying the idea of cause to the world.

Many, again, fasten on the alleged empirical basis of the Thomistic arguments. These are held to have 'roots in experience.' 'Thomists are confident that their arguments make ample

[1] R. W. Hepburn, *Christianity and Paradox*, p. 160.

concessions to empiricism, while going on to draw out explicitly what experience knows only in a confused way.'[1] How far this is true of Thomists is, I believe, very hard to determine. St Thomas himself appears at times very anxious to begin with certain facts about the world which no one can dispute, for example that there is movement and that things have worth; and this is apt to leave the impression that he wishes to build up an argument from these facts in the way an argument about finite things normally proceeds. I would not wish to dispute that St Thomas sometimes thought of his arguments in this way—or that, with a part of his mind, he conceived the matter thus. But it is very hard indeed to believe that this is the whole story, since he sets us so clearly on the course which leads out of ordinary thought about the world into the apprehension of what lies altogether beyond this.

It seems to be the case also that recent Thomists have been anxious to make the alleged concessions to empiricism. There is always a temptation to come to terms with prevailing fashion or to try to turn the tables on your opponent by starting with something he also stresses. A philosophy that has set itself traditionally the role of providing a synthesis of secular philosophy and theology, a bridge as it were between secular wisdom and religion, may be very susceptible to the temptation in question. The adoption, as a starting point, of the hard fact that some things exist and are presented to our senses may be attributable in this way to an over-accommodating attitude, and the subsequent contention may have been presented, for that reason, too much in terms of ordinary processes of thought. If so, it has certainly been a mistake.

On the other hand, there may be a quite different, and most legitimate, purpose to the stress on the fact that certain things do exist, namely as a technique for evoking the insight into the inevitability of ultimate self-subsistent being. In controversy with an agnostic one may well say: it is very plain that some things do exist here and now; whatever further view you take about them, we ourselves and the world exist and have a nature of some sort; but does not this induce you to ask how all this came to be, and if you answer in terms of causal antecedents you know that this

---

[1] *Op. cit.*, p. 158.

does not really touch your problem, it just pushes it a little back, and are you not forced in this way to recognize, in all our thinking, a background which is adequate as our thought, or the world as we grasp it, cannot be? The agnostic may be unimpressed, and we may have to try again, if he has patience, or start another tack, raising for example the questions of beginning or end in space or time. But we are not strictly arguing here. We are not indicating certain facts of experience of which a certain hypothesis provides the most likely explanation. We are noting features of experience, or presenting the world, in the way which best helps us to apprehend that limit to all explanation which yet calls for 'explanation' in some quite radically different way. The point of departure for this is strictly immaterial, and we need not, *pace* my Thomist friends, begin at all with the fact that some things exist.

We may, on the contrary, just ask ourselves whether it is conceivable to us that there should be nothing, and be induced in this way to apprehend that all which in fact we do find to be real is so in a way that is bound up with the inevitability of some mysterious self-subsistent being. The empirical anchorage is here very hard to detect and may well be logically nil, our thought having strictly nothing to do with the fact that we ourselves or other entities happen to be; for the point is that *nothing could* ultimately just happen. On the other hand, psychologically there is much to be gained by starting with the obvious; and in this respect to stress the fact that some things do exist is important. That is one of the points from which we come most cleanly to the need for the alleged ultimate 'explanation'.

For these reasons, one retort sometimes given to the sceptic is apt to be ambiguous. In reply to the question 'what would count for or against your belief in the existence of God', some have said, 'Nothing'. If this meant 'the existence of no entity of any kind', then I think it would be mistaken; for it entertains at least the possibility that there should be nothing and makes the existence of God a consequence of the fact that there is obviously something. But that breaks things up too much. For what we have is one insight into the inevitability of a very special wholeness of things in which all that in fact we encounter has part. If, however, by saying 'Nothing', in the context noted, we mean that no evidence, or other consideration of the way the world goes, counts for or against the existence of God, then we seem on very safe ground and are making a very proper move.

VII

In the light of these considerations we can understand much better how the cosmological argument and the ontological argument converge on the same initial insight. It is not a case that men have hit on two quite different approaches to the subject, each attractive in a way quite different from the other. It would be odd if that had happened when both arguments are independent of what we specifically find in the world; they are as 'abstract' as any arguments of this sort could be. But in fact they both stem from the same source, distorting in various measures according to their forms the same fundamental conviction which makes them plausible.

The weaknesses in the ontological argument, as usually presented, have often been exposed. Existence, we are told, is not a predicate, it is not a part of any concept; propositions affirming existence are synthetic. To this the reply has been made that the objection misses the point, for while it is true of all finite things that they do not exist by any necessity of their own nature, the case of God is peculiar. What holds of finite things does not here hold of him, and I submit that the conviction which initially set the ontological argument going, and revived it when it had been made quite clear that normally existence is not a predicate, is that of the inevitability of the universe having a character by which all things have an explanation that has not the radical inadequacy of explanations as we usually offer them.

It has always been tempting, and understandably so, to present this peculiar conviction as a proof or inference of the sort we normally base on some features of thought or experience. This may be seen to as good advantage in the case of Descartes as anywhere. It is also easy to point out many mistakes and strange assumptions which Descartes makes in the rationalistic proofs he attempts of the existence of God. But the persistence with which

Descartes holds to the view that it is a basic rational conviction that God must be is nonetheless impressive. One could say, of course, with the sceptic, that he is totally mistaken. But his persistence in holding to positions so palpably weak in themselves seems to me to derive from the way those positions borrowed a strength not their own from an initially clear and simple way in which the being of God impressed itself on Descartes' mind.

The conviction which Descartes has here is not to be easily attributed to religious orthodoxy. It is not at all as a matter of special revelation or part of the specific teaching of his Church that he speaks of the existence of God, but as an independently clear and ineradicable conviction he had as a rational being, and it is significant how firmly and repeatedly he states this. 'For is there anything', he writes, 'more manifest than that there is a God, that is to say, a Supreme Being, to whose essence alone existence pertains.'[1] 'It follows that existence is inseparable from him.'[2] These and kindred affirmations are made in the context of very doubtful arguments, and this might be thought to detract from the weight and impressiveness of Descartes' conviction; but it can also cut the other way and suggest that there is something here more than extreme confidence in faulty arguments, namely an insight which the arguments confuse but which has a firmness not derived from the arguments. That is what I take to be in fact the case here.

I think it also significant that Descartes, and others of like mind to him, should have presented their conviction as one made evident especially to their reason. That is what lent particular force to the temptation to formulate it as a straightforward rational argument. It had no strictly empirical foundation, and how in that case could we proceed except on the basis of certain limited insights and more elaborate arguments built up out of these. Descartes at least thought there was no other way. In this he was wrong, but he was not wrong in connecting the conviction of the necessary being of God with the distinctive operations of reason. For it is in the activity of providing rational explanations

---

[1] Meditation V, *The Philosophical Works of Descartes*, Vol. 1, trans. Haldane and Ross, p. 183.   [2] *Op. cit.*, p. 181.

of events, in a rudimentary or sophisticated fashion, that we come
to apprehend the limits of such explanations which call for their
completion in some way which goes altogether beyond them.

VIII

In saying this, however, we only sharpen an issue which has been
lurking in what I have been saying all along, namely that if God is
regarded as 'Ground' or 'Cause' or 'Ultimate Source' or 'Explanation' in some way quite radically different from the ordinary
meaning of these words, we are in danger of not saying anything
at all in our reference to him. Make God a total mystery and it
seems impossible even to say that he is; for how can you affirm
that anything is real if you do not know, at least in some very
general way, what sort of thing it is? This is the dilemma with
which our critics confront us. Either we think of the relation of
God to the world in some way resembling the finite relations we
can at any rate partly understand, and thus follow at least some
of the subtler forms of the traditional arguments and kindred
apologetics, or our contention becomes vacuous. The first
alternative exposes us to the objections already noted and which
are now quite familiar in the history of the subject. Anything we
proffer as a final explanation of things in the normal way will, by
parity of reasoning, call for explanation itself; the regress of
causes, if it is to do its business in the argument, cannot stop. But
if we drop right outside the ordinary processes of thinking, if we
qualify 'explanation' so that it does not in fact explain anything,
we seem impaled on the other horn of our dilemma and to be
saying nothing intelligible.

It is very good that recent controversy should have sharpened
this dilemma as much as it has. This is the main point, it seems to
me, where criticism has helped the apologist to understand his
own position and the way it should be commended to others. And
the first thing he must realize is that he must not run away from
the dilemma. Many subtle attempts to do so may be found in
recent philosophy of religion, the recourse for instance to the
notion of evidence counting without 'counting decisively'.
Evidence which does not count decisively is in itself no different

from other evidence, and indeed we may ask whether any evidence is altogether decisive. Nor are we helped by attempting subtle variations on the ploys common among theologians at this point, for example saying that revelation is not cognitive at all or making loose play with the idea of commitment or obscure 'existentialist' notions. If God is to be worshipped we must properly 'believe that he is'. How then do we cope with our obvious dilemma?

Only, it seems to me, by realizing, and boldly affirming, that we do here apprehend something of a positive character which cannot be properly set out or described. There is a content to our thought, otherwise it would not be thought at all, but it neverthe-less falls outside ordinary discourse; we are not affirming pre-dicates of an entity already characterized and recognized in some fashion, nor are we claiming existence for some entity with a nature in some way determined. Subject and predicate are not relevant here, yet our thought is not empty, it has, in a fashion, the richest content of all. But it is not the apprehension of distinct characteristics, but of the inevitability of there being the com-pletion which finite thought lacks or the perfection of the world as we find it. In what this completion consists we do not know at all, we are not having any glimpse behind the scenes—and we could not. Any light on things we can receive, as finite beings, is the sort of light they have partially already; what we can grasp is the kind of thing we now grasp. There can be no means therefore of determining what it is to be God. We have not even a partial reduction of that mystery. The nature of God is in this sense altogether hidden. We know him in the necessity of his being as the other and positive side to the impossibility of ultimate fortuitousness.

I repeat that it is insight or apprehension that we have here; it is not, as Tillich suggests, a case of anxiety or of frustration at the inadequacy of the sort of understanding we can attain, but the positive apprehension of supreme unconditioned being in the way noted. This does not depend on our being in a peculiar state where ordinary thought and understanding are altogether superseded; that is not in my view possible, although we may have odd experiences vastly different from our present ones. To be religious

P

is not to be in a strange state where true and false do not matter or where the laws of thought are annulled. It is to apprehend a 'beyond' which thought cannot reach but which thought itself requires as its completion.

It is for these reasons that we come to affirm that essence and existence are one in God. They are not so elsewhere. The nature of God can only be expressly known to us in the peculiar inevitability of his being. To claim to know his essence in any way that is divorced from the special necessity of his being is to fail to understand what this necessity properly involves and to belie the most express insight we have into the nature of God. We can, in other words, say nothing about the essence of God except in terms of the special way in which he must be.

Christians might object that, for them, God is love. But the sense in which God is love varies from one context to another, and deepens in mature religion. The relation of God to the world as its creator and sustainer, as the one who provides in himself what the world lacks, or as supreme perfection, may well be said to be love. But, in the Christian revelation, there is disclosed and made operative also a special concern which God has for men, and if we can accept this we can regard it as a manifestation of God's character in his dealings with us; in its unlimited nature, as we find it in Christ, it entitles us to say in this very special sense that God is love. But we could not get the proper import of this unless we understood what it meant for it to be God's love; and this we can only understand in terms of the insight into the being of God described already.

These are matters which were sadly, and I think surprisingly, overlooked in a comment which a very influential Oxford professor is alleged to have made recently on the celebrated passage in the Scriptures where God refuses to tell Moses even his name and simply declares 'I am'.[1] The professor observed, apparently, that if God just said to Moses 'I am', then the proper response to this should have been 'You are what?' Now, of course, if anyone approached us and just said 'I am' or 'He is' or 'It is', then we should be just mystified. We could have no notion what he meant unless something in his tone of voice or the context gave

[1] Or 'I am that I am', Exodus iii. 14.

us some clue. In answer to a question I might quite properly say 'I am' and no more.[1] I might also convey some mood by an incomplete phrase of this kind, boredom perhaps or extreme content. But unless there is some way of completing the sentence in this fashion it can have no meaning at all, and if we are guided by the rules of ordinary discourse and what is normally proper to say, and not to say, we must exclude the words 'I am' from the field of meaningful utterance.

This is, however, one of the many places where excessive pre-occupation with language is apt to be misleading and a mild witticism made to masquerade as philosophical insight. It is no doubt true that no one can mean anything normally by just 'I am'. There must be some predicate. But then the case of God is not a normal one, it falls altogether outside the ordinary rules of discourse; and it is a most impressive testimony to the exceptional religious sense of the Jews and the insights which shaped their destiny, that God should be represented in the story as simply saying 'I am'. The maturity reflected here, most of all when we consider the place of this narrative in Hebrew experience, is of great importance for our understanding of the Bible as a whole, and it is pitifully inadequate to brush it away with a linguistic jest.

IX

The question arises now of the relation of 'explanation', in the very peculiar sense in which God is the explanation or ground of all things, to explanations as we normally provide them in terms of the interrelations of finite events. There is plainly a relation of this kind, and a vital one; and it is this which licenses the move from ordinary explanation to the requirement that there be explanation in the peculiar sense in which God provides one. This move, as I have stressed, is not inferential; but the fact that we are impelled to look for explanations of one event in terms of others is not divorced from the need for the other and exhaustive

---

[1] One might also of course use 'He is' or 'I am' to confirm existence. Suppose, for instance, I had been reading a story, presumed to be fiction, about Mr X's escape from a prisoner-of-war camp. Someone then assures me that the story is not fiction, there was such a person; 'He exists' my friend might say. Similarly Mr X might settle the debate about his identity by bursting into the room with the words 'I exist!' It would indeed be unusual, but not altogether wrong, in English to substitute for 'He exists' here 'He is'.

explanation. We look for causes of events because we do not think that anything can just happen, and the need for the explanation which such relations do not provide arises because, if we could not get beyond these, there would remain a very final sense in which we would have to accept it that things 'just happen'. The demand for normal explanation is a mode of the demand for total explanation in God.

There is thus a religious side to the belief in cause and effect, and the failure to appreciate this has bedevilled a great deal of the discussion of the principle of causality and the problems of induction in the past. Nor has this occurred solely among secular thinkers. Religious persons have also failed to appreciate the expressly religious nature of the basic questions we raise about causality. The question of causality has, in short, been treated as an independent metaphysical or logical problem which might have a bearing on religious matters, but was not itself an expressly religious issue.

The place where this mistake shows itself is when some account is offered of the factor of necessity in causal explanation. It is notoriously difficult to find some empirical basis for this necessity. We do discover relations of things and can form general rules and hypotheses to cover what in fact we find to be the case about the events we observe. But we do not observe the necessity of their behaving in this way. We do not perceive necessity, and the attempt to derive it, as in some celebrated treatments of the ground of induction, from the concomitance of events and the regularities we do in fact discover in the world, is exceptionally hard to make without at some point begging the principle we are seeking to establish. I do not myself believe that such attempts can be successful. On the other hand I am equally certain that Hume is not right in maintaining that the necessity in causal relations is a merely psychological one, an expectation of a deep or ineradicable kind created in us by long experience such that we cannot but assume that explanation in terms of consistent behaviour is *bound* to be forthcoming, or must be there, even if we cannot at the moment provide it. It is not an assumption, I submit, that we have here, but certainty, and that of a cognitive, and not merely psychological, character. It seems initially and altogether impossible that there should be quite fortuitous occurrences. There may be drastic changes in the course of events, things may take a turn which wholly surprises us, but then there must somewhere be some explanation of that. We do not just hope, we know this must be.

The temptation now arises to say that we have an intuitive awareness of the principle of causality itself, although particular causal relations are known empirically. This is one of the ways in which a wholly secular metaphysical view of the subject might be offered, and I have myself been prone to adopt this intuitive account of causality. I still think that is very near the truth, but I would now wish to qualify it and say that what is apprehended here in a non-empirical and non-inferential way is the requirement that there should be ultimate explanation lending its necessary character to the way we find that things go in the world. The world might be different but only if God made it so; being as it is it must be as it is and events connected as we find them; for that is the sort of world God made. It could however be, or become, more opaque to our reason; but only if God wished this and intervened.

This enables us to counter a common objection to the cosmological argument which could be awkward if we did not see aright what lies behind the argument. It has been urged that if we could in fact come across wholly fortuitous or chance events, then we would have demolished the basis on which the cosmological argument is raised, namely the notion that every event must have a cause. The difficulty of providing a fool-proof instance is also stressed, for the fact that we find some situation quite bewildering does not prove that no explanation of it will ever be forthcoming; perhaps it is just the case that we have not found, or may not find, the cause in this instance; there may nonetheless be one. Users of the cosmological argument are sometimes taunted with being prone to shelter behind this difficulty. But what then if they should also believe in absolute free will? This is not like the alleged indeterminacy of some natural events, for the scientist may eventually be able to account for these and see that the 'indeterminacy' was relative to the state of his knowledge at some time. If, however, one holds that undetermined choice is a prerequisite of responsibility, and that we have experience of making such choices, the situation is disconcerting in a much more serious way for anyone who wishes to hold that every event has a cause.

There is, however, no serious difficulty here if the necessity of causal relations is seen to be lent to them by the way they are embedded in the ultimately self-explanatory character of the Universe. To put the matter in more expressly religious terms, it is no limitation on the power of God that he should grant me free will, or that I should exercise it in defiance of him. For I only defy him by his own consent. He could always take away this power from me, it is he that allows me to go my own way. I am never therefore properly outside his control, and if my action cannot be rationally explained in the sense of relating it to events that determine it, yet it does not affect the conviction that nothing happens in the last analysis without explanation in the sense of being within the ultimate control of God.

Some questions concerning the possibility of miracle admit of being treated in a similar way. But I shall not go into such questions now. Suffice it to say that it seems to me that considerable light may be thrown on many topics if we can properly appreciate the sense in which belief in causality, as a necessary principle, is tantamount to belief in God.

x

The reference to intuition in what I have just said about cause and effect raises the question whether the term 'intuition' is the proper one to apply to the apprehension we have of the necessary being of God. The term seems to me less misleading than most in this context, and I have used it so in the past. Some prefer to speak of apprehension of God, but apprehension is a fairly general term which might apply to many forms of knowledge. Intuition has the advantage of being sharply contrasted with inference, and, as I have stressed, there are no steps or stages into which our awareness of the being of God may be broken up. In the recourse to the arguments this is overlooked. For that reason there is much to be said for 'intuition' as our proper term here. But we must, all the same, be careful not to assimilate the intuition of God too closely to other intuitions, for these have their determinate finite content whereas the intuition of God, equally immediate though it is, is not the awareness of some distinct nature or relation but of something more elusive which goes beyond these.

There is a further and more important way in which 'intuition' may be misleading in its present use. For some have supposed that there may be obtained some awareness of God or union with him similar to the acquaintance which certain thinkers have supposed we have with one another's minds. I have already urged that acquaintance, in the sense intended in the technical use of this term in philosophy, is in no way possible here. We only learn about one another's minds from evidence, we do not reach across to one another independently of all observation as we introspect our own minds. Much less do we have acquaintance, in the present sense, with God; for, in addition to all other difficulties, that would imply that we saw altogether beyond finite things and apprehended the infinite in some way in itself.

The latter possibility has been ruled out as much by general religious thought and religious experience as by philosophical thinking. Few things are reiterated more in sacred Scriptures than the invisible character of God, the impenetrable nature of his mystery. He is a God that hides himself, no man hath seen him; he gives to Moses not even his name, but only the affirmation that he is. If the term 'intuition' suggests a reversal of this, and in some instances that appears certainly to have been the case, then it is most misleading. But the words 'direct awareness' might be misleading in the same way, and almost certainly have been; and we must have some way of indicating that the initial awareness we have of God is direct or immediate. It is so, not in the form of acquaintance or any other apprehension of some limited content, but in the peculiar undiversified awareness of there being some 'beyond' in which such limitations are superseded.

To understand the sense in which our awareness of God is direct, and the sense in which it is not, is very important. It will help much in our study of mysticism and keep us to a proper course in examining doctrines like that of ontologism. This doctrine has been condemned as a heresy, and very properly so if it implies strictly unmediated knowledge of God as he is in himself; that would be very presumptuous heresy and might have serious repercussions on theological thinking and religious practice. But I also much suspect that those who fell under the lure of this heresy did so because they rightly felt that there was some sense in which we did apprehend God directly and with complete certainty. Had the necessary distinctions been drawn a heretical thesis might not have presented itself.

This is one of many matters which become plainer as we understand better the sense in which it has to be affirmed that the idea of God is unique. Another is the way in which our knowledge of one another affords a clue to our knowledge of God. I censured earlier the contention that there is an 'I-Thou' relation between persons, or between persons and things, which involved no mode of 'knowledge about'. I added that these notions were even less plausible in the case of our knowledge of God. It may now appear that I have revoked or contradicted this in affirming that the initial knowledge we have of the being of God is some intuition of necessary being which has no content in the form of some specifiable item or items. I have, however, stressed that this knowledge, however peculiarly difficult it may be to indicate or describe it, is not devoid of content. It is knowledge, and knowledge of a very rich kind, although we cannot bring it under normal classifications of knowledge.

By contrast, the theory of 'I-Thou' relations, and the closely connected notion of 'encounter' with God, are apt to be represented as if they were not cognitive at all. At other times they seem to have affinity with the notion of 'acquaintance' with things and persons as a general possibility of establishing contact with those independently of our observations or in some character they have not disclosed to observation. This I have also ruled out. Even in noting the peculiar mystery that attaches to the otherness of another mind, I distinguished carefully between the apprehension of this and having the alleged acquaintance with other minds. I suspect, however, that, in these matters also, the fact that there is, in a very different way, a directness in our awareness of God has lent some plausibility to other notions of direct awareness so little tenable in themselves.

We have thus an additional clue to the attractiveness of the notion of an 'I-Thou' relation for many persons; and we also understand how misleading, in what seems to be the normal intention, this notion is as applied to our knowledge of God or our union with him. For what seems most certain is that we do not penetrate at all the mystery of the being of God, but only become confronted with it in the peculiar consciousness that it must be. This is a little like knowing that some entity must have another side although we have not the faintest notion what this is like; but the analogy must not be pressed too closely, for we know what it is like to have another side in a way in which we do not know at all what it is like to be God.

XI

A classical phrase which comes to mind here, and is most useful, is 'Something we know not what'. These are not terms which many will commend today, they are to be discarded along with other obscurantisms by which men have been deluded in the past. Indeed, no sooner had the phrase been put to philosophical use by Locke than Berkeley began the work of demolition. In the context which Locke had mainly in mind, namely the postulation of material substances, I, for one, have no quarrel with Berkeley, but gladly follow his lead. It appears quite proper to say here that our inability to form any clear notion of what such substances might be, is enough to disqualify them or rule the reference to them out from meaningful discourse. At the same time I do not think we can quite leave the matter there even where physical things are concerned.

For there is one sense in which the objects presented to our senses do refer beyond themselves to some mysterious source. They do this in the way everything else does so, and it is quite erroneous to represent that in terms of discrete substances in which qualities inhere in a fashion of which nothing can be known. It is the case, nonetheless, that something is left out in an account of the natural world in terms of our sensible experiences. Berkeley would of course agree and ascribe our experiences directly to God. This may be claiming to know too much. But he and Locke have this in common, that they consider objects of sense to require some ground or basis of which we can form no proper notion, and Berkeley's instinct was right to the extent that this is *ultimately* a postulation of God.

As applied to mental substances the phrase 'something I know not what' is more expressly apposite. I referred earlier to the difficulty of describing consciousness, although we knew quite well what it is in being minds ourselves. We cannot treat minds like the entities minds apprehend, or as part of the observable world. But few things are plainer to us all the same than that our minds are real, although we cannot say in what their reality consists; and this may again be a reference in which it may profit us to consider whether the words 'something I know not what' are as vacuous or absurd as is commonly thought today. We may find that they are, on the contrary, helpful and illuminating.

But the meaning which these words may have in respect to minds, important though it may be, is not the meaning they have when we think of God as the unfathomable mystery in which all things are rooted. For, as I have stressed, the difficulty here is not that of finding proper terms or comparisons for something which we know well in itself but is *sui generis*. It is that we know and do not know at the same time, or know without knowing what we know. The religious apologist must just not be daunted by this paradox, but rather realize how essential it is to maintain it and to indicate how it should be taken. Averse he may be to paradoxes and conscious of the ease with which they may be exploited or put into the service of tantalizing evasions of genuine difficulties or fair criticism. His concern as a philosopher for reasonableness and integrity may be in rebellion, yet this is just the point at which he must not waver; if he does so the sceptic triumphs and the changes are rung on the familiar critical themes. The knowledge to be claimed is knowledge, and as such it has a content, but only in a very peculiar way which cannot be properly specified even to ourselves. The knowledge we have topples over into what we cannot know, and we may talk of 'explanation', 'source', 'ultimate perfection', and know that these are the appropriate terms to use, and yet know that in using them we are speaking of 'something we know not what'. The beginning of wisdom in religious thought is to appreciate that.

It must be added that while we cannot specify properly what we apprehend in this basic insight or intuition of God, we may nonetheless do much to evoke the intuition. We cannot persuade the sceptic, at this point, by setting before him compelling considerations to which the existence of God is the answer. It is only other finite entities that could be established in that way. The move from the finite to the infinite is quite different, but there are pressures and practices which help us to make this move. Some of these are of a reflective or philosophical nature such as the notions discussed or mentioned in this paper, but there are other procedures, those of the prophet, the priest, or the poet for example, by which the mind is made to appreciate both its own inevitable limitations and the absolute unlimited reality which lies beyond these. These procedures will be more closely and expressly linked with reflective thought in a sophisticated and self-consciously critical culture like our own.

XII

A new and somewhat different type of difficulty may now, however, raise its head, and though it falls strictly outside the scope of this paper it must be mentioned in closing. It will be said: 'You seem to have struggled out of the cleft stick in which your antagonist seemed to hold you, but have you not done this at a very high price, namely that it is no longer possible to make any of the specific affirmations about God which typify particular religions?' That would indeed be an exacting price, and a Christian would find it impossible to pay it without surrender of allegiance to his own religion. He has some very determinate claims about God to defend.

Some modern theologians, impressed by the transcendence of God and the need to have this in mind at all points in theological controversy, have come very close to paying the ruinous price. They still retain the forms of Christian utterance, alleged to be guaranteed in some strange 'existentialist' way or deprived, unintelligibly it seems to me, of any claim to objectivity, but the precision and substance have gone out of them. Jesus is alleged to be the Son of God, but in a way which owes nothing to the reliability of the evidence we have about him as a man; risks of the latter sort must not be taken, not only because of the uncertainties of Biblical and historical criticism, but also because we must not bring the transcendent realities apprehended by faith to the level of human considerations.

This seems to me a counsel of despair, and a quite fatal one. Specific Christian claims must be defended more boldly; and here again our critics help by holding before us persistently the bogy of worthlessly vacuous assertions. Their challenge is met, in the case of the being of God, by firmly contending that it is not vacuous to claim his existence as an irreducibly mysterious being; and on that head enough has been said already. But on the second score we can come to better terms with our antagonist. For once the initial intuition of the being of God is granted, there are ways in which, it seems to me, further claims about him can be made.

These will not take the form of deductions from the way the world goes such as would be warranted if the idea of God were an explanatory hypothesis advanced to account for what we discover the world to be like. That is not the principle of religious symbolism. What we find, on the contrary, is that the sense of the overwhelming mystery of God, and the compelling way in which this presents itself to us in certain circumstances, associates itself with certain other insights and experiences and makes them its own. Out of these come the content of specific beliefs, sometimes confused and distorted and sometimes more plainly discerned. Of the course which this process takes, the place of imagination and thought in sustaining it, of the patterns by which it grows into a more explicit sense of divine intervention and the presence of God, this is not the place to write. I have made these matters the main themes of my book, *Our Experience of God*. To amplify what I said there would take long, but there is one comment which falls sufficiently within the scope of this paper to be made.

It is that where particular knowledge of God is concerned the analogy with our knowledge of one another's minds becomes close. I do not know the existence of God, as I know the existence of my neighbours, from evidence which I observe in the course of my experience. To suppose that would be to make a very misleading use of the analogy with 'other minds', and this unhappily has often occurred. But, knowing that there must be God, and through the domination of other experience by this knowledge, the details of what we learn specifically about God, his dealings with us and our intercourse with him, become very similar to the way we learn about one another, a mediation so unobtrusive as not to be noticed. To that extent, Berkeley, and others who made much of this analogy, were perfectly justified.

To steer our course properly through these and kindred issues, to know when the alleged 'I-Thou' relation may, and may not, be affirmed and deemed relevant, we need to be very alive to the different ways and measures in which we may be confronted with mystery in our experience; and this is moreover only one of many ways in which effective thinking depends on the ability, so little evidenced in recent philosophy, to cultivate, without jargon and avoidable obscurity, a due appreciation of mysteries.

INDEX